⊛ RAND MᶜNALLY

S0-BYC-004

the road atlas

MIDSIZE

CONTENTS

Photo Credits: ©Mary Lu Laffey/Rand Mc-Nally ii (#1&2), iii (#1,2&3), vi (#1,2&3), vii (#1); ©Nathalie Stassheim/Rand McNally iv (#1&2), v (#1&2), xv (#3); © Dreamcatcher Sailing Charters iv (#3); ©Laurie Bor-man/Rand McNally viii (#1&2), ix (#1,2&3); ©Rand McNally x (#1,2&3), xi (#1&2); ©Getty Images xii (#1), xiv (#1), xvi (#1&2), xvii (#3), xviii (#2), xix (#4), xx (#2), xxi (#2), 1 (#1), 59 (#1), 89 (#1); ©FoodPix/Burke/Tri-olo Productions xv (#1); ©Louisiana Shrimp & Petroleum Festival & Fair Association xv (#2), xix (#1); ©2007 Riverside County Fair & National Date Festival xv (#4); ©Courtesy Warren County Chamber of Commerce xvi (#2); ©Springfield Filbert Festival xvii (#1); ©Twillingate Fish, Fun & Folk Festival xvii (#2); ©2000 Town of Olathe Colorado xvii (#4); ©Tim Marsh/Pullman Lentil Festival xviii (#1); ©New Orleans MCVB/Carl Purcell xix (#3&4); ©Idaho Potato Commission xx (#1); ©Edward Savaria, Jr./Philadelphia CVB xx (#3); ©Skyline Chili xxi (#1); xxii (#1).

For licensing information and copyright permissions, contact us at licensing@randmcnally.com

If you have a question or even a compliment, please visit us at go.randmcnally.com/contact or e-mail us at consumeraffairs@randmcnally.com

or write to
Rand McNally Consumer Affairs
P.O. Box 7600
Chicago, Illinois 60680-9915

1 2 3 BN 08 07

Travel Information 2008

New! 2008 Best of the Road™........................... ii-xi
Our editors have mapped out five terrific road trips. Each trip features the best attractions, shops, and places to eat on the road.

Updated! Road Construction and Road Conditions Resources .... xii-xiii
Numbers to call and websites to visit for road information in each state and province.

Updated! Numbers to Know xiv
Toll-free phone numbers and websites for hotel chains.

New! Eat Your Way Across the U.S.A (and Canada, too) .... xv-xxii
30 food festivals, plus selected local dish side trips.

New! Numbers to Know 1
Rental car toll-free numbers and websites plus cell phone emergency numbers.

Updated! Border Crossing Information 59
What you need to know when driving to Mexico or Canada.

Updated! Tourism Concierge 89
Phone numbers and websites for tourism information in each state and province.

Mileage Chart...90
Driving distances between 77 North American cities.

Mileage and Driving Times Map ....inside back cover
Distances and driving times between hundreds of North American cities and national parks.

Maps and Indexes

Map legend 1
United States overview map 2-3
U.S. states 4-58
Canada overview map 60-61
Canadian provinces 62-71
Mexico overview map and Puerto Rico 72
U.S. and Canadian cities 73-88

State & Province Maps
United States

Alabama.................................... 4
Alaska....................................... 5
Arizona 6
Arkansas................................... 7
California 8-9
Colorado 10
Connecticut............................. 11
Delaware 12
Florida 13
Georgia 14
Hawaii 15
Idaho 16
Illinois 17
Indiana 18
Iowa 19
Kansas 20
Kentucky 21
Louisiana 22
Maine 23
Maryland 24
Massachusetts......................... 25
Michigan 26
Minnesota 27
Mississippi 28
Missouri................................... 29
Montana 30
Nebraska 31
Nevada 32
New Hampshire 33
New Jersey 34
New Mexico 35
New York 36-37
North Carolina......................... 38
North Dakota........................... 39
Ohio 40-41
Oklahoma 42
Oregon 43
Pennsylvania...................... 44-45
Rhode Island 46
South Carolina......................... 47
South Dakota........................... 48
Tennessee................................ 49
Texas.................................. 50-51
Utah 52
Vermont................................... 53
Virginia 54
Washington 55
West Virginia 56
Wisconsin 57
Wyoming 58

Canada

Alberta................................. 62-63
British Columbia................... 62-63
Manitoba 64-65
New Brunswick 70-71
Nova Scotia..........................70-71
Newfoundland & Labrador 71
Ontario................................ 66-67
Prince Edward Island.................71
Québec................................ 68-69
Saskatchewan 64-65

City Maps

Albuquerque 73
Atlanta 73
Austin 74
Baltimore 73
Birmingham 74
Boston 74
Buffalo 76
Chicago 75
Cincinnati................................ 76
Cleveland 76
Columbus 77
Dallas 76-77
Denver 77
Detroit 80
Fort Worth 76-77
Houston 80-81
Indianapolis 78
Kansas City 78
Las Vegas............................ 78-79
Los Angeles......................... 78-79
Louisville 82
Memphis 82
Mexico City 72
Miami 81
Milwaukee 82
Minneapolis 80-81
New Orleans 82
New York 83
Newark.................................... 83
Oakland 87
Orlando 82
Philadelphia............................ 84
Phoenix 82
Pittsburgh 85
Portland 84
St. Louis 85
St. Paul 80-81
St. Petersburg 86
Salt Lake City 85
San Antonio 86
San Diego................................ 86
San Francisco 87
Seattle 84
Tampa 86
Toronto 86
Vancouver 86
Washington 88

BEST of the Road

2008 BEST OF THE ROAD

Each year our editors drive five new road trips to share with you those special things we call Best of the Road™.

Simply Irresistible

Santa Barbara to Monterey, California

Driving north and west from Santa Barbara to Monterey, this route follows the El Camino Real Road and CA 1 as it wends its way through the core of coastal California. Following this course, the ocean is always on your left so you can't lose direction. But with the beauty that surrounds you, you may lose your heart south of San Francisco. Sunsets anchored by acres of blooming flowers are rivaled only by those setting over rolling vineyards, or melting into mammoth rock formations along the shore. Romance doesn't linger in the air, it permeates it. Along the way, you'll discover plenty of reasons to pull over into a small village, stroll along a sandy beach, or be mesmerized by the mystique that dusk brings to Monterey's Cannery Row.

Paseo Nuevo

Best known: Stearns Wharf in Santa Barbara and the flower seed fields of Lompoc; the charming Danish village of Solvang and the festivals found at Paso Robles; Hearst Castle; the wind-blown cypress trees and fog-laden cliffs that mark the coastline along the Big Sur.

See map on pg. 9

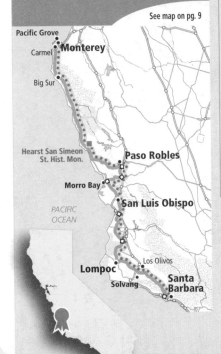

Pacific Grove
Carmel • **Monterey**
Big Sur
Hearst San Simeon St. Hist. Mon. ■
Paso Robles
Morro Bay
PACIFIC OCEAN
San Luis Obispo
Los Olivos
Lompoc
Solvang
Santa Barbara

EDITOR'S PICKS

▶ Paseo Nuevo (Santa Barbara)

Foodies and oenophiles know about Santa Barbara, but so should shoppers. Shopping at its best can be found along the winding pedestrian walks at this outdoor mall anchored by major retailers and Santa Barbara's main thoroughfare, State Street. Small shops offer wares from crystal, jewelry, and children's clothing like This Little Piggy Wears Cotton, to souvenirs, books, and flowers. The area brims with fountains, colorful arches, and casual al fresco dining spots like Pierre Lafond Paseo, a deli that serves wraps, sandwiches, soups, and salads. A classic grilled chicken Caesar Salad is generous enough for two. $8.95 on the luncheon menu.
de la Guerra and State St., (805) 963-2202

▶ Clairmont Lavender Farm (Los Olivos)

Walk through rows of lavender plants on this five-acre farm and then watch as 100-percent organic lavender oil is made using a copper still. The distilling demonstration is free. Once a horse farmer, the owner switched passions to flowers and grows enough product to stock a boutique of all things lavender—essential oils, candles, sachets, and personal products like shampoos and conditioners for people and pets, too. Shampoos for both start at $14.
2480 Roblar Ave., (805) 688-7505

tangent (San Luis Obispo)

Grab a chair at this tasting room before 5:30 p.m. or miss prime sunset seating. Outdoor tables, chairs, and chaises are lined up every day at the restored Independence Schoolhouse-turned-tasting room for tangent's crisp Pinot Gris and Sauvignon Blanc wines and Baileyana's, its sister brand, Pinot Noirs and Syrahs. The schoolhouse, now painted a creamy yellow, is set in the 2,500-acre Edna Valley, part of the Central Coast appellation. Tastings are $5. Open daily, 10 a.m. to 5 p.m.
5828 Orcutt Rd., (805) 269-8200

17-Mile Drive (Pacific Grove)

Located in the Del Monte Forest, this private toll road curves between the Pacific Ocean and multi-million-dollar estates and world-famous golf courses. Open sunrise to sunset, there's ample time to park the car, walk along the shoreline, even picnic. Pull-offs have intriguing names like #12 Spy Glass Hill or #17 the Ghost Tree, which is near Pescadero Point. The Point posts signs warning of "large unexpected waves that will sweep people off their feet." To visitors, just the sight of the Pacific crashing against the rocks does that trick. Enter at Pacific Grove gate. It's $9 per car—free if you ride in on a bicycle. At pull-off

#16, the Lone Cypress perches on rocks. The symbol of Pebble Beach, the wind-swept tree is estimated to be more than 250 years old.
CA 1 at Pebble Beach, Pacific Grove, (831) 624-3811

From Scratch (Carmel)

Breakfast service at this warm, friendly, and family-owned restaurant starts at 8 a.m. Arrive early and grab a newspaper as the locals do before heading toward their regular table. You'll want a paper to read as your order may take some time; it could be 20 minutes. From Hollandaise sauce to bakery goods, menu items are made fresh and from scratch. A fire in a stone fireplace foils the coastal morning chill for patrons wishing to dine inside; later in the day, an arbor protects outside diners from the warm California sun. Breakfast specialties include Roquefort Quiche and made-to-order omelets. Lunch service starts at 11 a.m. and offers Monte Cristo sandwiches that are grilled, not fried. Average price of an entrée: $9.
3626 The Barnyard Shopping Village, (831) 625-2448

MORE GREAT STOPS

Lompoc:
Mural tour, Lompoc Valley Chamber of Commerce
111 South St., (805) 736-4567
www.lompoc.com

Monterey:
Sea Harvest
Fish Market and Restaurant
598 Foam St., (831) 646-0547

Paso Robles:
Holiday Inn Express
Hotel and Suites
2455 Riverside Dr.
(805) 238-6500

San Luis Obispo:
Muzio's Grocery and Deli
870 Monterey St.
(805) 543-0800

Santa Barbara:
Franciscan Inn
109 Bath St., (805) 963-8845

For more romantic travel:

ARIZONA, Scottsdale: At the end of one of the 325 days of cloudless skies, stop what you are doing and catch the sunset as it melts over Camelback Mountain. Then watch as the stars light up the desert sky. *(480) 421-1004; www.experienceScottsdale.com*

CALIFORNIA, San Francisco: Ride a cable car to Ghirardelli Square and then share a chocolate bar while you stroll along Fisherman's Wharf. San Francisco is considered the most romantic of American cities. *(415) 391-2000; www.onlyinsanfrancisco.org*

NEW YORK, Niagara: See the majestic falls from the U.S. side at Prospect Point. Lovers might even catch a rainbow in the mist. *(716) 282-8992; www.niagara-usa.com*

PUERTO RICO, San Juan: Old San Juan's winding, narrow streets lined with pastel buildings exude romance. Visit the adjacent wharf to watch cruise ships glide in and out of the bay. No passport required. *(800) 866-7827; www.gotopuertorico.org*

SOUTH CAROLINA, Charleston: Visit Middleton Place, home of America's oldest landscape gardens (c. 1741) where the flowers, like love, bloom year-round. *(800) 868-8118; www.charlestoncvb.com*

North by Northwoods

Bayfield to Eagle River, Wisconsin

This drive through Wisconsin's Northwoods begins in Bayfield, perched on Lake Superior. Heading south, silky-smooth roads cut through forests once logged nearly bare but now nurtured, as densely green as they ever were. Pack the kids' gear to hike or ski the woods, listening for bird calls. Fish or kayak the waters—eagles may join the family. Ojibwe culture reveals time-honored ways to respect the woods while living in them. The Northwoods offer stops where everyone wants to get out of the car. The journey ends in Eagle River, nestled among a 28-lake chain.

Copper Falls State Park

Best known: Apostle Islands National Lakeshore cruises; Bayfield's Old Rittenhouse Inn; Lake of the Torches resort/casino in Lac du Flambeau; all things snowmobile, including the Snowmobiling Hall of Fame in St. Germain.

See map on pg. 57

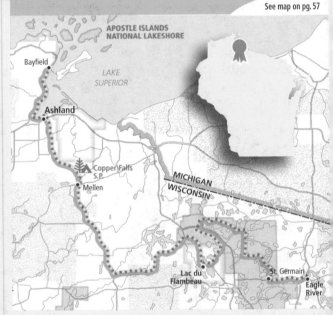

EDITOR'S PICKS

Dreamcatcher Sailing Charters (Bayfield)

Slip between the silent, wooded Apostle Islands aboard sailboats *Esprit* or *Dreamcatcher*. Captain John Thiel charts a course and offers tidbits about lake and island ecology while kids take the wheel and adults trim the jib. Island day trips ($110/person) feature craggy-shoreline exploration by dinghy and lunches of fresh turkey, ham, and hummus on locally baked bread, all washed down with Bayfield's signature apple cider. On the return leg of an afternoon sail ($55/person), the sun sinks toward Bayfield, warming your face as the hull slices through the swell. No worries—a 5,000-lb. keel keeps the boat upright. *City Dock, (715) 779-5561; (800) 262-4176*

Blue Vista Farm (Bayfield)

Northern Wisconsin: snow, lakes, and . . . agriculture with a view? On Blue Vista's slopes, soak up Lake Superior before plunging once more into raspberry canes heavy with plump red fruit ($3.25/lb.). Half-high bushes and dwarf trees invite toddlers to pick their fill of Patriot blueberries and Honeycrisp apples ($2.25/lb., $6/peck). Pick flowers, too. Ball-shaped dahlias, swaying sunflowers, and 300 other varieties grow well given the elevation and southern exposure. Purchase them fresh or dried, even arranged, in the shop tucked into the big red barn's fieldstone foundation. Dried Nigella buds, hanging from the support beams, go for $4/bunch. *34045 County J, (715) 779-5400*

Copper Falls State Park (Mellen)

High above the Bad River gorge, Civilian Conservation Corps-built log fences line the Doughboys' Trail. It was named for the WWI veterans who returned to the Northwoods and cleared the original loop. The current 1.7-mile trail winds through second-growth forest. It's quiet one minute then roaring the next when the Bad River or its tributary, Tyler Forks, plunges over outcroppings of lava on its way to Lake Superior. A disabled-access trail, broad with minimal rise, leads to the park's best outlook, a deck overlooking Brownstone Falls, where Tyler Forks rushes over a precipice to meet the Bad. On Sundays, visitors are treated to a pancake breakfast in the CCC-era concession cabin ($5.95/person). *36764 Copper Falls Rd., (715) 274-5123*

Wa-swa-goning (Lac du Flambeau)

Forest sounds—underbrush rustlings, nuthatches calling, leaves whispering—surround as you tread the path between re-created Ojibwe villages at this cultural exhibit. Small group tours can last 2.5 hours as volunteers explain how the Ojibwe used forest resources to survive outdoors, year-round. Birch bark roofs shed rain from bulrush-sided summer wigwams. Underground tubes carved from birch pipe in air to fuel fires, keeping windproof winter wigwams toasty. The trail ends at the sun-lit log gift shop—no electricity here—where locally made Ojibwe crafts (you're on the Lac du Flambeau reservation) are sold. A startlingly real duck decoy costs $35. *2750 County H, (715) 588-2615*

Chanticleer Inn (Eagle River)

Entire families return to the lakeside inn year after year; Jake and Sue Alward, the innkeepers, greet them by name. Even the chef has been there 30 years and counting. He dresses succulent 8-oz. filet mignon in green peppers, mushrooms, onions, and peppercorns ($27.95). Kids go for the pasta dishes (baked cheese ravioli: $14.50) or classic kids' menu items such as chicken strips ($5.95). Their elders enjoy an array of surf and turf, including a local favorite: walleye pike fillet ($17.95). Wood paneling glows in soft light, the rattle and crush of ice escapes from the bar, two leather sofas gather by the fireplace. Dining room tables overlook Voyageur Lake. *1458 E. Dollar Lake Rd., (715) 479-4486*

Northwoods Children's Museum and Discovery Store (Eagle River)

Even when it's not raining, kids, parents, and grandparents riffle through costumes in the dress-up attic, choose sundries in the old-time general store, and arrange furniture in the pioneer cabin. Twenty activity stations offer hands-on opportunities for families to learn together. If you really liked the catapult in the medieval castle, you can buy it ($20) and the other figurines at the store, which stocks all the activity station toys and then some. Check for events like July's Badger Mining Adventure: Kids uncover minerals common in Wisconsin. *346 W. Division St., (715) 479-4623*

MORE GREAT STOPS

Bayfield:
Apostle Islands Outfitters
10 S. Broad St.
(715) 779-3411

Ashland:
Northern Great Lakes
Visitor Center
29270 County G
(715) 685-9983
www.nglvc.org

Lac du Flambeau:
George W. Brown, Jr. Ojibwe
Museum & Cultural Center
603 Peace Pipe Rd.
(715) 588-3333
www.ldfojibwe.com

Lac du Flambeau:
Dillman's Bay Resort
13277 Dillman's Way
(715) 588-3143
www.dillmans.com

Eagle River:
Farmer's Wife Restaurant
1100 US 45 S.
(715) 479-7428

{ **For more family travel:** }

ARKANSAS, Murfreesboro: Pickings aren't slim at Crater of Diamonds State Park, the only place in the world where visitors may keep any diamonds they find. More than 75,000 sparklers have been uncovered in this 37-acre field. *(870) 285-3113; www.craterofdiamondsstatepark. com*

CALIFORNIA, Palm Desert: The 1,200 acres at The Living Desert zoo and botanical garden are home to more than 125 species of desert-dwelling animals, including meerkats, cinereous vultures, and Gila monsters, as well as 1,000 varieties of plants representing 10 desert ecosystems. *(760) 346-5694; www.livingdesert.org*

KENTUCKY, Louisville: Order your name on a wooden bat when starting a 30-minute tour of the Louisville Slugger Museum & Factory. It'll be finished when the tour is. Everyone receives a mini-bat (nonpersonalized) at tour's end. *(877) 775-8443; www.sluggermuseum.org*

MARYLAND, Tilghman: The *Rebecca T. Ruark,* a working 1886 skipjack, sails from Tilghman Island with waterman Captain Wade Murphy, Jr., as your two-hour tour guide. He invites kids and parents to take the helm. *(410) 886-2176; www.skipjack.org*

MICHIGAN, Grand Rapids: More than 550 carnivorous plants, the Venus flytrap included, inhabit the Carnivorous Plant House at the Frederik Meijer Gardens and Sculpture Park. The Children's Garden offers five acres of themed walkways through Midwest wildlife and geology. *(888) 957-1580; www.meijergardens.org*

Discover America's Past

Historic Jamestowne to Yorktown, Virginia

Curving its way through forested land with nary a billboard or telephone pole in sight, the Colonial Parkway connects America's Historic Triangle of Williamsburg, Jamestown, and Yorktown. Built by the Civilian Conservation Corps in the 1930s, the parkway serves as a time tunnel that leads travelers to the historic reenactment areas in Tidewater Virginia where freedom was won and America began.

The Revolutionary City

EDITOR'S PICKS

► The Revolutionary City (Colonial Williamsburg)

Introduce yourself to Thomas Jefferson and debate the cost of personal freedom with other patriots or loyalists as part of a three-day program called "Revolutionary City." Each interactive two-hour presentation (such as "Citizens at War") re-creates the confusion on the streets in the colonies as the idea of independence is realized. Join the revolution and march behind a fife and drum corps with the people who made it happen.
Duke of Gloucester Street, (800) 447-8679

► Riverfront Discovery (Jamestown Settlement)

Climb on board a replica of the *Susan Constant*, flagship of the three ships that carried colonists, supplies, and livestock to Virginia 400 years ago—but watch your head. The belowdecks quarters are much more cramped than today's passenger ships. Visit with a 17th-century Englishman as he loads and fires a matchlock musket, watch a Powhatan char a cypress tree to make a dugout canoe, and talk with settlers about their lives at James Fort.
VA 31 and Colonial Parkway, (888) 593-4682

► Yorktown Battlefield (Yorktown)

Walk reconstructed berms and original cannon lines built during the siege of Yorktown, which was led by General George Washington. Be sure to stop at the Moore House, often called the historic house that no one remembers. Unheralded Moore House was the location of British surrender negotiations. Ranger-led or self-guided auto tours end at Surrender Field, where the redcoats laid down their arms on October 19, 1781, signaling the end of the Revolutionary War.
Colonial Parkway, (757) 898-2410

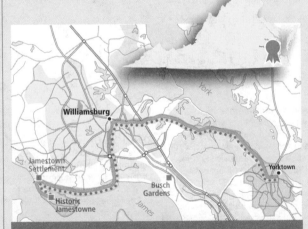

Best known: The elegant architecture of Colonial Williamsburg, the world's largest living history museum; 1607 fort at Historic Jamestowne; Surrender Field at Yorktown; tri-cornered hats and costumed interpreters; replicas of the *Susan Constant, Godspeed,* and *Discovery;* the legend of Pocahontas, and the campus of the College of William and Mary.

See map on pg. 54

Gabriel Archer Tavern at Williamsburg Winery (Williamsburg)

Fifty acres of vineyards provide a spectacular view for lunch or a weekend dinner. If you like to dine al fresco, this is the spot; the terrace is sheltered by a wisteria arbor. The French Country Platter of assorted patés, meats, cheeses, and breadstuffs serves two for lunch ($13) and reflects food choices of the 18th century.
5800 Wessex Hundred, (757) 229-0999

Abbey Stone Theatre at Busch Gardens Europe (Williamsburg)

The seats fill quickly for "Emerald Beat," a musical production of Celtic and contemporary Irish song and dance. While the rhythm and clacking of tap shoes entice the audience to get up and dance, clapping along has to do. Twenty members of Dublin-based O'Shea's School of Irish Dance perform fast-paced tapping and traditional Irish step dancing.
One Busch Gardens Blvd., (800) 343-7946

Riverwalk Landing (Yorktown)

Sun, shop, and dine in Yorktown along the shores of the York River. Shake off the sand from a morning at the beaches along Water Street before browsing the galleries and gift shops at the Landing. There's fine dining and fun food at Nick's Riverwalk Restaurant. Nick's houses three venues including The Rivah Café, which offers a menu of sandwiches from burgers ($8.50) to crab cakes ($9.50).
323 Water St., (757) 875-1522

MORE GREAT STOPS

Historic Jamestowne:
The Archaearium
Colonial Parkway
(757) 229-9776

Williamsburg:
Aromas Coffeehouse
Bakeshop & Café
431 Prince George St.
(757) 221-6676

Williamsburg:
King's Arms Tavern
Duke of Gloucester St.
(757) 229-2141

Yorktown:
Yorktown Waterfront Beach
423 Water St.
(757) 890-3500

Yorktown:
Yorktown Victory Center
VA 120
(757) 887-1776

For more travel through history:

FLORIDA, St. Augustine: Among the most intriguing of St. Augustine's Spanish-period structures are the Castillo de San Marcos, the Basilica of St. Augustine, and the San Agustin Antiguo or Spanish Quarter—a re-creation of an 18th-century Spanish Colonial village. *(800) 653-2489; www.getaway4florida.com*

ILLINOIS, Springfield: For those harboring a desire to have met Abraham Lincoln, a visit to The Abraham Lincoln Presidential Library and Museum is as close as you'll get. In two buildings, it houses the world's largest collection of Lincoln-related documents and artifacts. *(217) 782-5764; www.alplm.org/home.html*

OKLAHOMA, Oklahoma City: The Oklahoma City National Memorial remembers those who lost their lives in the bombing of the Alfred P. Murrah Building on April 19, 1995. The outdoor memorial is open 24 hours a day. *(405) 235-3313; www.oklahomacity nationalmemorial.org*

OREGON, Astoria: The 2,000-acre Lewis and Clark National Historical Park commemorates the arrival at the Pacific Ocean of the Lewis and Clark Expedition in mid-November 1805. Located at the mouth of the Columbia River, it includes the spring, the canoe landing, and a reconstruction of Fort Clatsop, where the expedition wintered. *(503) 861-2471; www.nps.gov/lewi*

PENNSYLVANIA, Gettysburg: Preserved on 5,989 acres, Gettysburg National Military Park is the site of the largest battle of the Civil War. Licensed Battlefield Guides lead two-hour tours; self-guided auto tours stop at key field exhibits and monuments. *(717) 334-1124; www.nps.gov/gett*

High Tide, Low Stress, Big Adventure

Prince Edward Island and the New Brunswick coast, Canada

Trailside Inn and Café

From pastoral green fields and gentle dunes on Prince Edward Island (PEI), across the Confederation Bridge and along New Brunswick's Bay of Fundy coast, this highly scenic drive means low stress and light traffic. Big adventures abound, including climbing PEI lighthouses and kayaking along national parks to hiking along Canada's version of the Appalachian Trail in New Brunswick's Fundy National Park. You can even drive across the ocean floor at low tide to visit Minister's Island. Just be sure to sneak back to the mainland before the tide captures your car!

Best-known: Tour Anne of Green Gables house in Cavendish, PEI; listen to bagpipers at the College of Piping in Summerside, PEI; watch for whales and seals all along the PEI coastline; walk around Hopewell Rocks at low tide in New Brunswick's most-photographed spot; sample smoked salmon and seafood shops just outside Saint Andrews, New Brunswick.

See map on pg. 70-71

EDITOR'S PICKS

Trailside Inn and Café (Mount Stewart, PEI)

Along the 270-km (168-mi.) Confederation Trail, which runs from Tignish to Elmira, the Trailside Inn and Café is housed in a former barn and filled with antiques. It offers four rustic accommodations above the café; tasty fare including chowder and seafood seasoned by herbs picked from the garden outside; and Canadian talent, entertaining on the very intimate stage. Rent bikes by the hour or day to explore the nearby bird sanctuary or to wheel along the trail. *109 Main St., (888) 704-6595*

East Point Lighthouse and Welcome Centre (East Point, PEI)

If the welcome centre's manager Nadine Cheverie seems to know everything about East Point, it's because she grew up here and loves the place. She'll take you up the steps to the top, for a view of cormorants diving and seals playing where the tides of the St. Lawrence and the Northumberland Strait meet in an X shape. If you go to the lighthouse at the other end of the island, you can collect a certificate proclaiming you've been tip to tip. *Rte. 16, (902) 357-2718; (902) 687-3489 October through May*

Lennox Island Ecotourism Complex (Lennox Island, PEI)

Drive over a small bridge into the heart of native Canadian Miq'mak culture on this Miq'mak-owned island. Try geocaching; stroll one of the island's three looped nature trails; taste Mik'maq traditional bread, local oysters, and seafood at the Minegoo Café. Hear about the history from the locals, such as how lightweight and insect-resistant their birch bark wigwams and canoes were. Up to 14 people can stay overnight in the hostel for just $20 CN ($17.60 US). *Rte. 163, off Rte. 12, (866) 831-2702*

Fundy National Park (Alma, NB)

The world's highest tides—as much as 12.2 m (40 ft.) between high and low tides—are the star attraction. Many spectacular hiking trails range from moderate to challenging in difficulty, offering Bay of Fundy views. You can even hike and camp on along the Fundy Trail—Canada's version of the Appalachian Trail—without any houses or roads to disturb your reverie. *Highway 114, (506) 887-6000*

Seascape Kayak Tours (Deer Island, NB)

Bruce Smith runs the original kayaking outfitter for the Canadian Pasamaquoddy Bay area. Guides teach about the high tides and local sea creatures such as lobster, crab, seals, and whales, as kayakers glide through water on 2-hour, 3-hour, or day-long adventures. *40 NW Harbour Branch Rd., (506) 747-1884; (866) 747-1884*

Ovenhead Salmon Smokers (Bethel, NB)

Not all smoked salmon tastes the same, and Ovenhead proves this point with a very smoky, not-too-sweet version of the local specialty. Cold-smoked under maple chip fires, the salmon can be bought at the smokers' headquarters on Ovenhead Road. The menu is simple: smoked salmon, salmon jerky, and salmon paté. *101 Ovenhead Rd., (506) 755-2507*

MORE GREAT STOPS

Winsloe, PEI:
PEI Sweater Shop
Rte. 10
(902) 621-0185

North Rustico, PEI:
Outside Expeditions
Kayaking Tours
370 Harbourview Drive
(902) 963-3366
www.getoutside.com

Saint Andrews, NB:
Fairmont Algonquin Hotel
184 Adolphus St.
(506) 529-8823
www.fairmont.com

Saint Andrews, NB:
Van Horne Estate on
Ministers Island
(506) 529-5081;
(800) 561-0123
www.gnb.ca/0007/Heritage/
ministers.asp

Blacks Harbour, NB:
Grand Manan Car and
Passenger Ferry
Wallace Cove Road
(506) 662-3724
www.coastaltransport.ca

For more adventurous travel:

CANADA, Alberta, Jasper: Strap on some crampons and gently tread over frozen ice flows, past waterfalls stopped by cold temperatures in Jasper National Park's Maligne Canyon. Hikers can hear the water rushing underneath their feet, and sheer granite cliffs rise up on either side. *(780) 852-5595; www.jasperadventurecentre.com*

FLORIDA, Tierra Verde: Fort De Soto Park routinely wins accolades for its sparkly white sand beach, but the marked 2.25-mile recreational canoe trail is the secret gem here for the adventurous. Experienced kayakers may prefer to paddle the 10 miles around Mullet Key. *(727) 464-3347; www.pinellascounty.org/park*

HAWAII, Moloka'i, Kalaupapa: Ride a mule along 26 switchback turns, down 2.9 miles of the world's highest sea cliffs to the Kalaupapa National Historical Park. Home to a former leper colony (only a few elderly residents remain), the real scare is how people with the disease were abandoned here starting in 1866. *(800) 567-7550; www.muleride.com*

UTAH, Springdale: Long, deep canyons and massive granite cliffs define the landscape of Zion National Park. Serious hikers relish the strenuous challenge of Walter's Wiggles on the trail up to Angels Landing, a 1,488-ft. elevation gain to 5,790 ft. on the five-mile round trip. *(435) 772-3256; www.nps.gov/zion*

WEST VIRGINIA, Beckley: Rafters head straight into whitewater exploring the New River Gorge National River or the Gauley River National Recreation Area. Rafting runs from gentle, family friendly sections of the upper New River to full-out rapids on the lower New and Gauley Rivers. *(800) 252-7784; www.class-vi.com*

Culture in Cowboyland

Fort Worth, Texas to Tulsa, Oklahoma

You'll find nary a tumbleweed on the route from Fort Worth to Tulsa. This drive—which passes through both green countryside and busy metropolises as it curves north, then east—is peppered with a surprising number of sleek museums, fine dining, and bijou-filled boutiques. From brimming arts districts to Art Deco architecture, the sights along this drive testify that culture and cowboys are more than compatible.

*Water Taxi,
Oklahoma City*

EDITOR'S PICKS

Kimbell Museum (Fort Worth, TX)

Museums as well respected as the Kimbell can be vast and wearying. But this gem of a collection, with works by Fra Angelico, El Greco, and others, is small enough to manage in an afternoon, with time left over for a game of Frisbee on the lawn, a snooze beside the outdoor fountain, or a bite in the award-winning restaurant. Admission is free.
*3333 Camp Bowie Blvd.,
(817) 332-8451*

Cierra Furniture (Dallas, TX)

Where does owner Tim Heard find the Mexican, Moroccan, traditional African, and Indian housewares, furniture, and art that fill this rabbit warren of a store? "He shops the world," a salesperson says. See (and buy) the fruits of his travels: Red Moroccan drinking glasses etched with gold go for $10 each, while $12 milagros crosses from Mexico line an entire wall.
*2920 N. Henderson Ave.,
(214) 887-8772*

Best known: Fort Worth Stockyards National Historic District; Sixth Floor Museum at Dealey Plaza, Dallas; National Cowboy and Western Heritage Museum and the Oklahoma City National Memorial, Oklahoma City; the Philbrook Museum of Art and the Gilcrease Museum, Tulsa.

See map on pg. 42 (OK) or pg. 51 (TX)

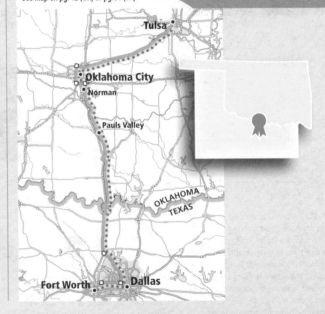

DeGolyer Garden Café (Dallas, TX)

This chic, friendly lunch spot, with white tablecloths and classical music playing on the patio, offers a bit of refined repast in the midst of the Dallas Arboretum's flowery profusion. One entrée: crustless tea sandwiches (cucumber, egg salad, and chicken salad) nestling against each other ($8). During the winter holidays and in the spring, visitors can splurge on high tea (which includes both tea sandwiches and dainty desserts) for $30.95 per person.
In the Dallas Arboretum, 8525 Garland Rd., (214) 515-6512

Bedre Fine Chocolate (Pauls Valley, OK)

Despite its Swedish name (it means "better"), this business is owned by Oklahoma's Chickasaw Nation—more evidence that chocolate is the universal language. Tours include the chance to watch liquid chocolate flow Willy Wonka-style before it solidifies into dark chocolate espresso crème Oklahoma Black Gold Bars ($3.50 each) and other treats that honor the area's heritage. Baskets of samples await in the gift shop. *2001 W. Airline Rd., (405) 207-9320 or (800) 367-5390*

▶ Water Taxi (Oklahoma City, OK)

A shallow, lovely canal winds through the city's historic Bricktown entertainment district (named for its WWI-era deep red brick buildings), and $6.50 grants all-day access to the small boats that glide along it. In the evenings, blues music from neighboring nightclubs drifts over the water. The round-trip ride takes about 40 minutes, but you're welcome to hop on and off throughout. *Buy tickets at dock below Mickey Mantle Boulevard, (405) 234-8294*

▶ Tulsa Gathering Place (Tulsa, OK)

With an hour's notice, glass artist Sarah Diggdon will help visitors to this small shop and studio make their own glass flower to take home. For $25, they'll learn how to swirl or "gather" glowing-hot liquid glass onto a metal rod and shape it into a delicate blossom to keep. Works for sale include vases as bright and flowery as the blooms they're meant to hold ($20 and up). *19 E. Brady, (918) 582-4527*

MORE GREAT STOPS

Dallas, TX:
Tom Tom Asian Grill
3699 McKinney Ave.
(214) 522-1237
www.tomtomasiangrill.com

Fort Worth, TX:
Lone Star Wines
140 E. Exchange Ave.
Ste. 108
(817) 626-1601

Norman, OK:
Fred Jones Jr. Museum of Art
555 Elm Ave.
(405) 325-4938
www.ou.edu/fjjma

Oklahoma City, OK:
Panaderia la Herradura
2235 SW 14th St.
(405) 232-3502

Tulsa, OK:
Linnaeus Teaching Garden
2435 S. Peoria Ave.
(918) 746-5125
www.tulsagardencenter.com

{ For more cultural travel: }

CANADA, Québec, Montréal: Vacationers don't have to go to Europe to have a French vacation. French is the official language of Québec. Montréal boasts a deep connection with its French forebears as a stroll through Old Montréal's narrow lanes attest.
(514) 873-2015;
www.tourism-montreal.org

LOUISIANA, Baton Rouge: To experience working life at a 19th-century plantation, visit Louisiana State University's Rural Life Museum. It re-creates plantation life using 28 buildings filled with artifacts and tools of the day.
(225) 765-2437; rurallife.lsu.edu

MINNESOTA, Minneapolis: While in Minneapolis, home to the acclaimed Guthrie Theater for regional productions, theater fans also can head to Hennepin Avenue for touring Broadway shows.
(888) 676-6757; www.minneapolis.org

NEW MEXICO, Santa Fe: A major culinary and art capital, Santa Fe is a repository of Spanish and Native American culture. Many top spots are within a short stroll of the Palace of the Governors, one of four facilities of the Museum of New Mexico.
(505) 955-6200; www.santafe.org

NORTH DAKOTA, Stanton: Knife River Indian Villages offers a glimpse of life for the Hidatsa Indian tribe on the northern plains before the advent of explorers, fur traders, and settlers. The Hidatsa may have arrived in this area as long ago as the early 1300s.
(701) 745-3300; www.nps.gov/knri

Road Work

Road construction and road conditions resources

Road closed. Single lane traffic ahead. Detour. When you are on the road, knowledge is power. Let Rand McNally help you avoid situations that can result in delays, or worse.

There are ways to prepare for construction traffic and avoid the dangers of poor road conditions. Read on:

1. Use the state and province websites and hotlines listed on this page for road construction and road conditions information.

2. Go to randmcnally.com/roadconstruction for current U.S. and Canadian road construction information.

Road Conditions

Road Construction

Both

Get the info from the 511 hotline

The U.S. Federal Highway Administration has begun implementing a national system of highway and road conditions/construction information for travelers. Under the new plan, travelers can dial 511 and get up-to-date information on roads and highways.

Implementation of 511 is the responsibility of state and local agencies.

For more details, visit: www.fhwa.dot.gov/trafficinfo/511.htm.

United States

Alabama
www.dot.state.al.us/docs ●

Alaska
511 ●
(866) 282-7577 ●
(907) 456-7623 ✿
(907) 269-0450 ⚒
511.alaska.gov ●
In AK: (800) 478-7675 ✿

Arizona
511 ●
(888) 411-7623 ●
www.az511.com ●

Arkansas
(800) 245-1672 ✿
(501) 569-2374 ✿
www.arkansashighways.com ●

California
(916) 445-7623 ⚒
www.dot.ca.gov ●
www.511.org ●
San Francisco Bay and
    Sacramento areas: 511 ●
In CA: (800) 427-7623 ✿

Colorado
511 ●
(303) 639-1111 ●
www.cotrip.org ●
In CO: (877) 315-7623 ●

Connecticut
(860) 594-2650 ✿
www.ct.gov/dot ⚒
In CT: (800) 443-6817 ●

Delaware
www.deldot.net ⚒
In DE: (800) 652-5600 ●
Out of state: (302) 760-2080 ●

Florida
511 ●
www.511tampabay.com ●
www.fl511.com ●

Georgia
(404) 635-8000 ●
(888) 635-8287 ●
www.dot.state.ga.us ●

Hawaii
(808) 536-6566 ⚒
www.hawaii.gov/dot/publicaffairs/
    roadwork/ ⚒

Idaho
511 ●
(888) 432-7623 ●
511.idaho.gov ●

Illinois
(800) 452-4368 ●
(312) 368-4636 ●
www.gettingaroundillinois.com ●

Indiana
(800) 261-7623 ✿
(317) 232-8298 ✿ (12/1-3/31)
www.in.gov/dot ●

Iowa
511 ●
(800) 288-1047 ●
www.511ia.org ●

Kansas
511 ●
(800) 585-7623 ●
511.ksdot.org ●

Kentucky
511 ●
(866) 737-3767 ●
www.511.ky.gov ●

Louisiana
www.511la.org ●

Maine
511 ●
(866) 282-7578 ●
(207) 624-3595 ●
www.511maine.gov ●

Maryland

(800) 327-3125
(800) 541-9595
(410) 582-5650
www.chart.state.md.us

Massachusetts

www.state.ma.us/eotc/
SmarTraveler, Greater Boston only:
   (617) 374-1234

Michigan

(800) 381-8477
www.michigan.gov/mdot/
West and Southwest Michigan:
   (888) 305-7283
Metro Detroit: (800) 641-6368

Minnesota

511
(800) 542-0220
www.511mn.org

Mississippi

(601) 987-1211
(601) 359-7301
www.mdot.state.ms.us

Missouri

(800) 222-6400
www.modot.mo.gov

Montana

511
(800) 226-7623
www.mdt.mt.gov/travinfo/511

Nebraska

511
(800) 906-9069
(402) 471-4533
www.nebraskatransportation.org/

Nevada

511
(877) 687-6237
www.nevadadot.com

New Hampshire

511
(866) 282-7579
www.nh.gov/dot/511

New Jersey

www.state.nj.us/transportation/
   commuter/
Turnpike: (732) 247-0900,
   then 2 , (800) 336-5875 ,
   www.state.nj.us/turnpike/
Garden State Parkway:
   (732) 727-5929

New Mexico

(800) 432-4269
www.nmshtd.state.nm.us

New York

www.dot.state.ny.us
Thruway: (800) 847-8929 ,
   www.thruway.state.ny.us

North Carolina

511
(877) 511-4662
www.ncdotorg/traffictravel

North Dakota

511
(866) 696-3511
www.dot.nd.gov/divisions/
   maintenance/511_nd.html

Ohio

(614) 644-7031
www.buckeyetraffic.org
Cincinnati/northern Kentucky area:
   511 , (513) 333-3333 ,
   www.artimis.org
Turnpike: (440) 234-2030 ,
   (888) 876-7453 ,
   www.ohioturnpike.org
In OH: (888) 264-7623

Oklahoma

(888) 425-2385
(405) 425-2385
www.okladot.state.ok.us

Oregon

511
(800) 977-6368
(503) 588-2941
www.tripcheck.com/Pages/
   AT511.asp

Pennsylvania

www.dot.state.pa.us
In PA: (888) 783-6783
SmarTraveler, Camden/Philadelphia
   area: (215) 567-5678

Rhode Island

511
www2.tmc.state.ri.us
Outside RI: (888) 401-4511

South Carolina

www.dot.state.sc.us

South Dakota

511
(866) 697-3511
www.sddot.com/travinfo.asp

Tennessee

511
www.tn511.com

Texas

(800) 452-9292
www.dot.state.tx.us

Utah

511
(800) 492-2400
(866) 511-8824
www.utahcommuterlink.com

Vermont

511
(800) 429-7623
www.aot.state.vt.us/
   travelinfo.htm
www.511vt.com

Virginia

511
(800) 367-7623
(800) 578-4111
www.511virginia.org

Washington

511
(800) 695-7623
www.wsdot.wa.gov/traffic/

Washington, D.C.

www.ddot.dc.gov

West Virginia

(877) 982-7623
www.wvdot.com

Wisconsin

(800) 762-3947
www.dot.state.wi.us

Wyoming

511
(888) 996-7623
www.dot.state.wy.us

Canada

Alberta

(403) 246-5853
www.trans.gov.ab.ca

British Columbia

(604) 660-9770
www.gov.bc.ca/tran/

Manitoba

(204) 945-3704
www.gov.mb.ca/roadinfo/
In MB: (877) 627-6237

New Brunswick

www1.gnb.ca/cnb/transportation/
   index-e.asp
In NB: (800) 561-4063

Newfoundland & Labrador

www.roads.gov.nl.ca/
   roadreport-information.stm

Nova Scotia

(902) 424-3933
www.gov.ns.ca/tran
In NS: (800) 307-7669

Ontario

www.mto.gov.on.ca
In ON: (800) 268-4686
In Toronto: (416) 235-4686

Prince Edward Island

(902) 368-4770
www.gov.pe.ca/roadconditions

Québec

(888) 355-0511
www.mtq.gouv.qc.ca/en/
   index.asp
In Québec: (877) 393-2363

Saskatchewan

www.highways.gov.sk.ca
Regina and surrounding areas,
   areas outside of province:
   (306) 787-7623
Saskatoon and surrounding areas:
   (306) 933-8333
All other areas: (888) 335-7623

Mexico

www.sct.gob.mx
(in Spanish only)

Numbers to Know

HOTEL RESOURCES

Adam's Mark
Hotels & Resorts
(800) 444-2326
www.adamsmark.com

America's Best Inns
& Suites
(800) 237-8466
www.americasbestinns.com

AmericInn
(800) 396-5007
www.americinn.com

Baymont Inns & Suites
(877) 229-6668
www.baymontinn.com

Best Western
(800) 780-7234
www.bestwestern.com

Budget Host
(800) 283-4678
www.budgethost.com

Clarion Hotels
(877) 424-6423
www.clarioninn.com

Coast Hotels & Resorts
(800) 716-6199
www.coasthotels.com

Comfort Inns
(877) 424-6423
www.comfortinn.com

Comfort Suites
(877) 424-6423
www.comfortsuites.com

Courtyard by Marriott
(888) 236-2427
www.courtyard.com

Crowne Plaza
Hotel & Resorts
(877) 227-6963
www.crowneplaza.com

Days Inn
(800) 329-7466
www.daysinn.com

Delta Hotels & Resorts
(888) 778-5050
(877) 814-7706
www.deltahotels.com

Doubletree Hotels
& Guest Suites
(800) 222-8733
www.doubletree.com

Drury Hotels
(800) 378-7946
www.druryhotels.com

Econo Lodge
(877) 424-6423
www.econolodge.com

Embassy Suites Hotels
(800) 362-2779
www.embassysuites.com

Exel Inns of America
(800) 367-3935
www.exelinns.com

Fairfield Inn by Marriott
(800) 228-2800
www.fairfieldinn.com

Fairmont Hotels & Resorts
(800) 257-7544
www.fairmont.com

Four Points Hotels
by Sheraton
(800) 368-7764
www.fourpoints.com

Four Seasons
Hotels & Resorts
(800) 819-5053
www.fourseasons.com

Hampton Inn
(800) 426-7866
www.hamptoninn.com

Hilton Hotels
(800) 445-8667
www.hilton.com

Holiday Inn
Hotels & Resorts
(800) 465-4329
www.holidayinn.com

Homewood Suites
(800) 225-5466
www.homewood-suites.com

Howard Johnson Lodges
(800) 446-4656
www.hojo.com

Hyatt Hotels & Resorts
(888) 591-1234
www.hyatt.com

InterContinental
Hotels & Resorts
(888) 424-6835
www.intercontinental.com

Jameson Inns
(800) 526-3766
www.jamesoninns.com

Knights Inn
(800) 843-5644
www.knightsinn.com

La Quinta Inn & Suites
(800) 642-4271
www.lq.com

Le Meridien Hotels
(800) 543-4300
www.lemeridien.com

Loews Hotels
(866) 563-9792
www.loewshotels.com

MainStay Suites
(877) 424-6423
www.mainstaysuites.com

Marriott International
(888) 236-2427
www.marriott.com

Microtel Inns & Suites
(800) 771-7171
www.microtelinn.com

Motel 6
(800) 466-8356
www.motel6.com

Omni Hotels
(888) 444-6664
www.omnihotels.com

Park Inn
(888) 201-1801
www.parkinn.com

Preferred Hotels & Resorts
(800) 323-7500
www.preferredhotels.com

Quality Inns & Suites
(877) 424-6423
www.qualityinn.com

Radisson Hotels & Resorts
(888) 201-1718
www.radisson.com

Ramada Inn/
Ramada Limited/
Ramada Plaza Hotels
(800) 272-6232
www.ramada.com

Red Lion Hotels
(800) 733-5466
www.redlion.com

Red Roof Inns
(800) 733-7663
www.redroof.com

Renaissance Hotels
& Resorts
(800) 468-3571
www.renaissancehotels.com

Residence Inn by Marriott
(800) 331-3131
www.residenceinn.com

The Ritz-Carlton
(800) 241-3333
www.ritzcarlton.com

Rodeway Inn
(877) 424-6423
www.rodeway.com

Sheraton Hotels & Resorts
(800) 325-3535
www.sheraton.com

Signature Inns
(800) 526-3766
www.signatureinns.com

Sleep Inn
(877) 424-6423
www.sleepinn.com

Super 8 Motel
(800) 800-8000
www.super8.com

Travelodge Hotels
(800) 578-7878
www.travelodge.com

WestCoast Hotels
(800) 325-4000
www.westcoasthotels.com

Westin Hotels & Resorts
(800) 937-8461
www.westin.com

Wyndham Hotels
& Resorts
(877) 999-3223
www.wyndham.com

NOTE: All toll-free reservation numbers are for the U.S. and Canada unless otherwise noted. These numbers were accurate at press time, but are subject to change. Find more listings or book a hotel online at randmcnally.com.

Eat Your Way Across the U.S.A.

and Canada too!

From gator bashes and annual spud days to the Great Wisconsin Cheese Festival, there are food hot spots all across the U.S.A. and Canada. Check out these 30 food festivals—plus a few suggestions for a side trip to savor a favorite local dish.

Shrimp and Petroleum Festival

Swamp Cabbage Festival

February
La Belle, Florida

As if regular cabbage wasn't bad enough, someone had to come up with swamp cabbage? Actually, this is just the local name for heart of palm. Tender, ivory-colored, and tasting somewhat like artichoke, it's harvested from the stem, or "heart," of Florida's state tree, the sabal palm. La Belle's festival honoring this delicacy features gospel music, armadillo races, and goods made by local Seminole Indians. And, of course, lots of swamp cabbage, served raw, stewed, or frittered. *(863) 675-0125, members.aol.com/browne/scf.html*

LOCAL DISH DETOUR

To: Tampa, Florida
(150 miles NW of La Belle)

Trying to order Spanish bean soup in Spain will get you nowhere, even if you ask nicely ("Garbanzo sopa, por favor"). This dish, made with garbanzo beans, ham and beef bones, salt pork, chorizo, and potatoes, is more or less available only in Florida, specifically Tampa, where it was invented at the Columbia Restaurant (2117 East 7th Ave.) around 1910. Enjoy a bowl while taking in one of the $6 flamenco shows here. Other Tampa soup spots: Carmine's Seventh Avenue (1802 E. 7th Ave.), which offers it with a half-sandwich on the side, and La Tropicana Café, just down the street (1822 E. 7th Ave.).

National Date Festival

February
Indio, California

Sorry, lonely hearts, the date we're talking about here is the fibrous fruit, not the romantic rendezvous. Some 250,000 date palms sway over California's Coachella Valley, producing 35 million pounds of dates annually. Witness the ceremonial Blessing of the Dates, stroll through a shady date palm garden, check out elaborate date exhibits in the "Taj Mahal," and sample more than 50 varieties of dates, including sweet medjools, delicate deglet noors, and caramel-like amer hajjs. *(760) 863-8247, www.datefest.org*

National Date Festival

World Catfish Festival

April
Belzoni, Mississippi

With more than 30,000 acres of land under water and more catfish acreage than any other state, Humphreys County has earned the nickname "Catfish Capital of the World." What better place, then, for the world's largest catfish fry? Sample a genuine Southern midday dinner of fried catfish, hush puppies, and coleslaw. Or save your appetite for the catfish-eating contest: Entrants have 10 minutes to devour three pounds of hot catfish fillets. Watch out for those whiskers! *(800) 408-4838, www.catfishcapitalonline.com*

xvi

Vidalia Onion Festival

April
Vidalia, Georgia

If the thought of biting into an onion brings tears to your eyes, you haven't tried a Vidalia. Not just anyone can grow a Vidalia—the Georgia legislature restricts production of this mild, sweet onion to a 20-county growing area. Munching on raw onions is common practice at this festival, but those who prefer 'em deep-fried can nosh on "blooming onions" and onion rings. There's also an onion cook-off and an onion-eating contest. BYOBM: Bring Your Own Breath Mints. *(912) 538-8687, www.vidaliaonionfestival.com*

Great Wisconsin Cheese Festival

June
Little Chute, Wisconsin

Cheeseheads of the world, this festival's for you. At the free Cheese Tasting, you can sample more than 30 types of cheese, including Wisconsin's native Colby. And no Dairy State experience would be complete without those peanut-sized munchies known as cheese curds. (Connoisseurs say they're best deep-fried.) Don't miss the cheese-carving demos, where barns, cows, and other sculptures take form out of behemoth blocks of cheddar. But please, don't eat the art! *(920) 788-7390, www.littlechutewi.org/calendar_events/cheesefest.html*

Stockton Asparagus Festival

April
Stockton, California

Stockton has asparagus to spare: Nearly 20 tons are cooked during this weekend extravaganza. Fried asparagus is the most popular dish, but asparagus nachos, asparagus pasta, and asparagus margaritas are also on the menu. Watch local celebrities hurl green projectiles through the air in the Spear Throwing Contest, then pose for pics with festival mascots Gus and Brit-Nee Spears. *(209) 644-3740, www.asparagusfest.com*

LOCAL DISH DETOUR
To: San Francisco, California (80 miles W of Stockton)

Cioppino (say chih-PEEN-oh), a fish and tomato stew, is said to have its origins in the early-1900s Italian fishing community of San Francisco. Try it at Cioppino's on Fisherman's Wharf (400 Jefferson St.), which serves it with grilled sourdough toast, or Scoma's (Pier 47 on Al Scoma Way), where you can have it with either a half or a whole crab. At the Tadich Grill (240 California St.) — open since 1849—diners can order a bowl of the house cioppino while sitting in the semi-private booths.

Pink Tomato Festival

Pink Tomato Festival

June
Warren, Arkansas

Bradley County's prize produce might look a little under-ripe, but this is one case where a tomato is supposed to be pink. Unfortunately, the fruit isn't usually shipped because it bruises easily, so southern Arkansas might be the only place to sample what local folks call "the world's tastiest tomato." Taste them for yourself at Warren's festival, which features a tomato-eating contest, pink salsa competition, and an all-tomato luncheon . . . tomato carrot cake, anyone? *(870) 226-5225, www.bradleycountychamberof commerce.com*

LOCAL DISH DETOUR
To: Racine, Wisconsin (144 miles S of Little Chute)

It takes three days to make kringle, the oval coffee cake that Danish immigrants brought to Racine, Wisconsin in the 1800s, the traditional way. Fortunately, the town brims with bakeries that will do the work for you. The O&H Danish Bakery (1841 Douglas Ave. and 4006 Durand Ave.) is a kringle addict's delight—not only can you buy the pastry on site, you can also sign up for the Kringle-of-the-Month Club. Other pastry enablers: Larsen's Bakery (3311 Washington Ave.), and Lehmann's Bakery (4900 Spring St.), which offers a banana-split version by special order.

International Horseradish Festival

June
Collinsville, Illinois

Not only is Collinsville home to the world's largest ketchup bottle, it's also the Horseradish Capital of the World! The bottomlands of the Mississippi are fertile ground for the zesty root, producing more than 60 percent of the world's horseradish each year. This annual celebration features a Root Toss, a recipe contest (mmm . . . horseradish apple pie!), and Root Golf, played with balls carved from horseradish. Pick up a jar of cranberry-horseradish relish or horseradish jelly to kick your next meal up a notch. *(618) 344-2884, www.horseradishfestival.com*

Fish, Fun & Folk Festival

July
Twillingate, Newfoundland & Labrador

There are many reasons to visit the tranquil village of Twillingate: the spectacular coastline, the towering blue icebergs that drift down from the Arctic, the humpback whales just offshore, the friendly people, and of course the annual Fish, Fun & Folk Festival. This celebration of Newfoundland culture and heritage draws top folk musicians and dancers from throughout the province. When the fiddling stops, festivalgoers head to the dining hall for traditional Newfoundland meals of cod, salmon, and lobster. *(709) 884-2678, www.fishfunfolkfestival.com*

Springfield Filbert Festival

Springfield Filbert Festival

August
Springfield, Oregon

In most places they're known as hazelnuts, but here in Oregon's Willamette Valley—which grows 99 percent of the U.S. total—they're called filberts. When you get to Springfield, just look for Phil, the giant papier-mâché nut who watches over the celebration. Munch on spiced, roasted, or chocolate-covered filberts while the kids go nuts in the Nutty Kingdom play area. Then come out of your shell for an old-fashioned ice cream social and live music on two stages. *(541) 746-6750, www.filbertfestival.com*

Olathe Sweet Corn Festival

August
Olathe, Colorado

Nothing says summer like fresh corn-on-the-cob, and in the tiny town of Olathe they've got plenty to give away on festival day (more than 70,000 free ears!). This isn't just any old corn either— it's Olathe Sweet, and it's extra sweet. This special strain grows best in the Uncompahgre Valley, where locals proclaim it "the best sweet corn on the planet." If you're an old pro at cleaning the cob, try chomping past the corn-eating contest record: 32 ears in 12 minutes. *(866) 363-2676, www.olathesweetcornfest.com*

Vermont State Zucchini Fest

August
Ludlow, Vermont

At festival time, Ludlow becomes a zucchini zoo. Kids zoom to the zucchini-carving, zucchini model car racing, and "Dress Your Zucchini Doll" contests, and green-thumbed locals produce their biggest produce for the squash weigh-in. At the "Taste of Zucchini," zuke zealots feast on dishes like zucchini-lemon sorbet and cold zucchini soup, while the less adventurous squash their appetites with fried zucchini and zucchini bread. So if you're zany for zucchini, Ludlow's the place to be this August. *(802) 228-5830, www.okemovalleyvt.org/news/zucchini.html*

Fish, Fun & Folk Festival

Olathe Sweet Corn Festival

Blackberry Festival

August
Powell River, British Columbia

Blackberry vines are as ubiquitous in coastal British Columbia as kudzu in Mississippi. *Rubus armeniacus* is generally considered a thorny nuisance, but the people of Powell River celebrate its plump, sweet fruit each summer with a street party, music, clowns, and, of course, lots of blackberries. Dessert contests for amateur and professional chefs yield delectable dishes like blackberry crème brûlé and blackberry dessert pizza. Winning chefs can usually be persuaded to share their recipes.
(604) 414-5232,
www.discoverpowellriver.com/
visitors/Blackberry.htm

National Lentil Festival

August
Pullman, Washington

Having trouble getting the kids to eat their lentils? Treat them to some of the leguminous delicacies at this festival, and they'll never know what hit 'em. In the past lentil chocolate cake, lentil cookies, and lentil ice cream have topped the list of unusual creations offered in Pullman, heart of the largest U.S. lentil-producing region. Festival highlights include a parade led by mascot Tase T. Lentil, a lentil cook-off, and 250 gallons of free lentil chili. Don't forget to bring home a lentil dog biscuit for Spike.
(800) 365-6948,
www.lentilfest.com

National Lentil Festival

LOCAL DISH DETOUR

To: Vancouver, British Columbia (108 miles SE of Powell River)

Wild salmon have inhabited the pristine Pacific Northwest waters for thousands of years. The five species of Pacific salmon are sold as delicacies in many international markets. The mighty Chinook, or king salmon can grow up to 120 pounds and is a rare catch; the other four are coho, sockeye, pink, and chum. In downtown Vancouver, Salmon Village (779 Thurlow) sells a variety of salmon products, including sockeye and king smoked salmon, Indian candy (smoked salmon marinated in pure Canadian maple syrup), and salmon jerky. The Liliget Feast House (1724 Davie St.) is a First Nations-owned-and-themed restaurant that serves authentic regional dishes and is acclaimed for its imaginative preparation of salmon.

AppleJack Festival

September
Nebraska City, Nebraska

More than 36,000 bushels of apples are picked from orchards around Nebraska City, which celebrates with an applefest each September. Held at different locations around town, activities include picking your own apples at local orchards, apple-pie eating contests, crafts vendors, and a parade. Try all sorts of apple-based goodies, including apple fritters, caramel apples, and apple cider.
(402) 873-6654,
www.nebraskacity.com/ajack.html

Applejack Festival

Shrimp and Petroleum Festival

Shrimp and Petroleum Festival

September
Morgan City, Louisiana

The name of this riverside blowout may conjure up images of dishes named "Shrimp Valdez," but have no fear: Cajun Country's two most important resources are kept separate at all times. Feast on shrimp cooked in so many ways it would "make Forrest Gump proud," then take in the Blessing of the Fleet and the Water Parade, where decorated shrimp trawlers and oil boats motor up and down the Atchafalaya River. *(985) 385-0703, www.shrimp-petrofest.org*

Hard Crab Derby and Fair

September
Crisfield, Maryland

Find a fast crab, because this event's all about pinching out the competition. About 350 of the clawed critters race down a wooden board, vying for trophies for their human cheerleaders. There's also a Governor's Cup race, where crabs representing all 50 states try to out-scuttle each other. (Winners are spared the pot.) A crab-picking contest and a crab-cooking contest round out the festivities. *(800) 782-3913, www.crisfieldchamber.com/ crabderby.htm*

Hatch Chile Festival

September
Hatch, New Mexico

The "Chile Capital of the World" celebrates the harvest with a Chile Queen contest, a cooking contest with everything from chile eggplant parmesan to chile chocolate cake, and literally tons of the famous Hatch chiles. Jalapeños, anchos, serranos, and other varieties are served in tamales, enchiladas, empañadas, burritos, chile rellenos, and chile con carne. If you can take the heat, head to Hatch for this fiery festival. It might take a few days, but the burning in your mouth will eventually fade away. *(505) 267-5050, www.hatchchilefest.com*

Beignets and chicory coffee

LOCAL DISH DETOUR

To: New Orleans, Louisiana (85 miles NE of Morgan City)

Only two things interrupt business at New Orleans's 146-year-old Café du Monde—Christmas Day and hurricanes. Otherwise, both locals and tourists come to the café's original French Quarter location (800 Decatur St.) 24 hours a day, seven days a week for beignets, the fried squares of dough blanketed with powdered sugar and best consumed with a cup of chicory coffee or a steaming café au lait. Nearby at 819 Decatur St., Café Beignet has shorter hours but a more extensive menu. In addition to beignets, here you can try other Cajun specialties such as gumbo. (Both Café du Monde and Café Beignet have other locations around the city, too.) Before the Morning Call Coffee Stand moved outside the city to Metairie (two locations: 3325 Severn Ave. and 4436 Veterans Memorial Blvd. in the Clearview Mall), it too lay in the French Quarter, where it opened in 1870. But its Severn Avenue location still serves beignets around the clock. Wherever you go, be prepared for the unavoidable powdered sugar fallout on your clothes.

Café du Monde

McClure Bean Soup Festival

September
McClure, Pennsylvania

Ever wondered what the Civil War tasted like? Find out at this festival, where ground beef, beans, and lard are slow-cooked in 35-gallon iron kettles just like they were back when the Blue fought the Gray. The festival began in 1891 when Civil War vets got together and cooked up their typical wartime fare at a public dinner. Today, descendants of those veterans and citizens of McClure stir the soup for more than 75,000 festivalgoers. Fireworks, parades, and Civil War reenactments top off the celebration. *(800) 338-7389, www.mcclurebeansoup.com*

Texas Gator Fest

September
Anahuac, Texas

Does alligator really taste like chicken? Find out at this three-day celebration in the Alligator Capital of Texas, where gators outnumber people three to one. Food booths offer such reptilian fare as alligator sausage, fried alligator, grilled alligator legs, and alligator jerky. The festival also features airboat rides, live music, vendors selling alligator products, and the Great Texas Alligator Roundup, in which hunters compete to bring in the biggest gator. (The winners are often longer than 13 feet!) *(409) 267-4190, www.texasgatorfest.com*

Okrafest

September
Checotah, Oklahoma

Notoriously slimy, okra is one of those veggies people either love or hate. Lovers won't want to miss this, one of the only okra celebrations in the United States. Okra cooking contest winners serve a variety of okra foods, which in the past have included pickled okra, okra-dogs, okra gumbo, okra bread, and even okra ice cream. Sample free fried okra from the Okra Pot, which cooks more than 400 pounds of the pod. Antique tractors, live music, and vendors round out the fest. *(918) 473-4178*

Idaho Spud Day

September
Shelley, Idaho

Bingham County is the top potato-growing county in the United States. So when harvest time comes around, there's good reason to celebrate—and to give out free baked potatoes. Spud Day isn't for couch potatoes. Competition is fierce in the Great Potato Games, which feature the World Spud-Picking Championships, and Spud Tug: After a cement mixer fills a pit with mashed potatoes, tug-of-war teams try to pull each other into the glop. There also are potato recipe contests and a kids' parade. *(208) 524-3880*

 LOCAL DISH DETOUR

To: Philadelphia, Pennsylvania (168 miles SE of McClure)

The proper components of a Philadelphia cheese steak are the subject of intense controversy. Is Cheez Whiz preferable to provolone? Should the steak be sliced thickly or chopped into a hash? The only thing everyone seems to agree on: the roll must be from Amoroso's Baking Company. The two best-known places, Pat's King of Steaks (1237 E. Passyunk) and Geno's Steaks (1219 South 9th St.), lie across the street from each other, making a personal taste-test very simple. Though Rick's Philly Steaks (in the Reading Terminal Market, 12th and Arch Sts.) offers chicken and vegetarian versions, no one can deny this place's authenticity—it's run by the grandson of Pat Olivieri, who claims to have invented the cheese steak in 1932. Wherever you go, be ready to give your order the right way—state your cheese choice first (usually "Whiz," provolone, or American), and say "with" or "without" to indicate your onion preference.

Philadelphia cheese steak

Persimmon Festival

September
Mitchell, Indiana

If you've never eaten a persimmon, you can make up for lost time at this weeklong event. The people of Mitchell offer persimmon fudge, bread, cookies, cake, and ice cream, but the most popular dish is pudding. In fact, the Persimmon Pudding Contest grabs more attention than the midway rides, arts and crafts, and candlelight tours of Spring Mill State Park. When the festival's over and withdrawal sets in, don't get caught stealing persimmons from anyone's tree. *(812) 849-4441, www.mitchellpersimmonfestival. org*

Barnesville Pumpkin Festival

September
Barnesville, Ohio

Maybe you've rolled a pumpkin before, but have you ever rolled one uphill with sticks? At Barnesville's fall extravaganza, you can compete against other pumpkin-pushers on a tough 50-foot course. After the race, treat yourself to pumpkin pancakes, pumpkin fudge, or maybe even a pumpkin shake. Don't miss the King Pumpkin contest—winning pumpkins have tipped the scales at more than 1,000 pounds. And FYI, that enormous orange thing looming overhead isn't the Great Pumpkin—it's the town's water tower. *(740) 425-2593, www.barnesvillepumpkinfestival. com*

LOCAL DISH DETOUR

To: Louisville, Kentucky (60 miles SE of Mitchell)

In 1923, chef Fred Schmidt of the Brown Hotel in Louisville got tired of making the same old ham and eggs in the wee hours of the morning for patrons who needed sustenance after the hotel's nightly dinner-dance. So he created the hot brown, an open-faced turkey sandwich with bacon and a creamy parmesan cheese sauce. The Brown Hotel still serves the classic hot brown in its J. Graham's Café (335 W. Broadway), but it's also available in various incarnations at other restaurants around town. The quirkily furnished Lynn's Paradise Café (984 Barret Ave.) serves its rendition, the "Paradise Hot Brown," with a slice of cheddar on top. While patrons wait for their orders here, they can survey the mural made out of beer caps.

LOCAL DISH DETOUR

To: Cincinnati, Ohio (213 miles SW of Barnesville)

It's said that Cincinnati has more chili parlors than it does McDonald's. Most of those are outposts of two chains—Gold Star and Skyline, which both have their fans—but plenty of others thrive as well. At Empress Chili (locations include 8340 Vine St.), you can try the original recipe. This is where, in 1922, Tom Kiradjieff, a Macedonian immigrant, invented Cincinnati-style chili-spiced ground beef in tomato sauce ladled over spaghetti. He's also the one who started the custom of ordering it "two-way" (with spaghetti only), "three-way" (add grated cheese), "four-way" (add chopped onions), or "five-way" (add kidney beans). For a spicier version and 24-hour service, head to Camp Washington Chili (3005 Colerain Ave.), which won a Regional Classics Award from the James Beard Foundation. On the city's west side, Price Hill Chili (4920 Glenway Ave.) reigns; locals often gather here after high school football games to celebrate (or mourn) with a plate of coneys—small hot dogs topped with chili, onions, mustard, and cheese.

Naples Grape Festival

September
Naples, New York

Move over, apple pie. Festivalgoers can't get enough of the famous grape pies introduced in Naples in the 1960s. Over the years, entrants in the World's Greatest Grape Pie Contest have shocked traditionalists with new twists on Irene Bouchard's original recipe, introducing such radical additions as peanut butter and meringue (gasp!). After the judging, try a slice of a competing pie, then kick off your shoes and join in the Grape Stompin' Contest—it's all about how much juice you produce. *(585) 374-2240, www.naplesvalleyny.com/ grapefestival.php*

Norsk Høstfest

October
Minot, North Dakota

North America's largest Scandinavian festival draws 60,000 people to Minot's sprawling All Seasons Arena, which is divided into separate halls representing Denmark, Finland, Iceland, Norway, and Sweden. Booths offer all things Norsk, from birch bark boxes and baskets to rosemaling, runestones, and reindeer skins. On stage there are yodelers, folk dancers, and top-name entertainers. For those who can't stomach lutefisk (cod that's soaked in lye and then boiled), there are other Scandinavian specialties like lefse and Swedish meatballs. *(701) 852-2368, www.hostfest.com*

Boggy Bayou Mullet Festival

October
Niceville, Florida

Elsewhere it might be scorned as a trash fish, or "roadkill with fins," but the people who live along Boggy Bayou love the mullet. And they're out to make converts of the rest of us. They'll serve some 10 tons of the humble bottom feeder—oops, make that "algae eater"—during three days of mullet mania. If smoked or fried mullet doesn't tempt your taste buds, try other local specialties like crawfish bread, boiled peanuts, and alligator-on-a-stick. *(850) 729-4008, www.cityofniceville.org*

Chatsworth Cranberry Festival

October
Chatsworth, New Jersey

You could strap on your waders and jump into one of the dozens of cranberry bogs at the third-largest U.S. cranberry harvest. There's a cornucopia of cranberry creations to sample—from cranberry mustard and cranberry vinegar to cranberry ice cream and cranberry upside-down cake. Just the right blend of sweet and tart to satisfy any palate. *(609) 726-9237, www.cranfest.org*

Kona Coffee Cultural Festival

November
Kailua Kona, Hawaii

There's enough joe here to give anyone the jitters. Hawaii is the only state where coffee is grown commercially, and the Big Island's Kona Coast is renowned for its particularly potent bean. Watch as local growers brew their best coffee at the Cupping Contest, then try your hand harvesting beans at the Kona-picking contest. Pooped after all that picking? Stay awake by sampling different island blends or indulging in a perked-up dessert at the Kona Coffee Recipe Contest. *(808) 326-7820, www.konacoffeefest.com*

Chitlin' Strut

November
Salley, South Carolina

Chitlin' is Southern slang for "chitterling"—a cleaned pig intestine floured and deep-fried in peanut oil. Folks stand in long lines to get their hands on the delicacy, which connoisseurs say tastes similar to pork rinds and has an addictive texture— a crunch followed by a savory chew. Even avid chitlin' eaters agree that the sizzling intestines smell something awful, yet more than 20,000 pounds are devoured on festival day. After dinner, listen to the champs serenade the swine with their best "Sooooey!" at the hog-calling contest. *(803) 258-3485, www.chitlinstrut.com*

LOCAL DISH DETOUR

To: Charleston, South Carolina (112 miles SE of Salley)

When slaves from West Africa arrived in Charleston, South Carolina, in the early 1700s, so did benne seeds, now more commonly known as sesame seeds. Benne seed wafers, now a local tradition, can be bought from many vendors in the downtown open-air shopping area known as the Market (Market St. between Meeting St. and E. Bay St.). One of the biggest purveyors of the treats: the Olde Colony Bakery (1391 B Stuart Engalls Blvd.) in nearby Mount Pleasant, which claims that its recipe is more than 100 years old. Back in Charleston, the Anson Restaurant (12 Anson St.) fancies up the tradition by forming the seed mixture into an edible basket and filling it with ice cream.

LOCAL DISH DETOUR

To: Atlantic City, New Jersey (41 miles S of Chatsworth)

Atlantic City was promoted in the 1800s as a resort for convalescents—a place where the salty sea breezes were reputed to cure everything from consumption to insanity. Now the city's reputation as the home of sticky-sweet saltwater taffy makes any health claims a little harder to justify. James' Candy Company (the Boardwalk at New York Avenue) has been in business since 1880. Its taffy purportedly doesn't stick to candy wrappers (or teeth). Flavors such as cinnamon and coconut can be purchased packaged in a retro souvenir papier-mâché barrel that doubles as a bank. James' also makes chocolate-covered taffy. Fralinger's Original Salt Water Taffy (two locations including 1325 Boardwalk) came along in 1885. The original flavors—chocolate, vanilla, and molasses—are still available, along with others such as peppermint, root beer, and lime. Both companies offer gift packages featuring saltwater taffy alongside other treats such as macaroons, peanut butter chews, and creamy after-dinner mints.

Numbers to Know

RENTAL CAR RESOURCES

**Advantage
Rent-a-Car**
(800) 777-5500
www.arac.com

Alamo
(800) 462-5266
www.alamo.com

Avis
(800) 331-1212
www.avis.com

Budget Rent-a-Car
(800) 527-0700 (U.S.)
www.budget.com

Enterprise Rent-a-Car
(800) 261-7331
www.enterprise.com

Hertz
(800) 654-3131 (U.S.)
(800) 654-3001
(International)
www.hertz.com

National Car Rental
(800) 227-7368
www.nationalcar.com

Payless Car Rental
(800) 729-5377
(U.S., Canada & Mexico)
www.800-payless.com

Thrifty Car Rental
(800) 847-4389
www.thrifty.com

CELL PHONE EMERGENCY NUMBERS

Alabama *47
Alaska 911
Arizona 911
Arkansas 911
California 911
Colorado 911; *277; (303) 329-4501
Connecticut 911
Delaware 911
District of Columbia 911
Florida 911

Georgia 911
Hawaii None
Idaho *477
Illinois 911
Indiana 911
Iowa 911; *55
Kansas *47
Kentucky (800) 222-5555 (in KY)
Louisiana 911
Maine 911

Maryland 911
Massachusetts 911
Michigan 911
Minnesota 911
Mississippi 911
Missouri *55
Montana 911
Nebraska 911
Nevada *647
New Hampshire 911
New Jersey 911
New Mexico 911
New York 911
North Carolina 911
North Dakota *2121
Ohio 911

Oklahoma 911
Oregon 911
Pennsylvania 911
Rhode Island 911
South Carolina 911
South Dakota 911
Tennessee 911
Texas 911
Utah 911
Vermont 911
Virginia 911
Washington 911
West Virginia 911
Wisconsin 911
Wyoming 911

Map Legend

Roads and related symbols
Free limited-access highway
Toll limited-access highway
New road (under construction as of press time)
Other multilane highway
Principal highway
Other through highway
Other road (conditions vary — local inquiry suggested)
Unpaved road (conditions vary — local inquiry suggested)
One way route; ferry
Interstate highway; Interstate highway business route
U.S. highway; U.S. highway business route
Trans-Canada highway; Autoroute
Mexican highway or Central American highway
State or provincial highway
Secondary state, secondary provincial, or county highway
County trunk highway
Toll booth or fee booth
Tunnel; mountain pass
Interchanges and exit numbers (For most states, the mileage between interchanges may be determined by subtracting one number from the other.)
Highway miles between arrows (Segments of one mile or less not shown.)
Comparative distance
1 mile = 1.609 kilometers   1 kilometer = 0.621 mile

Cities & towns (size of type on map indicates relative population)
National capital; state or provincial capital
County seat or independent city
City, town, or recognized place; neighborhood
Urbanized area
Separate cities within metropolitan area

Parks, recreation areas, & points of interest
U.S. or Canadian national park
U.S. or Canadian national monument, other National Park Service facility, state or provincial park, or recreation area
Park with camping facilities; park without camping facilities
National forest, national grassland, or city park; wildlife refuge
Point of interest, historic site or monument
Airport
Campsite; golf course or country club
Hospital or medical center
Indian reservation
Information center or Tourist Information Center (T.I.C.)
Military or governmental installation; military airport

Physical features
Dam
Mountain peak; highest point in state/province
Lake; dry lake
River; intermittent river
Desert; glacier
Swamp or mangrove swamp

Other symbols
Area shown in greater detail on inset map
Inset map page indicator
Intracoastal waterway
County or parish boundary and name
State or provincial boundary
National boundary
Continental divide
Time zone boundary

Population figures are from the latest available census or are Census Bureau or Rand McNally estimates.
For a complete list of abbreviations that appear on the maps, visit go.randmcnally.com/ABBR.
©2008 Rand McNally & Company

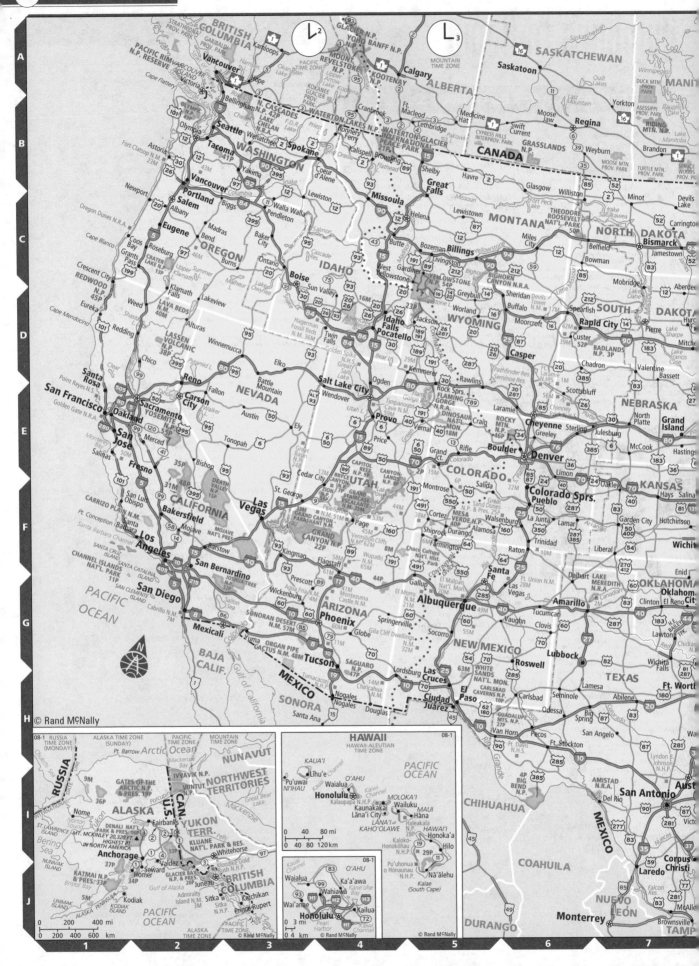

© Rand McNally

National Monuments and Memorials

1M	Agate Fossil Beds	E-6
2M	Alibates Flint Quarries	G-7
3M	Admiralty Island	J-3
4M	Agua Fria	G-4
5M	Aniakchak	J-1
6M	Aztec Ruins	F-5
7M	Cabrillo	G-2
8M	Canyon de Chelly	F-4
9M	Cape Krusenstern	I-1
10M	Capulin Volcano	F-6
11M	Casa Grande Ruins	G-4
12M	Castillo de San Marcos	H-12
13M	Cedar Breaks	F-4
14M	Chiricahua	H-4
15M	Colorado	E-5
16M	Craters of the Moon	D-4
17M	Devils Tower	D-6
18M	Dinosaur	E-5
19M	Effigy Mounds	D-9
20M	El Malpais	G-5
21M	El Morro	G-5
22M	Florissant Fossil Beds	F-6
23M	Fort Clatsop	B-2
24M	Fort Frederica	H-12
25M	Fort Matanzas	H-12
26M	Fort Pulaski	H-12
27M	Fort Sumter	G-12
28M	Fort Union	G-6
29M	Fossil Butte	D-5
30M	George Washington Carver	F-8
31M	Giant Sequoia	F-2
32M	Gila Cliff Dwellings	G-5
33M	Grand Canyon-Parashant	F-3
34M	Grand Portage	C-9
35M	Grand Staircase-Escalante	F-4
36M	Hagerman Fossil Beds	D-4
37M	Homestead	E-8
38M	Hovenweep	F-5
39M	Jewel Cave	D-6
40M	Lava Beds	D-2
41M	Montezuma Castle	G-4
42M	Mount Rushmore	D-6
43M	Mount St. Helens	B-2
44M	Natural Bridges	F-4
45M	Navajo	F-4
46M	Newberry Volcanic	C-2
47M	Ocmulgee	H-11
48M	Organ Pipe Cactus	G-3
49M	Petroglyph	F-5
50M	Pinnacles	E-1
51M	Pipe Spring	F-4
52M	Pipestone	D-8
53M	Rainbow Bridge	F-4
54M	Russell Cave	G-10
55M	Salinas Pueblo Missions	G-5
56M	Scotts Bluff	E-6
57M	Sonoran Desert	G-3
58M	Sunset Crater Volcano	F-4
59M	Timpanogos Cave	E-4
60M	Tonto	G-4
61M	Tuzigoot	G-4
62M	Vermillion Cliffs	F-4
63M	White Sands	H-5
64M	Wright Brothers	F-13
65M	Wupatki	F-4

National Parks

1P	Acadia	C-14
2P	Arches	E-5
3P	Badlands	D-7
4P	Big Bend	H-6
5P	Biscayne	J-13
6P	Black Canyon	F-5
7P	Bryce Canyon	F-4
8P	Canyonlands	F-4
9P	Capitol Reef	F-4
10P	Carlsbad Caverns	H-6
11P	Channel Islands	F-1
12P	Congaree	G-12
13P	Crater Lake	C-2
14P	Cuyahoga Valley	E-11
15P	Death Valley	E-3
16P	Denali	I-2
17P	Dry Tortugas	J-12
18P	Everglades	J-12
19P	Gates of the Arctic	I-1
20P	Glacier Bay	J-2
21P	Glacier	B-4
22P	Grand Canyon	F-4
23P	Grand Teton	D-5
24P	Great Basin	E-3
25P	Great Sand Dunes	F-6
26P	Great Smoky Mts.	G-11
27P	Guadalupe Mts.	H-5
28P	Haleakala	I-4
29P	Hawai'i Volcanoes	J-5
30P	Hot Springs	G-8
31P	Isle Royale	C-9
32P	Joshua Tree	G-3
33P	Katmai	J-1
34P	Kenai Fjords	J-2
35P	Kings Canyon	E-2
36P	Kobuk Valley	I-1
37P	Lake Clark	J-1
38P	Lassen Volcanic	D-2
39P	Mammoth Cave	F-10
40P	Mesa Verde	F-5
41P	Mt. Rainier	B-3
42P	North Cascades	B-3
43P	Olympic	B-2
44P	Petrified Forest	G-4
45P	Redwood	C-1
46P	Rocky Mountain	E-6
47P	Saguaro	H-4
48P	Sequoia	F-2
49P	Shenandoah	E-12
50P	Theodore Roosevelt	C-6
51P	Voyageurs	C-8
52P	Wind Cave	D-6
53P	Wrangell-St. Elias	C-5
54P	Yellowstone	D-5
55P	Yosemite	E-2
56P	Zion	F-4

08-1

Alabama

Population: 4,557,808
Land area: 50,744 sq. mi.
Capital: Montgomery

Cities and Towns

Abbeville	H-6
Alabaster	D-3
Albertville	B-4
Alexander City	E-5
Aliceville	E-1
Andalusia	H-4
Anniston	C-5
Arab	B-4
Ashland	D-5
Ashville	C-4
Athens	A-3
Atmore	I-2
Attalla	C-4
Auburn	E-6
Bay Minette	I-2
Bessemer	D-3
Birmingham	D-3
Boaz	B-4
Brent	E-3
Brewton	H-3
Bridgeport	A-5
Brundidge	G-5
Butler	G-1
Calera	E-3
Camden	G-3
Carbon Hill	C-2
Carrollton	D-1
Centre	C-5
Centreville	E-3
Chatom	H-1
Childersburg	D-4
Citronelle	H-1
Clanton	E-4
Clayton	G-6
Columbiana	D-4
Cottondale	D-2
Cullman	C-3
Dadeville	E-5
Daleville	H-5
Decatur	B-3
Demopolis	F-2
Dothan	H-6
Double Springs	C-2
East Brewton	H-3
Elba	H-5
Enterprise	H-5
Eufaula	G-6
Eutaw	E-2
Evergreen	H-3
Fairfield	D-3
Fairhope	J-1
Fayette	C-2
Florala	I-4
Florence	J-2
Foley	J-2
Fort Payne	B-5
Gadsden	C-5
Geneva	I-5
Greensboro	E-2
Greenville	G-4
Grove Hill	G-2
Guin	C-2
Gulf Shores	J-2
Guntersville	B-4
Haleyville	B-2
Hamilton	C-1
Hanceville	C-3
Hartford	H-5
Hartselle	B-3
Hayneville	F-4
Hazel Green	A-4
Headland	H-6
Heflin	D-5
Homewood	D-3
Hoover	D-3
Huntsville	A-4
Jackson	H-2
Jacksonville	C-5
Jasper	C-3
Lafayette	E-6
Lanett	E-6
Leeds	D-4
Lincoln	D-4
Linden	F-2
Lineville	D-5
Livingston	F-1
Luverne	G-4
Marion	E-2
Mobile	I-1
Monroeville	H-2
Montevallo	E-3
Montgomery	F-4
Moulton	B-3
Mountain Brook	D-4
Muscle Shoals	A-2
Northport	D-2
Oneonta	C-4
Opelika	E-6
Opp	H-4
Orange Beach	J-2
Oxford	D-5
Ozark	H-5
Pell City	D-4
Phenix City	F-6
Piedmont	C-5
Point Clear	J-1
Prattville	F-4
Prichard	I-1
Rainbow City	C-5
Rainsville	B-5
Red Bay	B-1
Reform	D-1
Roanoke	D-6
Robertsdale	J-2
Russellville	B-2
Samson	H-5
Saraland	I-1
Scottsboro	B-5
Selma	F-3
Sheffield	A-2
Spanish Fort	I-1
Stevenson	A-5
Sumiton	C-3
Sylacauga	D-4
Talladega	D-5
Tallassee	F-5
Tarrant	D-3
Theodore	J-1
Thomasville	G-2
Troy	G-5
Tuscaloosa	D-2
Tuscumbia	A-2
Tuskegee	F-5
Union Springs	F-5
Valley	E-6
Vernon	C-1
Warrior	C-3
Wedowee	D-5
Wetumpka	F-4
Winfield	C-2
York	F-1

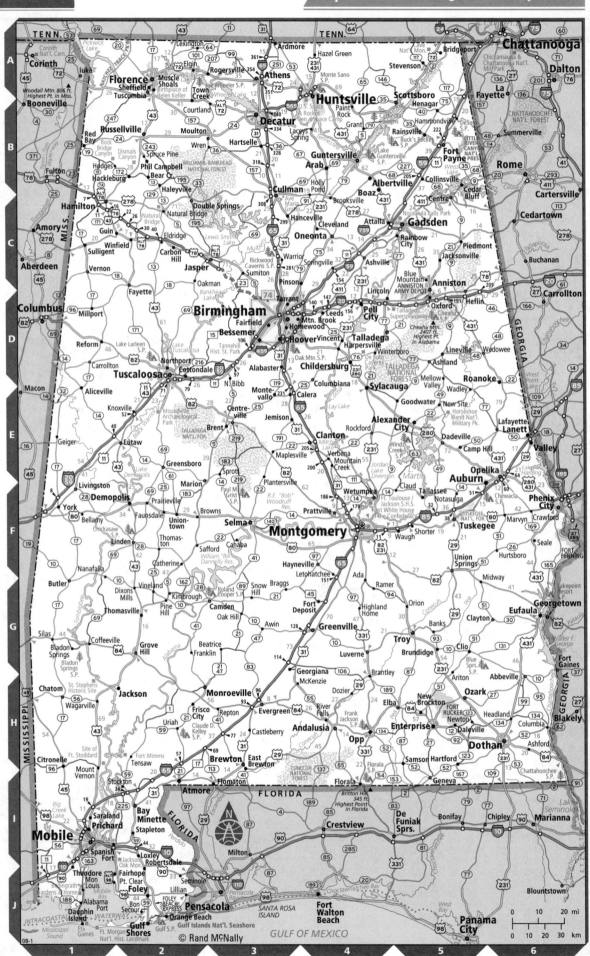

© Rand McNally

08-1

Alaska

Population: 663,661
Land area: 571,951 sq. mi.
Capital: Juneau

Cities and Towns

Akiachak	D-3
Akutan	F-1
Alakanuk	C-2
Ambler	B-4
Anchor Point	D-5
Anchorage	D-5
Anderson	C-5
Angoon	E-7
Aniak	D-3
Barrow	A-4
Bethel	D-3
Big Delta	C-5
Buckland	B-3
Cantwell	C-5
Chevak	C-2
Circle	C-6
Circle Hot Springs	C-5
College	C-5
Copper Center	D-6
Cordova	D-6
Craig	F-8
Delta Junction	C-5
Dillingham	E-3
Douglas	E-7
Eagle	C-6
Elim	C-3
Emmonak	C-2
Fairbanks	C-5
Fort Yukon	B-5
Galena	C-4
Gambell	C-1
Glennallen	D-6
Gustavus	E-7
Haines	E-7
Healy	C-5
Homer	D-5
Hoonah	E-7
Hooper Bay	D-2
Hydaburg	F-8
Idaitarod	D-3
Juneau	E-7
Kake	E-7
Kenai	D-5
Ketchikan	F-8
King Cove	F-1
King Salmon	E-3
Kipnuk	D-2
Kivalina	B-3
Klawock	F-8
Kodiak	E-4
Kotlik	C-2
Kotzebue	B-3
Koyuk	C-3
Kwethluk	D-3
Kwigillingok	D-2
Manokotak	E-3
McGrath	C-4
Metlakatla	F-8
Mountain Village	C-2
Naknek	E-3
Nenana	C-5
New Stuyahok	D-3
Nikiski	D-5
Ninilchik	D-5
Noatak	B-3
Nome	C-2
Noorvik	B-3
North Pole	C-5
Nulato	C-4
Palmer	D-5
Perryville	E-3
Petersburg	E-7
Pilot Station	C-2
Point Hope	B-2
Prudhoe Bay	A-5
Quinhagak	D-2
Ruby	C-4
St. Michael	C-3
Sand Point	F-2
Savoonga	C-1
Scammon Bay	C-2
Selawik	B-3
Seward	D-5
Shaktoolik	C-3
Shungnak	B-4
Sitka	E-7
Skagway	E-7
Soldotna	D-5
Stebbins	C-2
Talkeetna	D-5
Tanana	C-4
Teller	C-2
Togiak	E-3
Tok	C-6
Toksook Bay	D-2
Umiat	B-4
Unalakleet	C-3
Unalaska	F-1
Valdez	D-6
Venetie	B-5
Wainwright	A-3
Wasilla	D-5
Willow	D-5
Wrangell	E-7
Yakutat	E-6

For border crossing information,
please see p. 59

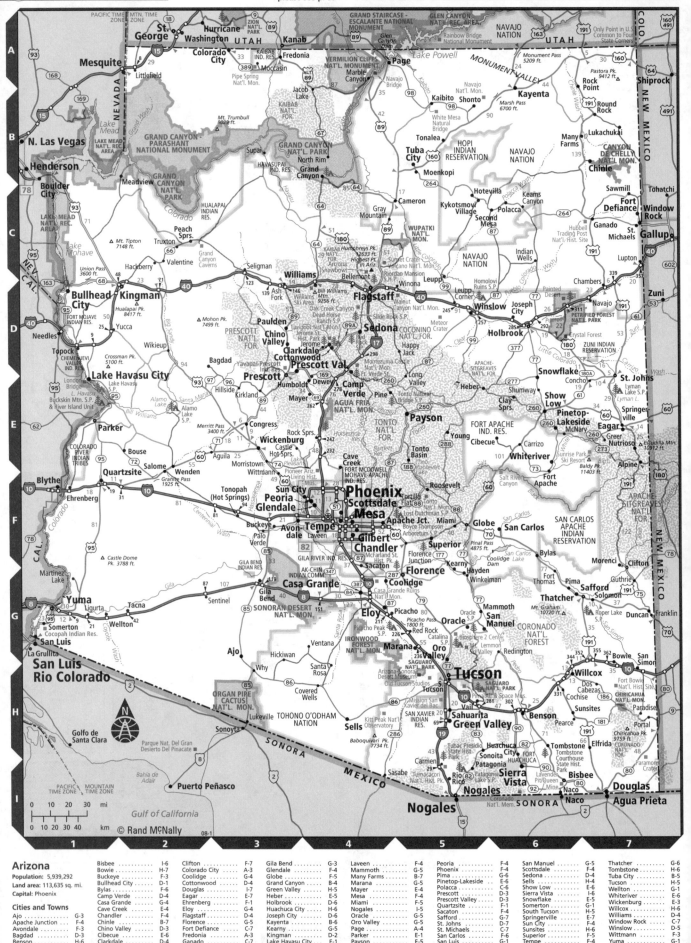

Arizona

Population: 5,939,292
Land area: 113,635 sq. mi.
Capital: Phoenix

Cities and Towns

Ajo	G-3	Bisbee	I-6
Apache Junction	F-4	Bowie	H-7
Avondale	F-3	Buckeye	F-3
Bagdad	D-3	Bullhead City	D-1
Benson	H-6	Bylas	F-6
		Camp Verde	D-4
		Casa Grande	G-4
		Cave Creek	E-4
		Chandler	F-4
		Chinle	B-7
		Chino Valley	D-3
		Clarkdale	D-4
Clifton	F-7
Colorado City	A-3
Coolidge	G-4
Cottonwood	D-4
Douglas	I-7
Eagar	E-7
Ehrenberg	F-1
Eloy	G-4
Flagstaff	D-4
Florence	G-5
Fort Defiance	C-7
Fredonia	A-3
Ganado	C-7
Gila Bend	G-3
Glendale	F-4
Globe	F-5
Grand Canyon	B-4
Green Valley	H-5
Heber	E-5
Holbrook	D-6
Huachuca City	H-6
Joseph City	D-6
Kayenta	B-6
Kearny	G-5
Kingman	D-2
Lake Havasu City	E-1
Laveen	F-4
Mammoth	G-5
Many Farms	B-7
Marana	G-5
Mayer	E-4
Mesa	F-4
Miami	F-5
Nogales	I-5
Oracle	G-5
Oro Valley	G-5
Page	A-4
Parker	E-1
Payson	E-5
Peoria	F-4
Phoenix	F-4
Pima	G-6
Pinetop-Lakeside	E-6
Polacca	C-6
Prescott	D-3
Prescott Valley	D-3
Quartzsite	F-1
Sacaton	F-4
Safford	G-7
San Carlos	F-6
San Luis	G-1
San Manuel	G-5
Scottsdale	F-4
Sedona	D-4
Sells	H-4
Show Low	E-6
Sierra Vista	I-6
Snowflake	D-6
Somerton	G-1
South Tucson	H-5
Springerville	E-7
St. Johns	D-7
St. Michaels	C-7
Sun City	F-4
Sunsites	H-6
Superior	F-5
Tempe	F-4
Thatcher	G-6
Tombstone	H-6
Tuba City	B-5
Tucson	H-5
Wellton	G-1
Whiteriver	E-6
Wickenburg	E-3
Willcox	H-6
Williams	D-4
Window Rock	C-7
Winslow	D-5
Wittmann	F-3
Yuma	G-1

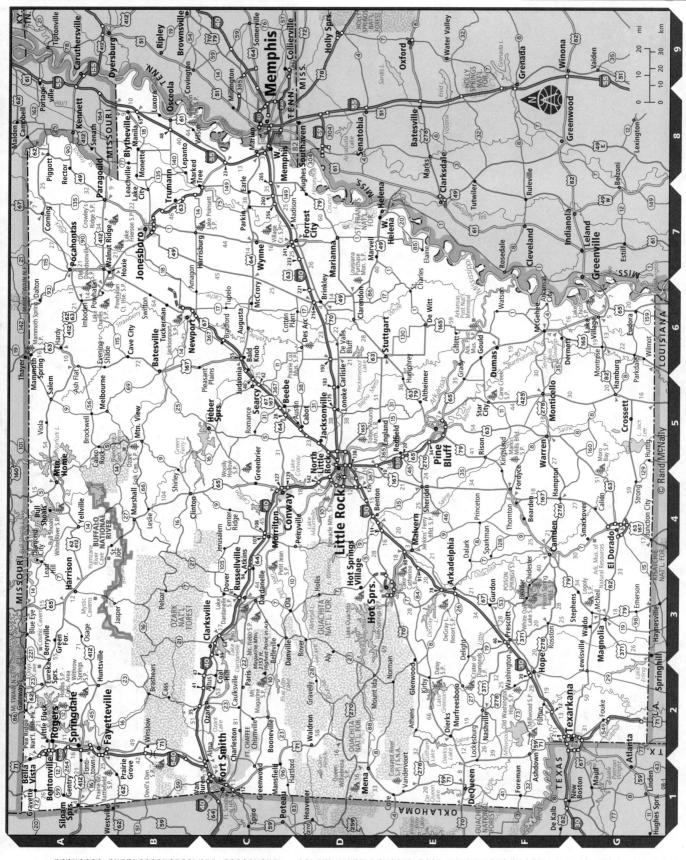

© Rand McNally

Arkansas

Population: 2,779,154
Land area: 52,068 sq. mi.
Capital: Little Rock

Cities and Towns

Arkadelphia	E-3
Arkansas City	F-6
Ash Flat	A-6
Ashdown	G-2
Augusta	C-6
Bald Knob	C-6
Beebe	C-5
Bella Vista	A-1
Benton	D-4
Bentonville	A-2
Berryville	A-2
Blytheville	B-8
Brinkley	D-6
Bull Shoals	A-4
Cabot	D-5
Camden	F-4
Charleston	C-2
Clarendon	D-6
Clinton	C-4
Conway	D-4
Corning	A-7
Crossett	F-6
Danville	D-3
Dardanelle	C-3
De Queen	E-2
De Valls Bluff	D-6
De Witt	D-6
Des Arc	D-6
Dumas	E-6
El Dorado	F-4
Eureka Springs	A-2
Evening Shade	B-6
Fayetteville	B-2
Fordyce	E-4
Forrest City	C-7
Fort Smith	C-1
Greenwood	C-1
Hamburg	F-6
Hampton	F-4
Harrisburg	B-7
Harrison	A-3
Heber Springs	C-5
Helena	D-7
Hope	F-3
Hot Springs	D-3
Huntsville	B-2
Jacksonville	D-5
Jasper	B-3
Jonesboro	B-7
Lake City	B-7
Lake Village	F-6
Lewisville	F-3
Little Rock	D-4
Lonoke	D-5
Magnolia	F-3
Malvern	E-4
Marianna	D-7
Marion	C-8
Marshall	B-4
McGehee	E-6
Melbourne	B-5
Mena	D-2
Monticello	E-5
Morrilton	C-4
Mount Ida	D-3
Mountain Home	A-4
Mountain View	B-5
Murfreesboro	E-2
Nashville	E-2
Newport	B-6
North Little Rock	D-5
Osceola	B-8
Ozark	C-2
Paragould	A-7
Paris	C-2
Perryville	D-4
Piggott	A-7
Pine Bluff	E-5
Pocahontas	A-6
Prescott	F-3
Rison	E-5
Rogers	A-2
Russellville	C-3
Salem	A-5
Searcy	C-5
Sheridan	E-4
Siloam Springs	A-1
Springdale	A-2
Star City	E-5
Stuttgart	D-6
Texarkana	G-2
Trumann	B-7
Van Buren	C-1
Viola	A-5
Waldron	D-2
Walnut Ridge	A-7
Warren	F-5
West Helena	D-7
West Memphis	C-8
Wynne	C-7
Yellville	A-4

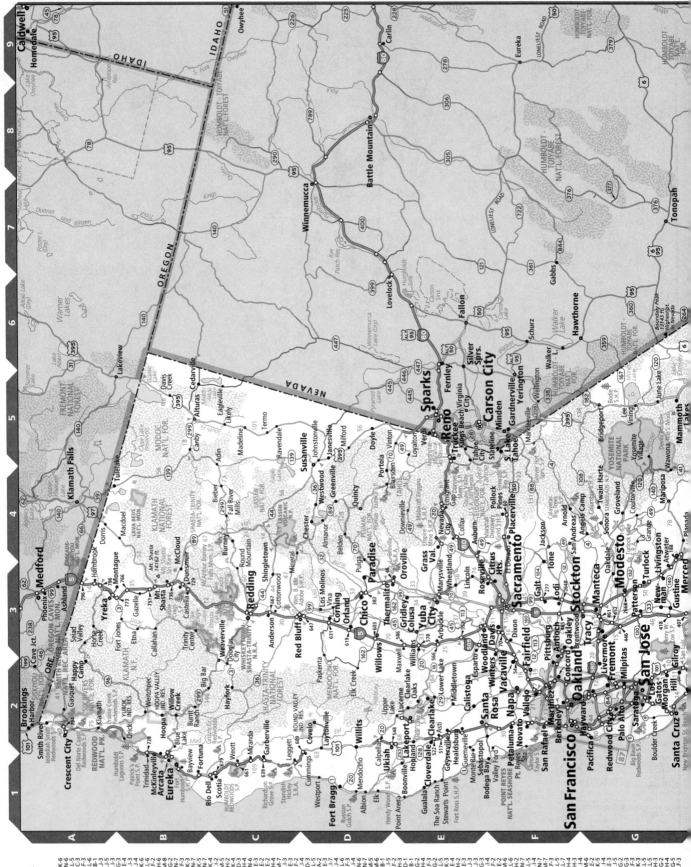

California
Population: 36,132,147
Land area: 155,959 sq. mi.
Capital: Sacramento

Cities and Towns

Adelanto	K-6
Alpine	N-6
Anaheim	L-5
Anderson	C-3
Antioch	F-3
Apple Valley	L-6
Arcata	B-1
Arroyo Grande	J-5
Arvin	K-4
Atascadero	J-4
Atwater	H-3
Auburn	E-3
Avenal	J-4
Bakersfield	K-5
Barstow	L-6
Beaumont	M-6
Berkeley	F-2
Bishop	H-6
Blythe	M-8
Boulder Creek	G-2
Brawley	N-7
Brentwood	F-3
Buellton	J-4
California City	K-6
Calexico	N-7
Calipatria	N-7
Camarillo	K-5
Cambria	J-4
Carlsbad	M-6
Carmel	H-2
Carpinteria	K-5
Chico	D-3
Chowchilla	H-4
Chula Vista	N-6
Citrus Heights	E-3
Clearlake	F-2
Cloverdale	F-2
Clovis	H-4
Coachella	M-7
Coalinga	J-4
Colusa	E-2
Concord	F-2
Corcoran	J-4
Corning	D-2
Corona	L-6
Crescent City	A-2
Davis	E-2
Death Valley	J-7
Delano	K-5
Desert Hot Springs	M-7
Dixon	F-2
Earlimart	J-5
El Cajon	N-6
El Centro	N-7
Encinitas	M-5
Escondido	M-6
Eureka	B-1
Exeter	J-5
Fairfield	F-2
Firebaugh	H-3
Fort Bragg	E-1
Fortuna	B-1
Fremont	G-2
Fresno	H-4
Galt	F-3
Gilroy	G-2
Glendale	L-5
Goleta	K-4
Grass Valley	E-3
Greenfield	H-3
Gridley	D-3
Grover Beach	J-4
Guadalupe	J-4
Gustine	H-3
Hanford	J-4
Hayward	G-2
Healdsburg	F-2
Hemet	M-6
Hesperia	L-6
Hollister	H-3
Holtville	N-7
Huron	J-4
Imperial	N-7
Indio	M-7
Irvine	L-6
Joshua Tree	M-7
Kerman	H-4
King City	H-3
Lake Elsinore	M-6
Lakeport	F-2
Lancaster	K-5
Lemoore	J-4
Lincoln	E-3
Lindsay	J-5
Livermore	G-2
Livingston	H-3
Lodi	F-3
Lompoc	K-4
Long Beach	L-5
Los Angeles	L-5
Los Banos	H-3
Madera	H-4
Mammoth Lakes	H-5

© Rand McNally

Marina ... H-2
Martinez ... F-2
Marysville ... E-3
McFarland ... J-4
McKinleyville ... B-1
Mendota ... H-3
Milpitas ... G-2
Modesto ... G-3
Mojave ... K-5
Montecito ... L-4
Monterey ... H-2
Moreno Valley ... L-6
Morgan Hill ... G-2
Morro Bay ... J-2
Murrieta ... M-6
Napa ... F-2
Needles ... K-9
Newman ... G-3
Newport Beach ... L-5
Novato ... F-2
Oakdale ... G-3
Oakland ... G-2
Oakley ... G-2
Oceanside ... M-6
Oildale ... J-4
Ontario ... L-5
Orland ... D-2
Oroville ... E-3
Oxnard ... L-4
Pacific Grove ... H-2
Pacifica ... G-2
Palm Desert ... L-7
Palm Springs ... L-6
Palo Alto ... G-2
Paradise ... D-3
Pasadena ... L-5
Paso Robles ... J-3
Patterson ... G-3
Perris ... L-6
Petaluma ... F-2
Pittsburg ... F-2
Placerville ... F-3
Planada ... G-3
Pollock Pines ... F-3
Pomona ... L-5
Porterville ... J-4
Quincy ... D-4
Ramona ... M-6
Red Bluff ... C-3
Redding ... C-3
Redlands ... L-6
Redwood City ... G-2
Reedley ... H-4
Ridgecrest ... J-5
Riverside ... L-6
Rosamond ... K-5
Roseville ... F-3
Sacramento ... F-3
Salinas ... H-2
San Bernardino ... L-6
San Clemente ... M-5
San Diego ... N-6
San Francisco ... G-2
San Jose ... G-2
San Juan Capistrano ... M-5
San Luis Obispo ... J-3
San Rafael ... F-2
Santa Ana ... L-5
Santa Barbara ... L-4
Santa Clarita ... K-4
Santa Cruz ... H-2
Santa Maria ... K-3
Santa Monica ... L-4
Santa Paula ... L-4
Santa Rosa ... F-2
Saratoga ... G-2
Seaside ... H-2
Selma ... H-4
Shafter ... J-4
Simi Valley ... L-4
Solvang ... K-3
Sonora ... F-4
South Lake Tahoe ... E-4
Stockton ... G-3
Susanville ... C-4
Taft ... K-4
Tehachapi ... K-5
Temecula ... M-6
Thermalito ... E-3
Thousand Oaks ... L-4
Torrance ... L-4
Truckee ... E-4
Tulare ... H-4
Turlock ... G-3
Twentynine Palms ... L-7
Ukiah ... D-2
Vacaville ... F-3
Vallejo ... F-2
Ventura ... L-4
Victorville ... K-6
Visalia ... H-4
Vista ... M-6
Wasco ... J-4
Watsonville ... H-2
Willows ... D-2
Winters ... E-3
Woodlake ... H-4
Woodland ... E-3

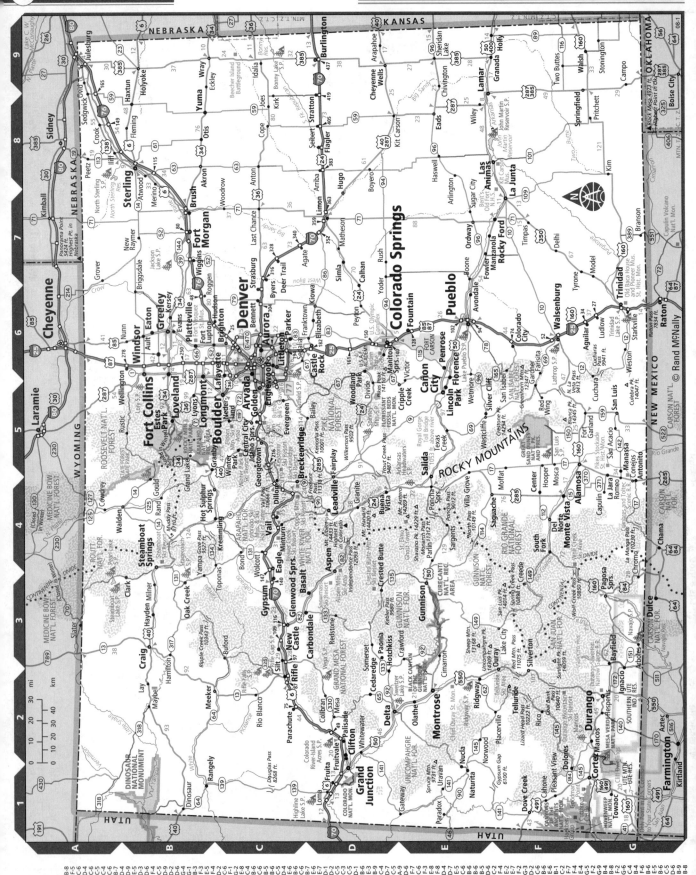

Colorado

Population: 4,665,177
Land area: 103,718 sq. mi.
Capital: Denver

Cities and Towns

Akron B-8
Alamosa F-5
Arvada D-6
Aspen D-4
Aurora C-6
Boulder C-6
Breckenridge D-5
Brighton C-6
Brush B-7
Buena Vista D-4
Burlington C-9
Cañon City E-5
Carbondale D-3
Castle Rock D-6
Cedaredge E-3
Central City C-5
Cheyenne Wells ... C-9
Clifton D-2
Colorado Springs .. D-6
Conejos F-5
Cortez F-2
Craig B-3
Creede E-4
Cripple Creek D-5
Del Norte F-4
Delta E-3
Denver C-6
Durango F-3
Eads D-8
Eagle D-4
Eaton B-6
Englewood C-6
Estes Park C-5
Evergreen C-5
Fairplay D-5
Florence E-5
Fort Collins B-6
Fort Lupton C-6
Fort Morgan B-7
Fountain D-6
Fowler E-7
Fruita D-2
Fruitvale D-2
Georgetown C-5
Glenwood Springs . D-3
Golden C-6
Granby C-5
Grand Junction ... D-2
Greeley B-6
Gunnison E-4
Holyoke B-9
Hugo D-7
Hot Sulphur Sprs. . C-5
Idaho Springs C-5
Julesburg A-9
Kiowa C-6
Kit Carson D-8
La Junta E-7
La Jara F-5
Lafayette C-6
Lake City E-4
Lamar D-8
Las Animas E-8
Leadville D-4
Limon D-7
Lincoln Park E-5
Littleton C-6
Longmont C-6
Loveland B-6
Lyons C-5
Manitou Sprs. D-6
Meeker C-3
Monte Vista F-4
Montrose E-3
Ordway E-7
Ouray E-3
Pagosa Springs F-4
Parker C-6
Platteville C-6
Pueblo E-6
Rangely B-2
Rifle D-3
Rocky Ford E-7
Saguache E-4
Salida E-5
Silverton F-3
Springfield F-8
Steamboat Sprs. ... B-4
Sterling B-8
Telluride F-3
Trinidad F-6
Vail D-4
Walden B-4
Walsenburg F-6
Wellington B-6
Windsor B-6
Winter Park C-5
Woodland Park D-6
Wray B-9

Connecticut
Population: 3,510,297
Land area: 4,845 sq. mi.
Capital: Hartford

Cities and Towns

Ansonia E-4
Avon C-5
Beacon Falls D-5
Berlin D-5
Bethel E-2
Bloomfield C-5
Bridgeport F-3
Bristol D-4
Brooklyn C-8
Canaan A-3
Cheshire D-4
Clinton E-6
Colchester D-7
Coventry C-7
Cromwell D-5
Danbury E-2
Danielson C-8
Darien G-2
Deep River E-6
Derby E-4
East Hartford C-5
East Haven E-4
Enfield B-6
Fairfield F-3
Farmington C-5
Georgetown F-2
Glastonbury C-6
Goshen B-3
Granby B-5
Greenwich G-1
Groton E-8
Guilford E-5
Hamden E-4
Hartford C-5
Litchfield C-3
Madison E-5
Manchester C-6
Mariborough D-6
Meriden D-5
Middlebury D-3
Middletown D-5
Milford F-4
Moodus D-6
Moosup C-9
Mystic E-8
Naugatuck D-4
New Britain D-5
New Canaan F-2
New Fairfield E-2
New Hartford B-4
New Haven E-4
New London E-8
New Milford D-2
Newington C-5
Newtown E-3
North Woodstock B-8
Norwalk F-2
Norwich D-8
Old Mystic E-8
Old Saybrook E-6
Pawcatuck E-9
Phoenixville C-7
Plainfield C-8
Plainville D-5
Portland D-6
Putnam B-8
Ridgefield E-2
Salisbury A-2
Sandy Hook E-3
Seymour E-4
Shelton E-4
Simsbury C-5
Somers B-6
South Canaan A-3
South Windsor C-6
Southbury E-3
Southington D-5
Southport F-3
Stamford G-2
Stafford Springs B-7
Sterling Hill C-9
Storrs C-7
Stratford F-3
Terryville D-4
Thomaston C-4
Torrington C-3
Trumbull F-3
Unionville C-4
Vernon C-6
Wallingford D-5
Waterbury D-4
Watertown C-4
Weatogue C-5
West Hartford C-5
West Haven E-4
Wethersfield C-5
Willimantic C-7
Wilton F-2
Windsor C-5
Windsor Locks B-5

© Rand McNally

08-1

ATLANTIC OCEAN

LONG ISLAND SOUND

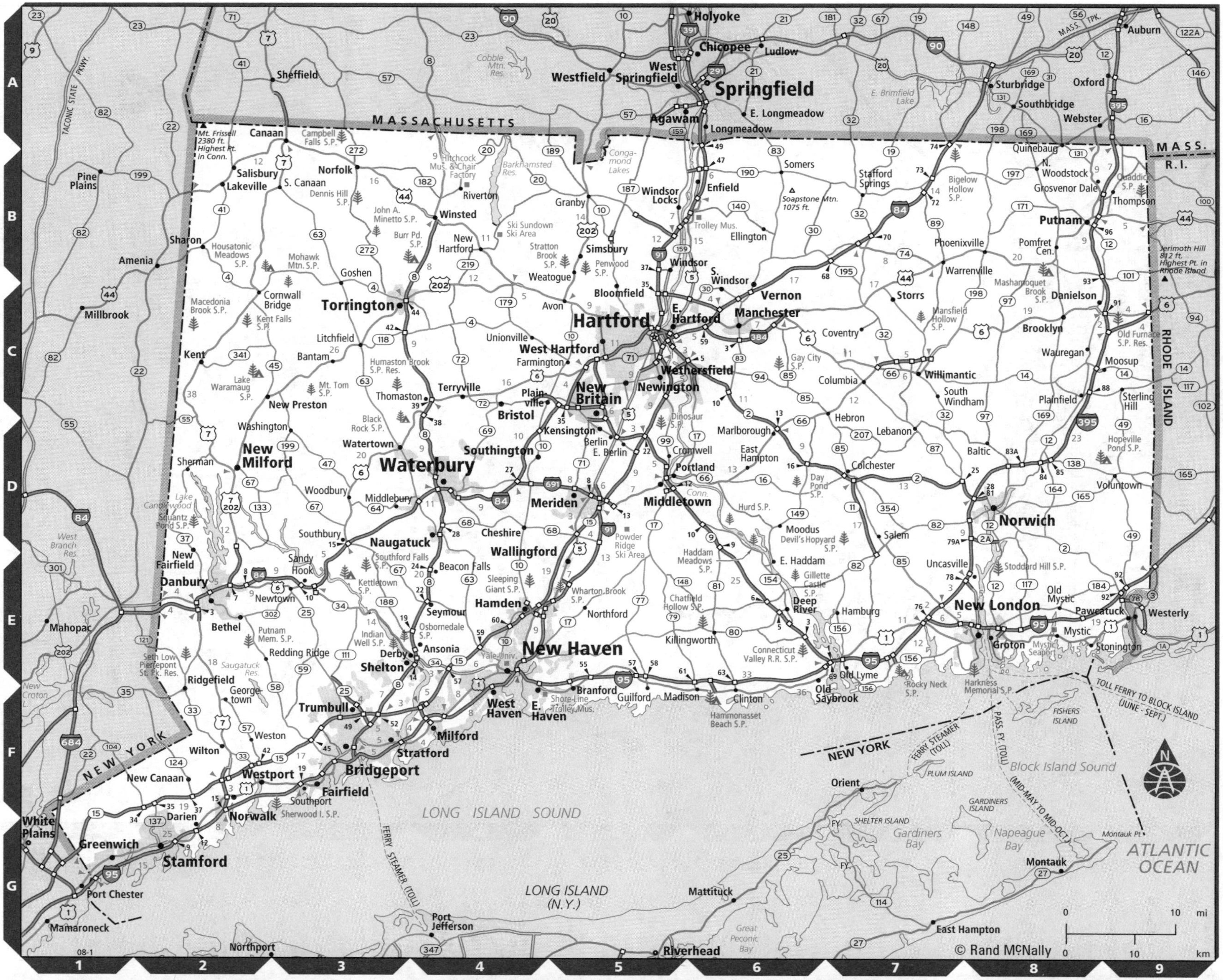

Delaware

Population: 843,524
Land area: 1,954 sq. mi.
Capital: Dover

Cities and Towns

Bear	C-2
Belltown	H-4
Bethany Beach	J-5
Bethel	I-2
Big Stone Beach	G-4
Blades	I-2
Bowers Beach	F-3
Bridgeville	H-2
Broadkill Beach	H-4
Camden	F-3
Cannon	I-2
Canterbury	G-3
Cheswold	F-2
Christiana	C-2
Claymont	B-3
Clayton	E-2
Concord	I-3
Dagsboro	I-4
Delaware City	C-3
Delmar	J-2
Dewey Beach	I-5
Dover	F-3
Dupont Manor	F-3
Ellendale	H-3
Elsmere	B-2
Farmington	H-2
Felton	G-2
Fenwick Island	J-5
Frankford	J-4
Frederica	G-3
Georgetown	I-3
Glasgow	C-2
Gravel Hill	I-4
Greenville	B-2
Greenwood	H-2
Gumboro	J-3
Harbeson	H-4
Harrington	G-2
Hartly	F-2
Hickman	H-2
Hockessin	B-2
Houston	G-3
Kenton	F-2
Kitts Hummock	F-3
Laurel	I-2
Leipsic	E-3
Lewes	H-4
Lincoln	H-3
Little Creek	F-3
Little Heaven	G-3
Lynch Heights	G-3
Magnolia	F-3
Marydel	F-2
Middleford	I-2
Middletown	D-2
Midway	H-5
Milford	G-3
Millsboro	I-4
Millville	I-5
Milton	H-4
Mount Pleasant	D-2
Nassau	H-4
New Castle	C-3
Newark	C-2
Newport	C-2
North Star	B-2
Oak Orchard	I-4
Ocean View	I-5
Odessa	D-2
Port Penn	D-2
Primehook Beach	H-4
Rehoboth Beach	I-5
Rising Sun	F-3
Riverdale	I-4
Rodney Village	F-3
Roxana	J-4
St. Georges	D-2
Seaford	I-2
Selbyville	J-4
Shawnee Acres	G-3
Slaughter Beach	G-4
Smyrna	E-2
South Bethany	J-5
Staytonville	H-3
Sycamore	I-3
Talleyville	B-3
Townsend	E-2
Viola	G-2
Whitesville	J-3
Williamsville	J-4
Wilmington	B-3
Woodland Beach	E-3
Woodside	F-2
Wyoming	F-2

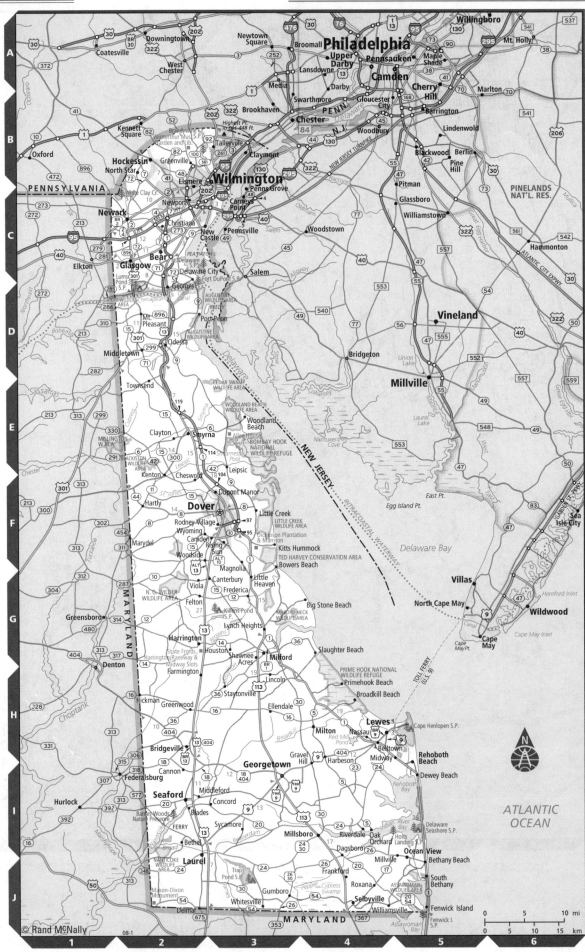

© Rand McNally

08-1

Florida

Population: 17,789,864
Land area: 53,927 sq. mi.
Capital: Tallahassee

Cities and Towns

Altamonte Sprs. D-4
Apalachicola J-4
Arcadia F-4
Atlantic Beach B-4
Avon Park F-4
Bartow E-4
Belle Glade G-5
Big Pine Key J-4
Blountstown I-4
Boca Raton G-6
Bonifay I-3
Bradenton F-3
Brandon E-3
Brooksville D-3
Bunnell C-5
Bushnell D-4
Cape Canaveral D-5
Cape Coral G-4
Chipley I-3
Clearwater E-3
Clermont D-4
Cocoa Beach E-5
Coral Gables H-6
Crawfordville B-1
Crestview I-2
Cross City C-2
Dade City E-3
Dania Beach H-6
Daytona Beach D-5
Debary D-4
De Funiak Springs I-2
DeLand D-4
Deerfield Beach G-6
Delray Beach G-6
Dunedin E-3
East Naples H-4
Edgewater D-5
Englewood F-3
Eustis D-4
Fort Lauderdale G-6
Fort Myers G-4
Fort Myers Beach G-4
Fort Pierce F-6
Fort Walton Beach I-2
Gainesville C-3
Green Cove Sprs. C-4
Haines City E-4
Hallandale Beach H-6
Hialeah H-6
Holly Hill C-5
Hollywood H-6
Homestead H-6
Hudson E-3
Immokalee G-4
Inverness D-3
Jacksonville B-4
Jacksonville Bch. B-4
Jasper B-3
Jensen Beach F-6
Jupiter F-6
Key Largo I-6
Key West J-4
Kissimmee E-4
La Belle G-4
Lady Lake D-4
Lake Butler B-3
Lake City B-3
Lake Wales E-4
Lake Worth G-6
Lakeland E-3
Largo E-3
Leesburg D-4
Lehigh Acres G-4
Live Oak B-3
Lutz E-3
Macclenny B-4
Madeira Beach E-3
Madison B-2
Marathon I-5
Marco H-4
Marianna I-3
Mayo B-2
Melbourne E-5
Miami H-6
Miami Beach H-6
Milton I-1
Monticello B-2
Moore Haven G-5
Mount Dora D-4
Naples H-4
New Port Richey E-3
New Smyrna Bch. D-5
North Palm Beach G-6
Ocala D-4
Okeechobee F-5
Orlando D-4
Ormond Beach C-5
Palatka C-4
Palm Bay E-5
Palm Beach G-6
Palmetto F-3
Panama City J-3
Pensacola I-1
Perrine H-6
Perry B-2
Plant City E-4
Pompano Beach G-6
Port Charlotte F-4
Port Orange D-5
Port St. Joe J-3
Port St. Lucie F-6
Punta Gorda G-4
Quincy B-1
St. Augustine C-4
St. Cloud E-4
St. Petersburg E-3
St. Petersburg Bch. E-3
Sanford D-5
Sanibel G-4
Sarasota E-5
Sebastian E-5
Sebring F-5
Starke C-4
Stuart F-6
Tallahassee B-1
Tampa E-3
Tarpon Springs E-3
Tavares D-4
The Villages D-4
Titusville D-5
Treasure Island E-3
Trenton C-3
Venice F-3
Vero Beach F-6
Warrington I-1
Wauchula F-4
West Palm Beach G-6
Winter Garden E-4
Winter Haven E-4
Yulee B-4
Zephyrhills E-3

© Rand McNally

08-1   08-1

Explore Georgia at go.randmcnally.com/GA

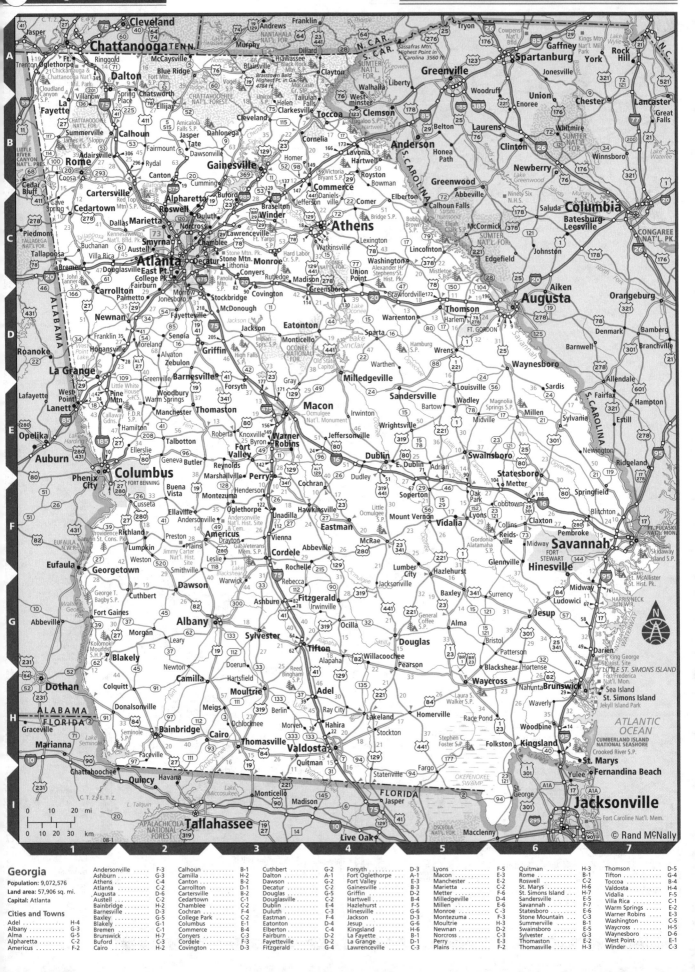

Georgia

Population: 9,072,576
Land area: 57,906 sq. mi.
Capital: Atlanta

Cities and Towns

Adel	H-4
Albany	G-3
Alma	G-5
Alpharetta	C-2
Americus	F-2

Andersonville	F-3
Ashburn	G-3
Athens	C-4
Atlanta	C-2
Austell	C-2
Bainbridge	H-2
Barnesville	D-3
Baxley	G-5
Blakely	G-2
Brunswick	H-7
Buford	C-3

Calhoun	B-1
Camilla	H-2
Canton	C-2
Carrollton	D-1
Cartersville	B-2
Cedartown	C-1
Chamblee	C-2
Cochran	F-4
College Park	C-2
Columbus	E-1
Commerce	B-4
Conyers	C-3
Cordele	F-3
Covington	D-3

Cuthbert	G-2
Dalton	A-1
Dawson	G-2
Decatur	C-2
Douglas	G-5
Douglasville	C-2
Dublin	E-4
Duluth	C-3
Eastman	F-4
Eatonton	D-4
Elberton	C-5
Fairburn	D-2
Fayetteville	D-2
Fitzgerald	G-4

Forsyth	D-3
Fort Oglethorpe	A-1
Fort Valley	E-3
Gainesville	B-3
Griffin	D-2
Hartwell	B-4
Hazlehurst	F-5
Hinesville	G-6
Jackson	D-3
Jesup	G-6
Kingsland	H-6
La Fayette	B-1
La Grange	D-1
Lawrenceville	C-3

Lyons	F-5
Macon	E-3
Manchester	E-2
Marietta	C-2
Metter	F-6
Milledgeville	D-4
Millen	E-6
Monroe	C-3
Montezuma	F-3
Moultrie	H-3
Newnan	D-2
Norcross	C-2
Perry	E-3
Plains	F-2

Quitman	H-3
Rome	B-1
Roswell	C-2
St. Marys	H-6
St. Simons Island	H-7
Sandersville	E-5
Savannah	F-7
Statesboro	E-6
Stone Mountain	C-3
Summerville	B-1
Swainsboro	E-5
Sylvester	G-3
Thomaston	E-2
Thomasville	H-3

Thomson	D-5
Tifton	G-4
Toccoa	B-4
Valdosta	H-4
Vidalia	F-5
Villa Rica	C-1
Warm Springs	E-2
Warner Robins	E-3
Washington	C-5
Waycross	H-5
Waynesboro	D-6
West Point	E-1
Winder	C-3

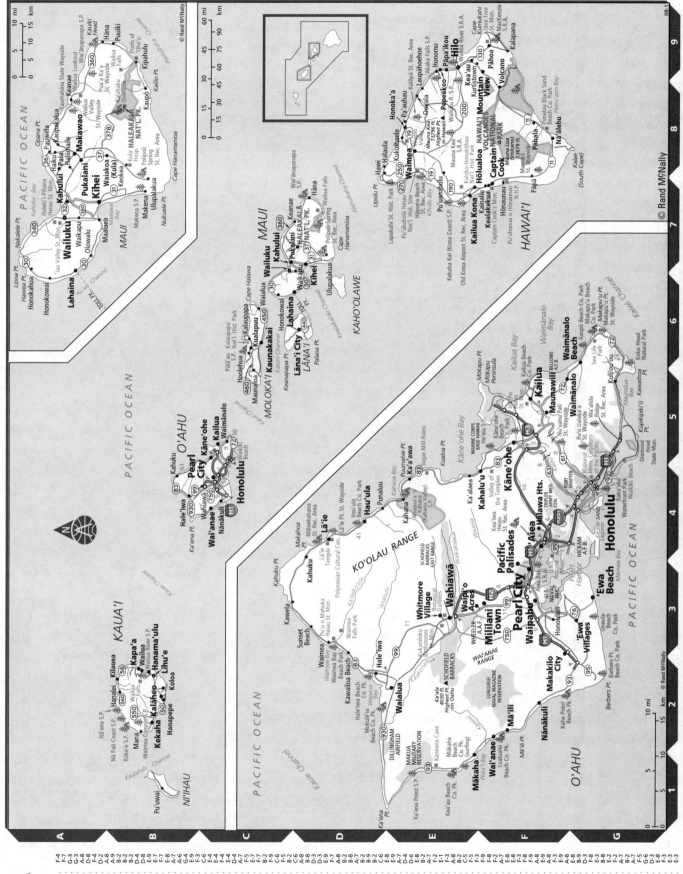

Hawaii

Population: 1,275,194
Land area: 6,423 sq. mi.
Capital: Honolulu

Cities and Towns

'Aiea	F-4
Captain Cook	F-7
'Ewa Villages	G-3
Haiku	D-8
Halaula	G-8
Haleiwa Heights	D-2
Hale'iwa	A-8
Haliimaile	C-8
Hana	C-9
Hanama'ulu	B-2
Hanapepe	B-2
Hau'ula	D-4
Hawi	G-8
Hilo	E-9
Holualoa	F-7
Honaunau	F-7
Honoka'a	A-7
Honokahua	C-6
Honolulu	G-4
Honomu	E-9
Hoolehua	C-6
Ka'a'awa	C-8
Ka'alaea	E-4
Kahalu'u	E-4
Kahana	D-4
Kahuku	A-7
Kahului	F-5
Kailua	C-8
Kailua Kona	F-7
Kalaheo	B-2
Kalapana	E-9
Kalaupapa	C-6
Kapa'a	B-2
Kaunakakai	C-6
Kaupo	D-9
Kawaihae	A-8
Kawela	D-3
Kea'au	E-9
Kealakekua	F-7
Keanae	B-9
Keokea	D-8
Kihei	F-5
Kilauea	A-2
Kipahulu	C-9
Koloa	B-2
Kualapuu	C-6
Kukuihaele	A-7
Kurtistown	E-9
Lahaina	C-6
Lana'i City	D-6
Laupahoehoe	A-7
Lihue	B-2
Ma'ili	F-2
Maalaea	E-1
Makaha	F-2
Makakilo City	G-3
Makawao	C-8
Mana	B-2
Maunaloa	C-6
Mililani Town	F-3
Mountain View	E-9
Nanakuli	F-2
Na'alehu	G-8
Pa'auhau	A-7
Pa'auilo	A-7
Pahala	F-8
Pahoa	E-9
Paia	C-8
Papa'ikou	E-9
Pauwela	B-8
Pearl City	F-3
Pepeekeo	E-9
Pukalani	C-8
Pu'uanahulu	A-7
Puuiki	F-5
Volcano	F-9
Wahiawa	F-3
Waiakoa (Kula)	D-8
Waialua	D-3
Wai'anae	F-2
Waikapu	F-5
Wailua	B-2
Wailuku	F-5
Waimanalo	G-5
Waimanalo Beach	G-5
Waimea	A-2
Waimea	A-7
Waipahu	F-3
Waipi'o Acres	F-3
Whitmore Village	E-3

Idaho

Population: 1,429,096
Land area: 82,747 sq. mi.
Capital: Boise

Cities and Towns

Aberdeen I-5
Albion I-4
American Falls I-5
Arco H-4
Ashton G-6
Athol B-1
Bancroft I-6
Bellevue H-3
Blackfoot H-5
Bloomington I-6
Boise H-2
Bonners Ferry A-2
Bovill D-2
Buhl I-3
Burley I-4
Caldwell H-1
Cambridge G-1
Carey H-4
Cascade G-2
Cataldo C-2
Challis G-3
Chester G-6
Clark Fork B-2
Coeur d'Alene C-1
Cottonwood E-2
Council F-1
Craigmont D-1
Culdesac D-1
Dayton J-5
Deary D-1
Downey I-6
Driggs H-6
Dubois G-5
Eden I-3
Elk City E-2
Emmett G-1
Fairfield H-3
Fernwood C-2
Filer I-3
Firth H-5
Fort Hall H-5
Franklin J-6
Fruitland G-1
Geneva I-6
Georgetown I-6
Glenns Ferry I-2
Gooding I-3
Grace I-6
Grand View I-2
Grangeville E-2
Hagerman I-3
Hailey H-3
Hammett I-2
Hansen I-3
Harrison C-1
Homedale H-1
Horseshoe Bend G-2
Idaho City G-2
Idaho Falls H-5
Inkom I-5
Jerome I-3
Kamiah D-2
Kellogg C-2
Kendrick D-1
Ketchum H-3
Kimberly I-3
Kooskia E-2
Kootenai B-2
Lava Hot Springs I-5
Lewiston D-1
Mackay G-4
Malad City J-5
Malta I-4
Marsing H-1
McCall F-2
McCammon I-5
Melba H-1
Montpelier I-6
Moreland H-1
Moscow D-1
Mountain Home H-2
Moyie Springs A-2
Mud Lake G-5
Mullan C-2
Murphy H-1
Nampa H-1
Naples A-2
New Meadows F-2
New Plymouth G-1
Newdale G-6
Nezperce D-2
North Fork E-4
Oakley I-4
Orofino D-2
Osburn C-2
Paris I-6
Paul I-4
Payette G-1
Pierce D-2
Pinehurst C-2
Pleasantview J-5
Plummer C-1
Pocatello I-5
Post Falls C-1
Potlatch D-1
Preston J-6
Priest River B-1
Rathdrum B-1
Rexburg G-6
Richfield H-3
Rigby H-6
Riggins E-2
Ririe H-6
Roberts H-5
Rockland I-5
Rupert I-4
St. Anthony G-6
St. Maries C-1
Salmon F-4
Sandpoint B-1
Shelley H-5
Shoshone I-3
Silverton C-2
Soda Springs I-6
Spirit Lake B-1
Star H-1
Sugar City G-6
Sun Valley H-3
Swan Valley H-6
Terreton G-5
Troy D-1
Twin Falls I-3
Victor H-6
Wallace C-2
Weippe D-2
Weiser G-1
Wendell I-3
Weston J-6

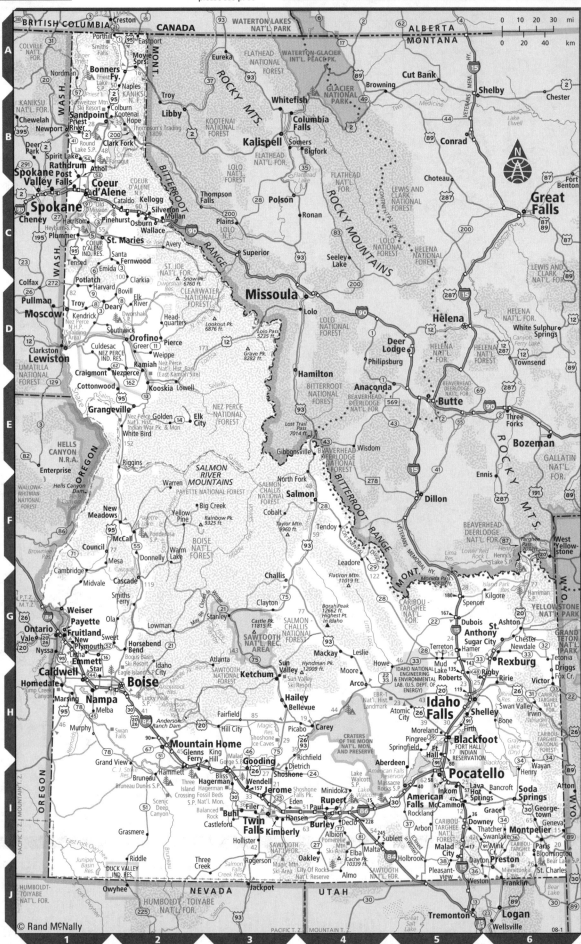

© Rand McNally

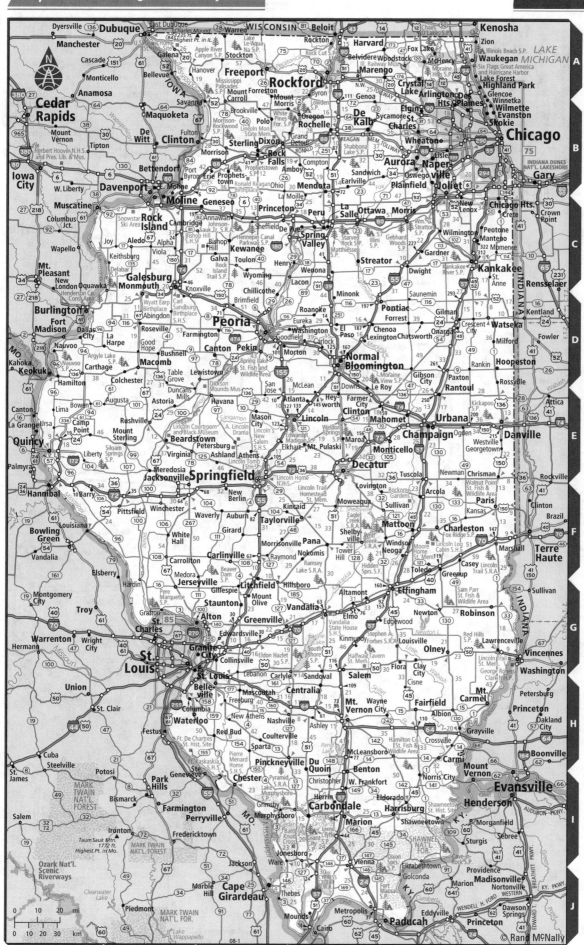

Illinois
Population: 12,763,371
Land area: 55,584 sq. mi.
Capital: Springfield

Cities and Towns

Albion H-5
Aledo C-2
Alton G-3
Arlington Heights A-6
Aurora B-5
Belleville H-3
Belvidere A-4
Bishop Hill C-2
Bloomington D-4
Cairo J-4
Cambridge C-2
Canton D-3
Carbondale I-4
Carlinville F-3
Carlyle H-4
Carmi H-5
Carrollton F-2
Carthage D-1
Centralia H-4
Champaign E-5
Charleston F-5
Chester I-3
Chicago B-6
Chicago Heights C-6
Clinton E-4
Collinsville G-3
Crystal Lake A-5
Danville E-6
De Kalb B-4
Decatur E-4
Dixon B-3
Du Quoin H-4
Dwight C-5
East Moline B-2
East St. Louis G-3
Edwardsville G-3
Effingham G-5
Elgin B-5
Eureka D-4
Evanston B-6
Fairfield H-5
Freeport A-3
Galena A-3
Galesburg C-2
Granite City G-3
Greenville G-3
Hardin F-2
Harrisburg I-5
Havana D-3
Herrin I-4
Highland Park A-6
Hillsboro G-3
Jacksonville F-2
Jerseyville G-2
Joliet B-5
Jonesboro I-4
Kankakee C-5
Kewanee C-3
La Salle C-4
Lacon C-3
Lake Forest A-6
Lawrenceville G-6
Lewistown D-3
Lincoln E-4
Lisle B-5
Louisville G-5
Macomb D-2
Marion I-4
Marshall F-6
Mattoon F-5
McHenry A-5
McLeansboro H-5
Meredosia E-2
Metropolis J-4
Moline B-2
Monmouth D-2
Monticello E-5
Morris C-5
Morrison B-3
Morton D-3
Mount Carmel H-6
Mount Carroll B-3
Mount Pulaski E-4
Mount Sterling E-2
Mount Vernon H-4
Murphysboro I-4
Naperville B-5
Nashville H-4
Nauvoo D-1
Newton G-5
Normal D-4
Olney G-5
Oquawka D-2
Oregon B-4
Ottawa C-4
Pana F-4
Paris F-6
Paxton D-5
Pekin D-3
Peoria D-3
Peru C-4
Petersburg E-3
Pinckneyville H-4
Pittsfield F-2
Pontiac D-4
Princeton C-3
Quincy E-1
Rantoul E-5
Robinson G-6
Rock Island C-2
Rockford A-4
Rushville E-2
St. Charles B-5
Salem H-4
Shawneetown I-5
Shelbyville F-4
Skokie B-6
Springfield F-3
Sterling B-3
Streator C-4
Sullivan F-5
Sycamore B-4
Taylorville F-4
Toledo F-5
Toulon C-3
Tuscola E-5
Urbana E-5
Vandalia G-4
Vienna I-4
Viola C-2
Virginia E-3
Washington D-3
Waterloo H-2
Watseka D-5
Waukegan A-5
Wheaton B-5
Wilmette B-6
Winchester F-2
Winnetka B-6
Woodstock A-5
Zion A-6

Plan an Indiana trip at go.randmcnally.com/IN

Indiana

Population: 6,271,973
Land area: 35,867 sq. mi.
Capital: Indianapolis

Cities and Towns

Albion	B-5
Alexandria	E-5
Anderson	E-5
Angola	A-6
Attica	D-2
Auburn	B-6
Batesville	G-6
Bedford	H-3
Berne	D-6
Bloomfield	G-3
Bloomington	G-3
Bluffton	C-6
Boonville	I-2
Brazil	F-2
Bremen	B-4
Brookville	F-6
Brownsburg	E-4
Brownstown	H-4
Cannelton	J-3
Carmel	E-4
Cedar Lake	B-2
Charlestown	I-5
Chesterton	A-2
Clarksville	I-5
Columbia City	C-5
Columbus	G-4
Connersville	F-6
Corydon	I-4
Covington	E-2
Crawfordsville	E-3
Crown Point	B-2
Danville	F-3
Decatur	C-6
Delphi	D-3
East Chicago	A-2
Elkhart	A-4
Elwood	D-5
English	I-3
Evansville	J-1
Fort Wayne	C-6
Fowler	D-2
Frankfort	D-3
Franklin	F-4
French Lick	H-3
Garrett	B-6
Gary	B-2
Gas City	D-5
Goshen	B-5
Greencastle	F-3
Greenfield	F-5
Greensburg	G-5
Greenwood	F-4
Hammond	A-2
Hartford City	D-5
Hebron	B-2
Hobart	B-2
Huntingburg	I-3
Huntington	C-5
Indianapolis	F-4
Jasper	I-3
Jeffersonville	I-5
Kendallville	B-5
Kentland	C-2
Knox	B-3
Kokomo	D-4
La Porte	A-3
Lafayette	D-3
Lagrange	A-5
Lawrenceburg	G-6
Lebanon	E-3
Liberty	F-6
Ligonier	B-5
Linton	G-2
Logansport	C-4
Loogootee	H-3
Lowell	B-2
Madison	H-5
Marion	D-5
Martinsville	F-4
Michigan City	A-3
Mishawaka	A-4
Mitchell	H-3
Mooresville	F-4
Mount Vernon	J-1
Muncie	E-5
Munster	B-2
Nappanee	B-4
Nashville	G-4
New Albany	I-5
New Castle	E-5
New Haven	C-6
Newport	E-2
Noblesville	E-4
North Terre Haute	F-2
North Vernon	G-5
Paoli	H-3
Peru	C-4
Petersburg	H-2
Plainfield	F-4
Plymouth	B-4
Portage	B-2
Portland	D-6
Princeton	I-1
Rensselaer	C-2
Richmond	E-6
Rising Sun	G-6
Rochester	C-4
Rockport	J-2
Rockville	F-2
Rushville	F-5
Salem	H-4
Schererville	B-2
Scottsburg	H-5
Sellersburg	I-5
Seymour	G-4
Shelbyville	F-5
Shoals	H-3
South Bend	A-4
Spencer	G-3
Sullivan	G-2
Tell City	J-3
Terre Haute	F-2
Tipton	D-4
Valparaiso	B-2
Veedersburg	E-2
Vernon	G-5
Versailles	G-6
Vevay	H-6
Vincennes	H-2
Wabash	C-5
Warsaw	B-4
Washington	H-2
West Lafayette	D-3
Westville	B-3
Whiting	A-2
Williamsport	D-2
Winamac	C-3
Winchester	E-6
Wingate	E-2

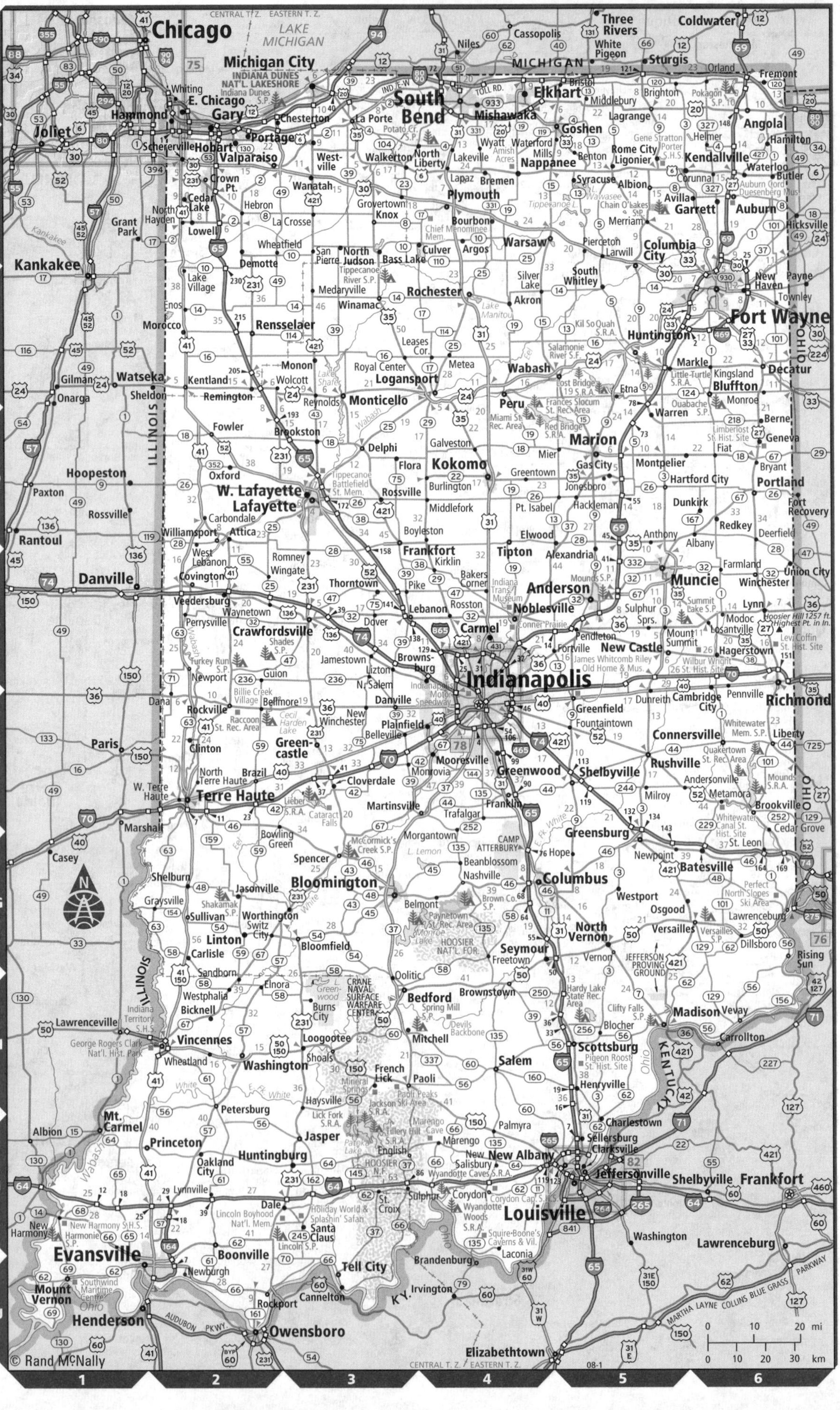

© Rand McNally

08-1

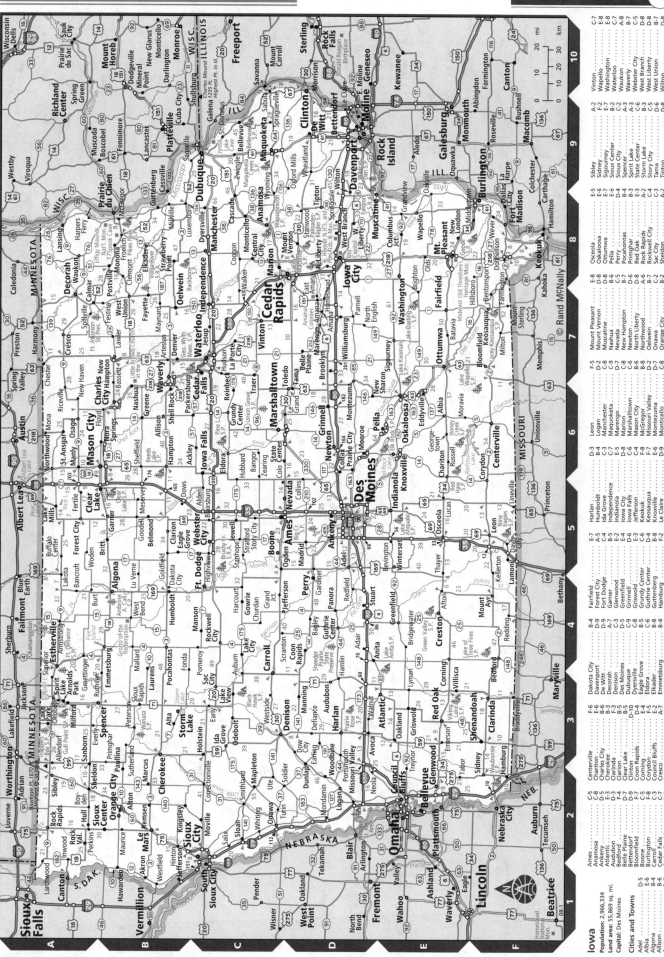

Vinton C-7
Wapello E-8
Washington E-8
Waterloo B-7
Waukon A-8
Waverly B-7
Webster City C-5
West Branch C-8
West Liberty C-8
West Union B-8
Wilton D-8
Winterset D-6

Sibley A-2
Sidney F-2
Sigourney D-7
Sioux Center B-2
Sioux City B-2
Spencer A-3
Spirit Lake A-3
State Center C-6
Storm Lake B-3
Story City C-5
Tama C-7
Tipton C-8
Toledo C-7

Mount Pleasant E-8
Mount Vernon C-8
Muscatine D-8
Nashua B-6
Nevada C-6
New Hampton B-7
Newton C-6
North English D-7
North Liberty C-8
Oelwein B-7
Onawa C-2
Orange City B-2
Osage A-6

Osceola E-5
Oskaloosa D-7
Ottumwa D-8
Pella D-7
Perry C-5
Pocahontas B-4
Primghar A-3
Red Oak E-2
Rock Rapids A-2
Rock Valley City B-2
Sac City B-3
Shenandoah F-3

Leon E-5
Logan D-3
Manchester B-7
Maquoketa C-8
Marengo C-7
Marion C-8
Marshalltown C-6
Mason City B-6
Missouri Valley D-2
Monticello C-8
Montezuma D-7
Mount Ayr F-5

Harlan E-7
Humboldt A-5
Ida Grove C-4
Independence B-7
Indianola D-6
Iowa City C-8
Iowa Falls B-6
Jefferson C-4
Keokuk F-8
Keosauqua E-8
Knoxville D-6
Le Claire C-9
Le Mars B-2

Fairfield E-7
Forest City A-5
Fort Dodge B-5
Garner B-5
Glenwood E-2
Greenfield D-4
Grinnell C-6
Grundy Center C-6
Guthrie Center D-4
Guttenberg B-8
Hamburg F-2
Hampton B-6

Dakota City F-6
Davenport B-6
De Witt C-8
Decorah A-7
Denison F-3
Des Moines B-5
Dubuque D-10
Dyersville D-4
Eagle Grove E-6
Eldora C-7
Elkader B-8
Emmetsburg A-7
Estherville B-8

Centerville C-5
Chariton C-8
Charles City D-5
Cherokee D-3
Clarinda D-2
Clarion F-4
Clear Lake D-7
Clinton C-7
Coon Rapids C-5
Corydon C-3
Council Bluffs E-2
Cresco A-7
Creston D-7

Iowa

Population: 2,966,334
Land area: 55,869 sq. mi.
Capital: Des Moines

Cities and Towns

Adel D-5
Albia E-6
Algona B-4
Allison B-6
Ames C-5
Anamosa C-8
Ankeny D-5
Audubon D-4
Bedford F-4
Bettendorf B-9
Bloomfield E-7
Boone C-5
Burlington E-8
Carroll C-4
Cedar Falls B-7
Cedar Rapids C-8

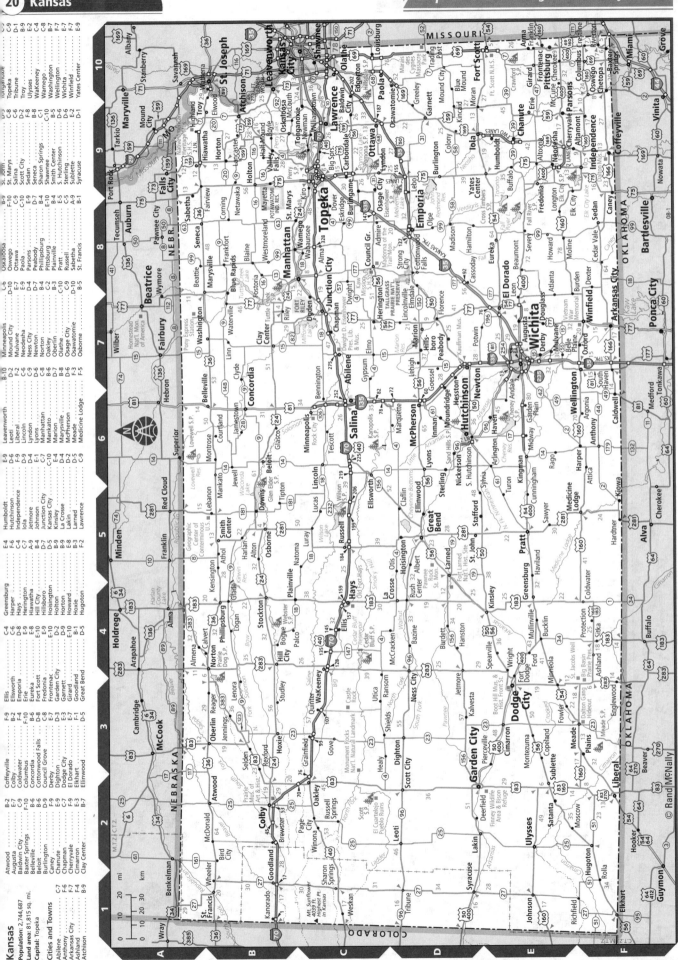

Kentucky

Population: 4,173,405
Land area: 39,728 sq. mi.
Capital: Frankfort

Cities and Towns

City	Grid
Albany	F-5
Alexandria	B-6
Ashland	C-9
Auburn	E-4
Barbourville	D-7
Bardstown	D-5
Bardwell	B-2
Benton	B-3
Berea	D-7
Bowling Green	E-4
Brandenburg	D-4
Burkesville	E-6
Burnside	D-6
Cadiz	C-7
Campbellsville	D-5
Carlisle	C-7
Carrollton	B-5
Catlettsburg	C-9
Cave City	E-4
Central City	D-3
Clinton	B-2
Columbia	E-5
Columbus	B-2
Corbin	D-7
Covington	B-6
Cumberland	D-9
Cynthiana	C-6
Danville	D-6
Dawson Springs	D-3
Dry Ridge	B-6
Earlington	D-3
Eddyville	C-2
Edmonton	E-5
Elizabethtown	D-4
Elkton	E-4
Falmouth	B-6
Flemingsburg	C-7
Florence	B-6
Fort Thomas	B-6
Frankfort	C-5
Fulton	B-2
Georgetown	C-6
Gilbertsville	B-3
Glasgow	E-5
Grayson	C-8
Greensburg	D-5
Greenville	D-3
Hardin	B-3
Hardinsburg	D-4
Harlan	D-8
Harrodsburg	D-6
Hartford	D-4
Hawesville	D-4
Hazard	D-8
Henderson	C-3
Hickman	B-2
Hodgenville	D-5
Hopkinsville	E-3
Horse Cave	E-5
Irvine	D-7
Irvington	D-4
Jackson	D-8
Jamestown	E-5
Jeffersontown	C-5
Jenkins	D-9
La Grange	C-5
Lancaster	D-6
Lebanon	D-5
Leitchfield	D-4
Lexington	C-6
Liberty	D-6
Livermore	D-4
London	D-7
Louisa	C-9
Louisville	C-5
Madisonville	D-3
Manchester	D-7
Marion	C-2
Mayfield	B-2
Maysville	C-7
Middlesboro	D-8
Monticello	E-6
Morehead	C-8
Morganfield	C-2
Morgantown	D-4
Mount Sterling	C-7
Mount Vernon	D-6
Munfordville	E-5
Murray	B-3
Newport	B-6
Nicholasville	C-6
Nortonville	D-3
Olive Hill	C-8
Owensboro	D-4
Owenton	B-5
Paducah	B-3
Paintsville	C-8
Paris	C-6
Perryville	D-6
Pikeville	C-9
Pine Knot	E-6
Pineville	D-8
Prestonsburg	C-9
Princeton	C-2
Providence	D-3
Radcliff	D-4
Richmond	D-6
Russell Springs	E-5
Russellville	E-3
Salyersville	C-8
Scottsville	E-4
Sebree	D-3
Shelbyville	C-5
Shepherdsville	D-5
Shively	C-5
Somerset	D-6
Springfield	D-5
Stanford	D-6
Sturgis	D-1
Tompkinsville	F-5
Tri City	B-2
Vanceburg	B-8
Versailles	C-6
Warsaw	B-5
West Liberty	C-8
Whitesburg	D-9
Wickliffe	B-2
Williamsburg	D-8
Wilmore	C-6
Winchester	D-7

© Rand McNally

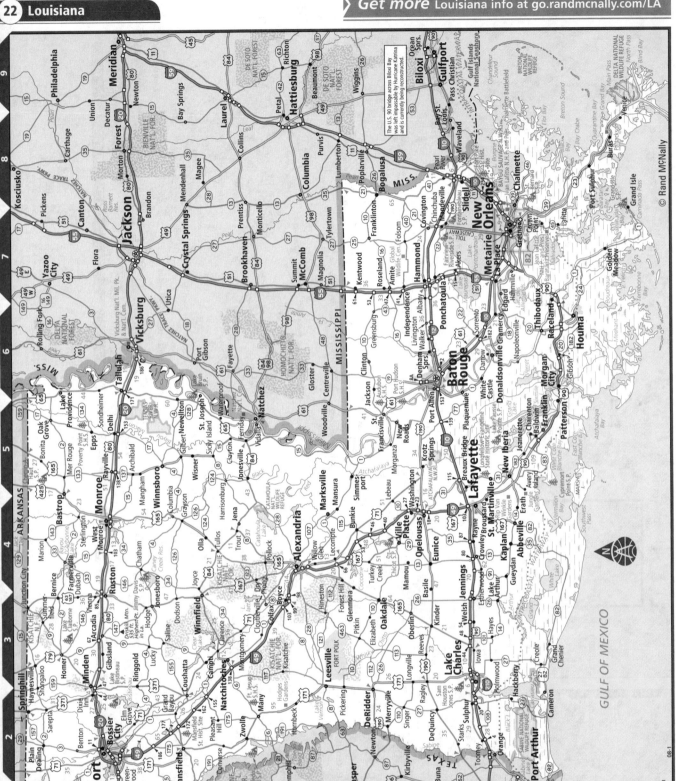

© Rand McNally

Louisiana

Population: 4,523,628
Land area: 43,562 sq. mi.
Capital: Baton Rouge

Cities and Towns

Abbeville	F-4
Alexandria	D-4
Amite	E-7
Arcadia	A-3
Baldwin	A-5
Bastrop	E-6
Baton Rouge	E-6
Benton	D-8
Bogalusa	A-2
Bossier City	E-5
Breaux Bridge	D-4
Bunkie	D-6
Chalmette	C-3
Colfax	B-4
Columbia	B-2
Coushatta	C-3
Covington	B-2
Crowley	E-4
De Quincy	E-2
De Ridder	E-2
Delhi	D-2
Denham Springs	D-6
Donaldsonville	D-6
Erath	E-4
Eunice	E-4
Farmerville	A-5
Ferriday	C-5
Franklin	A-3
Franklinton	B-7
Grand Isle	G-7
Gramercy	D-6
Greensburg	F-6
Gretna	D-2
Hahnville	D-6
Hammond	B-2
Harrisonburg	C-5
Haynesville	F-7
Homer	D-4
Houma	A-4
Iowa	F-2
Jeanerette	D-4
Jena	C-4
Jennings	E-3
Jonesboro	B-3
Kaplan	E-4
Kentwood	A-7
Kinder	E-3
La Place	D-6
Lafayette	E-4
Lake Arthur	E-3
Lake Charles	E-2
Lake Providence	A-6
Leesville	D-2
Livingston	D-6
Mamou	E-4
Mandeville	B-2
Many	C-2
Marksville	D-5
Metairie	C-3
Minden	A-3
Monroe	B-2
Morgan City	A-4
Napoleonville	D-6
Natchitoches	C-3
New Iberia	E-4
New Orleans	C-3
New Roads	D-5
Oak Grove	D-2
Oakdale	E-3
Oberlin	E-3
Opelousas	D-4
Patterson	A-4
Plaquemine	D-6
Ponchatoula	B-2
Port Allen	D-6
Port Sulphur	B-3
Raceland	A-4
Rayne	E-4
Rayville	B-2
Ruston	A-3
St. Francisville	D-6
St. Joseph	C-5
St. Martinville	D-4
Scotlandville	A-1
Shreveport	E-6
Slidell	B-2
Springhill	E-6
Tallulah	A-2
Thibodaux	A-4
Vidalia	C-5
Ville Platte	D-4
Vivian	E-6
Walker	E-6
Welsh	E-3
West Monroe	B-2
Winnfield	B-3
Winnsboro	B-5

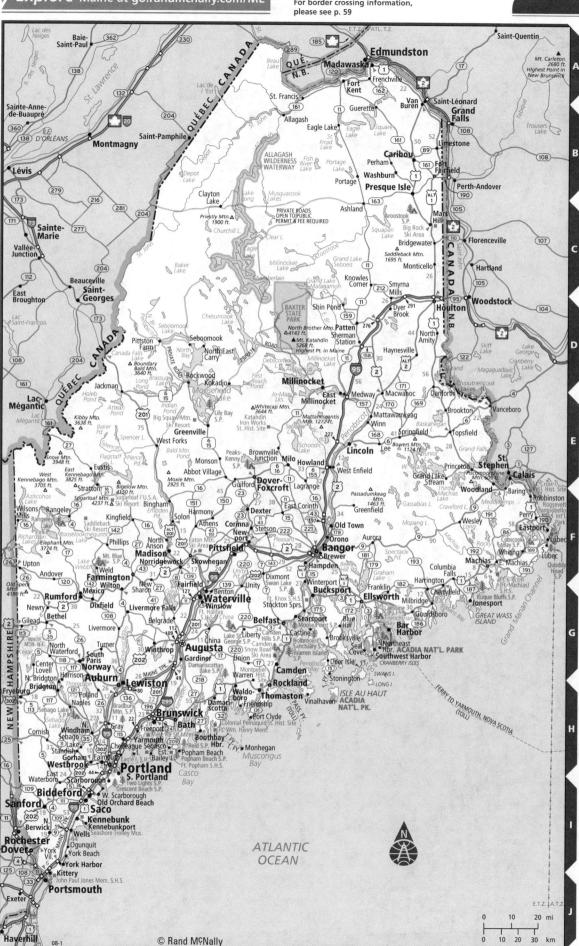

© Rand McNally

Maine

Population: 1,321,505
Land area: 30,862 sq. mi.
Capital: Augusta

Cities and Towns

Andover . . . . F-
Ashland . . . . C-
Auburn H-2
Augusta . . . . G-
Bailey Island . . . . H-
Bangor F-4
Bar Harbor . . . . G-
Bath H-2
Belfast . . . . G-
Bethel . . . . G-
Biddeford . . . . I-
Bingham . . . . F-
Blue Hill G-4
Boothbay Harbor . . . . . H-
Brewer F-4
Bridgewater . . . . C-
Bridgton . . . . H-
Brownville Jct. . . . . E-
Brunswick H-2
Bucksport G-4
Calais E-6
Camden . . . . G-
Caribou B-5
Castine G-4
Chebeague Island H-2
Corinna F-3
Cornish . . . . H-
Damariscotta H-3
Danforth . . . . D-
Deer Isle G-4
Dexter F-3
Dixfield G-1
Dover-Foxcroft E-2
Eagle Lake B-4
East Corinth F-3
East Machias F-6
East Millinocket E-4
Eastport F-6
Ellsworth G-4
Fairfield G-3
Falmouth H-2
Farmington F-2
Fort Fairfield B-5
Fort Kent A-4
Freeport H-2
Frenchville A-4
Friendship H-3
Fryeburg H-1
Gardiner G-2
Gorham H-1
Gray H-2
Greenville E-3
Guilford E-3
Hampden F-4
Harrington G-5
Harrison H-1
Houlton D-5
Howland E-4
Jackman E-2
Jonesport G-6
Kennebunk I-1
Kennebunkport I-1
Kingfield F-2
Kittery J-1
Lewiston H-2
Limestone B-5
Lincoln E-4
Livermore Falls G-2
Lubec F-6
Machias F-6
Madawaska A-4
Madison F-2
Mars Hill C-5
Mattawamkeag E-4
Medway E-4
Mexico G-1
Milbridge G-5
Millinocket D-4
Milo E-3
Monson E-3
Monticello C-5
Naples H-1
Newport F-2
Norridgewock F-2
North Anson F-2
North Berwick I-1
North Bridgton H-1
Northeast Harbor G-5
Norway H-2
Ogunquit I-1
Old Town F-4
Orono F-4
Patten D-4
Phillips F-1
Pine Point I-2
Pittsfield F-3
Poland H-2
Port Clyde H-3
Portage B-4
Portland H-2
Presque Isle B-5
Princeton E-6
Rangeley F-1
Rockland H-3
Rumford G-1
Saco I-1
Sanford I-1
Searsport G-4
Sebago Lake H-1
Sherman Station D-4
Skowhegan F-2
Solon F-2
South China G-3
South Paris H-2
Standish H-1
Stockton Springs G-4
Stonington G-4
Stratton E-2
Thomaston H-3
Turner G-2
Union G-3
Unity G-3
Van Buren B-5
Vinalhaven H-3
Waldoboro H-3
Washburn B-5
Waterville G-3
Wells I-1
West Enfield E-4
Westbrook H-2
Wilton G-2
Windham H-1
Winslow G-3
Winterport F-4
Winthrop G-2
Woodland E-6
Yarmouth H-2
York Beach I-1
York Harbor I-1

Maryland

Population: 5,600,388
Land area: 9,774 sq. mi.
Capital: Annapolis

Cities and Towns

Aberdeen	B-8
Annapolis	C-7
Baltimore	B-7
Bel Air	B-7

Bel Alton	E-6
Berlin	E-10
Bethesda	C-6
Boonsboro	B-5
Bowie	C-7
Cambridge	D-8
Centreville	C-8
Chesapeake City	B-9
Chestertown	C-8
Church Hill	C-8
Churchville	B-8

Clear Spring	A-4
Cockeysville	B-7
College Park	C-6
Conowingo	A-8
Cooksville	B-6
Cornersville	D-8
Corriganville	A-2
Crisfield	F-8
Crocheron	E-8
Cumberland	A-2
Darlington	A-8

Denton	C-8
Easton	D-8
Edgewood	B-8
Elkridge	C-7
Elkton	B-9
Ellicott City	C-6
Emmitsburg	A-5
Fair Hill	A-8
Fairbank	E-8
Flintstone	A-2
Frederick	B-5

Frostburg	D-9
Gaithersburg	C-6
Germantown	C-6
Grantsville	A-1
Grasonville	C-8
Hampstead	B-6
Hancock	A-4
Havre de Grace	B-8
Honga	E-8

Ingleside	C-8
James	C-6
Keyers Ridge	A-1
Kingsville	B-7
La Plata	D-6
Leonardtown	E-7
Level	B-8
Lexington Park	E-7
Libertytown	B-6
Lothian	C-7

Mount Airy	B-6
Nanticoke	D-8
Newburg	F-7
Oakland	B-1
Ocean City	D-10
Olney	C-6
Oxford	D-8
Pocomoke City	F-9
Point Lookout	F-7
Prince Frederick	D-7
Princess Anne	D-9

Queenstown	C-8
Reisterstown	B-6
Ridge	F-7
Riverside	E-6
Rock Hall	C-8
Rockville	C-6
Romancoke	D-8
St. Marys City	F-9
St. Michaels	E-7
Salisbury	D-9
Scotland	F-7

Shawsville	C-8
Silesia	B-6
Silver Spring	C-6
Snow Hill	E-9
Solomons	E-7
Sudlersville	C-8
Suitland	C-6
Sunderland	D-7
Taneytown	B-6
Taylors Island	D-8
Thurmont	A-5

Tilghman	D-7
Towson	B-7
Tuscarora	C-5
Upper Marlboro	D-7
Waldorf	D-6
Wenona	F-8
Westernport	B-2
Westminster	B-6
White Plains	D-6
Williamsport	B-4
Woodsboro	B-5

District of Columbia

Population: 550,521
Land area: 61 sq. mi.

City
Washington C-6

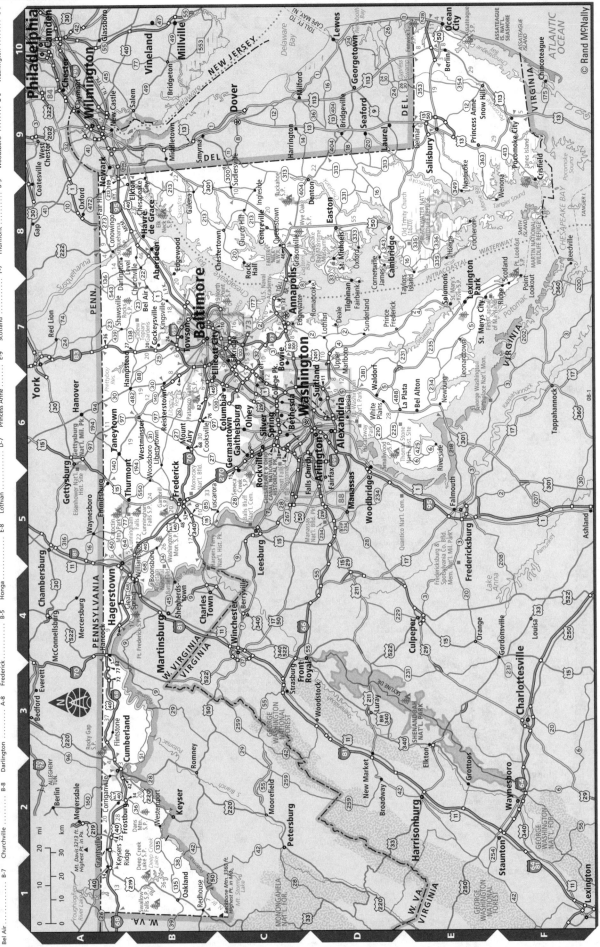

© Rand McNally

08-1

West Springfield	C-3
Westfield	C-3
Westport	E-7
Weymouth	B-7
Whitman	C-8
Williamstown	A-2
Wilmington	B-7
Winchendon	A-5
Woburn	B-7
Woods Hole	D-5
Worcester	C-7
Wrentham	C-5

Taunton	D-7
Truro	D-10
Tyringham	B-8
Vineyard Haven	C-7
Wakefield	B-3
Walpole	D-7
Waltham	A-2
Ware	B-7
Wareham	C-5
Webster	C-8
Wellesley	B-8
Wellfleet	C-7
West Brookfield	A-5

Saugus	C-4
Scituate	B-8
Shelburne Falls	D-8
Somerset	C-9
South Hadley	C-7
South Yarmouth	B-7
Southbridge	C-8
Spencer	C-5
Springfield	A-8
Stoughton	B-4
Sandwich	A-9

Palmer	C-6
Peabody	E-8
Pittsfield	A-8
Plymouth	C-7
Provincetown	A-7
Quincy	B-8
Randolph	D-7
Revere	A-8
Rockland	C-8
Rockport	A-8
Salisbury	B-9
Salem	B-4
Saxonville	F-10

Natick	B-7
New Bedford	C-4
Newburyport	D-7
Newton	C-6
North Adams	C-1
North Andover	A-9
North Attleborough	A-7
Northampton	D-7
Norwood	A-8
Middleboro	B-2
Milford	B-2
Orange	C-6
Oxford	C-5

Lowell	B-3
Ludlow	E-10
Lynn	C-6
Mansfield	A-7
Marblehead	B-5
Marlborough	C-1
Maynard	E-9
Methuen	A-8
Middleton	B-2
Lexington	A-8

Greenfield	E-9
Harwich Port	C-4
Haverhill	D-10
Holliston	C-3
Holyoke	F-9
Housatonic	E-8
Hudson	B-5
Hyannis	E-7
Ipswich	B-5
Lawrence	C-6
Leominster	B-5
Lenox	B-8

East Falmouth	C-7
East Longmeadow	C-7
Eastham	D-10
Easthampton	C-3
Edgartown	B-6
Fairhaven	D-8
Fall River	E-7
Fitchburg	B-5
Framingham	B-2
Gardner	B-7
Gloucester	B-3
Great Barrington	D-8

Brockton	B-4
Brookline	D-7
Cambridge	C-5
Chatham	B-7
Chicopee	E-9
Clinton	B-6
Cohasset	B-7
Concord	B-7
Dalton	C-5
Danvers	B-7
Dedham	C-7
Deerfield	D-1
Duxbury	D-8

Massachusetts	
Population: 6,398,743	
Land area: 7,840 sq. mi.	
Capital: Boston	
Cities and Towns	
Adams	B-2
Agawam	A-7
Amesbury	A-7
Athol	B-2
Attleboro	C-3
Auburn	C-5
Ayer	B-6
Barnstable	E-9
Bedford	B-7
Bellingham	B-1
Billerica	B-7
Boston	B-7
Braintree	B-7
Brewster	D-1

For border crossing information, please see p. 59

Explore Michigan at go.randmcnally.com/MI

© Rand McNally

Michigan

Population: 10,120,860
Land area: 56,804 sq. mi.
Capital: Lansing

Cities and Towns

Adrian J-4
Albion I-4
Allegan I-2
Alma G-4
Alpena D-5
Ann Arbor I-5
Bad Axe F-6
Baldwin F-2
Battle Creek I-3
Bay City G-4
Bellaire E-3
Benton Harbor I-1
Benton Heights I-2
Berrien Springs B-5
Bessemer B-5
Big Rapids G-3
Birmingham I-5
Boyne City D-3
Brighton I-5
Burton H-5
Cadillac F-3
Caro G-5
Cass City G-5
Cassopolis J-2
Cedar Springs H-3
Centreville J-3
Charlevoix D-3
Charlotte I-3
Cheboygan D-4
Chelsea I-4
Clare G-4
Clio H-5
Coldwater J-3
Corunna H-4
Croswell G-6
Crystal Falls B-6
Davison H-5
Dearborn I-5
Detroit I-5
Dowagiac J-2
East Tawas F-5
Escanaba C-1
Evart F-3
Fenton H-5
Flint H-5
Frankenmuth G-5
Frankfort E-2
Fremont G-2
Garden City I-5
Gaylord E-4
Gladstone C-1
Gladwin F-4
Grand Haven H-2
Grand Ledge H-2
Grand Rapids H-2
Grayling E-3
Greenville H-3
Hancock A-6
Harbor Beach F-6
Harbor Springs D-3
Harrison F-3
Hart G-2
Hastings H-3
Hillsdale J-4
Holland H-2
Holly H-5
Houghton A-6
Howell H-4
Hudson J-4
Hudsonville H-2
Imlay City H-5
Ionia H-3
Iron Mountain C-6
Iron River B-6
Ironwood B-5
Ishpeming B-6
Ithaca G-4
Jackson I-4
Jonesville I-4
Kalamazoo I-3
Kalkaska E-3
L'Anse B-6
Lake City F-3
Lansing H-4
Lapeer H-5
Livonia I-5
Ludington F-1
Mackinaw City C-3
Manistee F-2
Manistique C-2
Marlette G-5
Marquette B-6
Marshall I-3
Marysville H-6
Mason H-4
Menominee C-6
Midland G-4
Monroe J-5
Mount Clemens H-6
Mount Pleasant G-3
Munising B-1
Muskegon G-2
Muskegon Heights . . . H-2
Negaunee B-6
New Buffalo J-1
Newberry B-3
Niles J-2
Norway C-6
Ontonagon B-5
Owosso H-4
Paw Paw I-2
Petoskey D-3
Plainwell I-3
Pontiac H-5
Port Huron H-6
Portage I-3
Reed City F-3
Rockford H-3
Rogers City D-4
Saginaw G-4
St. Clair H-6
St. Ignace C-3
St. Johns H-4
St. Joseph I-1
Saline I-5
Sault Ste. Marie B-4
South Haven I-1
Sparta H-2
Standish F-4
Sturgis J-3
Tawas City F-5
Tecumseh I-4
Three Rivers J-2
Traverse City E-2
Trenton I-5
Vassar G-5
Wakefield B-5
Warren I-6
West Branch F-4
Westland I-5
Wyandotte I-5
Wyoming H-2
Ypsilanti I-5
Zeeland H-2

Plan a Minnesota trip at go.randmcnally.com/MN

For border crossing information, please see p. 59

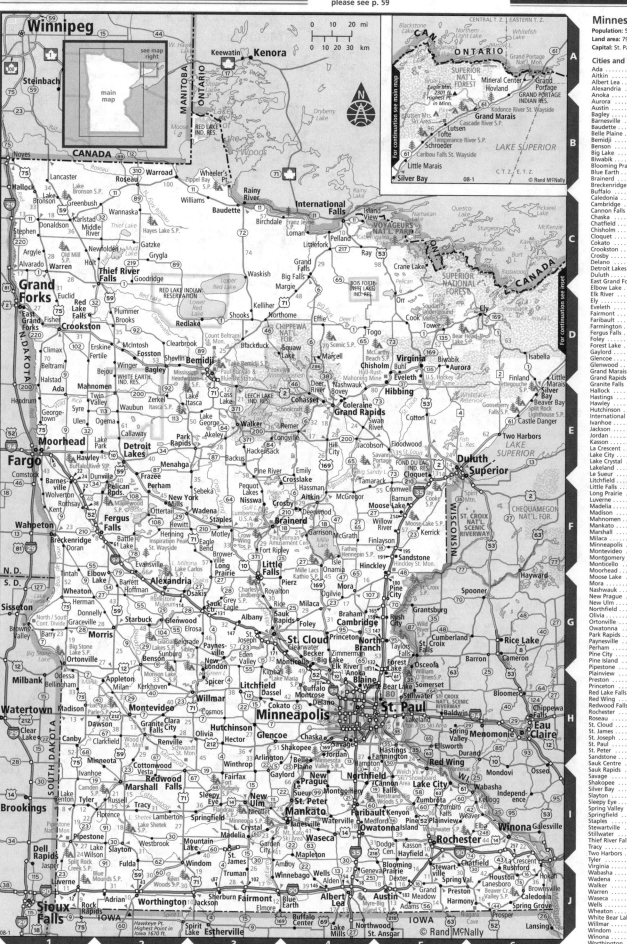

Minnesota

Population: 5,132,799
Land area: 79,610 sq. mi.
Capital: St. Paul

Cities and Towns

Ada E-1
Aitkin F-4
Albert Lea J-4
Alexandria G-3
Anoka H-4
Aurora D-6
Austin J-4
Bagley D-2
Barnesville F-1
Baudette C-3
Belle Plaine H-4
Bemidji D-3
Benson G-2
Big Lake H-4
Biwabik D-6
Blooming Prairie J-4
Blue Earth J-3
Brainerd F-4
Breckenridge F-1
Buffalo H-4
Caledonia J-6
Cambridge G-4
Cannon Falls H-5
Chaska H-4
Chatfield J-5
Chisholm D-5
Cloquet E-5
Cokato H-3
Crookston D-1
Crosby F-4
Delano H-4
Detroit Lakes E-2
Duluth E-5
East Grand Forks D-1
Elbow Lake G-2
Elk River H-4
Ely D-6
Eveleth D-5
Fairmont J-3
Faribault H-4
Farmington H-4
Fergus Falls F-2
Foley G-4
Forest Lake H-4
Gaylord H-3
Glencoe H-3
Glenwood G-2
Grand Marais C-7
Grand Rapids E-5
Granite Falls H-2
Hallock B-1
Hastings H-5
Hawley E-1
Hutchinson H-3
International Falls .. C-4
Ivanhoe I-1
Jackson J-2
Jordan H-4
Kasson J-5
La Crescent J-6
Lake City I-5
Lake Crystal I-3
Lakeland H-5
Le Sueur I-4
Litchfield H-3
Little Falls G-3
Long Prairie G-3
Luverne J-1
Madelia I-3
Madison H-1
Mahnomen E-2
Mankato I-4
Marshall I-2
Milaca G-4
Minneapolis H-4
Montevideo H-2
Montgomery I-4
Monticello G-4
Moorhead E-1
Moose Lake F-5
Mora G-4
Nashwauk D-5
New Prague H-4
New Ulm I-3
Northfield H-4
Olivia H-2
Ortonville G-1
Owatonna I-4
Park Rapids E-3
Paynesville G-3
Perham F-2
Pine City G-5
Pine Island I-5
Pipestone I-1
Plainview I-5
Preston J-6
Princeton G-4
Red Lake Falls D-1
Red Wing H-5
Redwood Falls I-2
Rochester I-5
Roseau B-2
St. Cloud G-4
St. James I-3
St. Joseph G-3
St. Paul H-5
St. Peter I-4
Sandstone F-5
Sauk Centre G-3
Sauk Rapids G-3
Savage H-4
Shakopee H-4
Silver Bay E-6
Slayton I-2
Sleepy Eye I-3
Spring Valley J-5
Springfield I-3
Staples F-3
Stewartville J-5
Stillwater H-5
Thief River Falls ... D-2
Tracy I-2
Two Harbors E-6
Tyler I-1
Virginia D-5
Wabasha I-5
Wadena F-3
Walker E-3
Warren C-1
Waseca I-4
Wells J-3
Wheaton G-1
White Bear Lake H-5
Willmar H-3
Windom I-6
Winona I-6
Worthington J-2
Zimmerman G-4

08-1
© Rand McNally

Mississippi
Population: 2,921,088
Land area: 46,907 sq. mi.
Capital: Jackson

Cities and Towns

Aberdeen C-5
Ackerman C-6
Amory C-6
Anguilla E-2
Baldwyn B-5
Batesville B-3
Bay Springs G-4
Bay St. Louis J-4
Beaumont H-5
Belmont B-6
Belzoni D-3
Biloxi J-5
Booneville B-5
Brandon F-3
Brookhaven G-3
Brooksville C-4
Bruce C-4
Bude H-2
Byhalia A-4
Calhoun City C-4
Canton F-3
Carthage E-4
Centreville H-2
Charleston C-3
Clarksdale C-2
Cleveland C-2
Clinton F-3
Coffeeville C-4
Collins G-4
Columbia H-4
Columbus D-6
Como B-3
Corinth A-6
Crystal Springs G-3
D'Iberville J-5
De Kalb E-5
Decatur F-5
Drew C-2
Durant E-3
Edwards F-2
Ellisville G-5
Eupora D-4
Fayette G-2
Forest F-4
Fulton C-6
Gautier J-5
Greenville D-2
Greenwood D-3
Grenada C-4
Gulfport J-5
Hattiesburg H-4
Hazlehurst G-3
Hernando A-3
Hollandale D-2
Holly Springs B-4
Horn Lake A-3
Houston C-5
Indianola D-2
Itta Bena D-3
Iuka B-6
Jackson F-3
Kosciusko E-4
Laurel G-5
Leakesville H-5
Leland D-2
Lexington E-3
Long Beach J-5
Louisville E-5
Lucedale I-5
Lumberton H-4
Macon E-5
Madison F-3
Magee G-4
Magnolia H-3
Marks C-3
Mathiston D-5
McComb H-3
Mendenhall G-3
Meridian F-5
Mississippi State D-5
Monticello G-3
Morton F-4
Moss Point J-6
Mount Olive G-4
Natchez G-1
Nettleton C-5
New Albany B-5
Newton F-5
Ocean Springs I-5
Okolona C-5
Olive Branch A-4
Oxford B-4
Pascagoula J-6
Pass Christian J-4
Pearl F-3
Petal H-4
Philadelphia E-5
Picayune I-4
Pickens E-3
Pontotoc C-5
Poplarville I-4
Port Gibson G-2
Prentiss G-3
Purvis H-4
Quitman G-5
Raleigh F-3
Raymond F-3
Richton H-5
Richland F-3
Ridgeland F-3
Ripley B-5
Rolling Fork E-2
Rosedale C-2
Ruleville D-2
Sardis B-3
Seminary G-4
Shannon C-5
Shaw D-2
Shelby C-2
Southaven A-3
Starkville D-5
Summit H-3
Tchula D-3
Terry F-3
Tunica B-3
Tupelo C-5
Tutwiler C-3
Tylertown H-3
Union F-5
Utica F-2
Vancleave I-5
Vicksburg F-2
Water Valley C-4
Waynesboro G-5
Webb C-3
West Point D-5
Wiggins I-5
Winona D-4
Woodville H-1
Yazoo City E-3

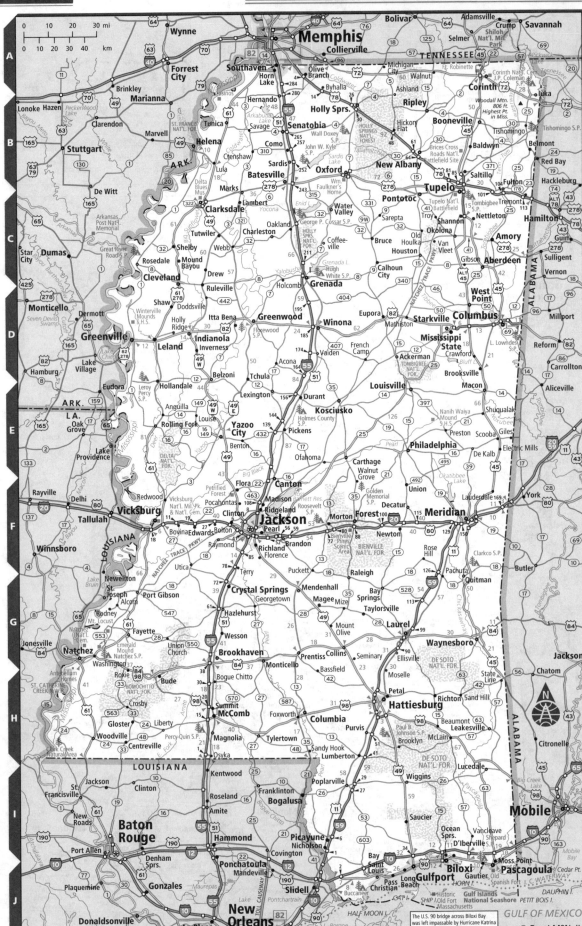

The U.S. 90 bridge across Biloxi Bay was left impassable by Hurricane Katrina and is currently being reconstructed.

© Rand McNally

Missouri

Population: 5,800,310
Land area: 68,886 sq. mi.
Capital: Jefferson City

Cities and Towns

Arnold	D-7
Aurora	F-3
Ava	F-4
Belton	C-2
Bethany	A-3
Blue Springs	C-3
Bolivar	E-4
Bonne Terre	E-7
Boonville	C-4
Bowling Green	B-6
Branson	F-4
Brookfield	B-4
Butler	D-2
California	D-4
Cameron	B-3
Cape Girardeau	E-8
Carthage	F-2
Caruthersville	G-8
Centralia	C-5
Charleston	F-8
Chillicothe	B-3
Clinton	D-3
Columbia	C-5
Crystal City	D-7
De Soto	D-7
Dexter	F-8
East Prairie	F-8
El Dorado Springs	E-3
Eldon	D-4
Eureka	D-7
Eveningshade	E-5
Excelsior Springs	B-3
Farmington	E-7
Festus	D-7
Fredericktown	E-7
Fulton	C-5
Grandview	C-2
Hannibal	B-6
Harrisonville	C-2
Hayti	G-8
Independence	C-2
Jackson	E-8
Jefferson City	D-5
Joplin	F-2
Kansas City	C-2
Kennett	G-7
Kirksville	A-4
Lamar	E-3
Lebanon	E-4
Lexington	C-3
Liberty	C-2
Louisiana	B-6
Macon	B-5
Malden	F-8
Marshall	C-4
Marshfield	E-4
Maryville	A-2
Mexico	C-5
Moberly	B-5
Monett	F-3
Mount Vernon	E-3
Mountain Grove	F-5
Neosho	F-2
Nevada	E-2
New Madrid	F-8
Nixa	F-4
Odessa	C-3
Osage Beach	D-4
Ozark	F-4
Pacific	D-7
Palmyra	B-6
Perryville	E-8
Platte City	B-2
Pleasant Hill	C-3
Poplar Bluff	F-7
Potosi	E-7
Republic	F-3
Richmond	C-3
Rolla	E-5
St. Charles	C-7
St. Clair	D-6
St. James	D-6
St. Joseph	B-2
St. Louis	C-7
Ste. Genevieve	D-7
Salem	E-6
Savannah	B-2
Sedalia	C-4
Sikeston	F-8
Springfield	F-4
Sullivan	D-6
Trenton	A-3
Troy	C-6
Union	D-6
Warrensburg	C-3
Warrenton	C-6
Washington	D-6
Waynesville	E-5
Webb City	F-2
Wentzville	C-6
West Plains	F-5
Windsor	D-3

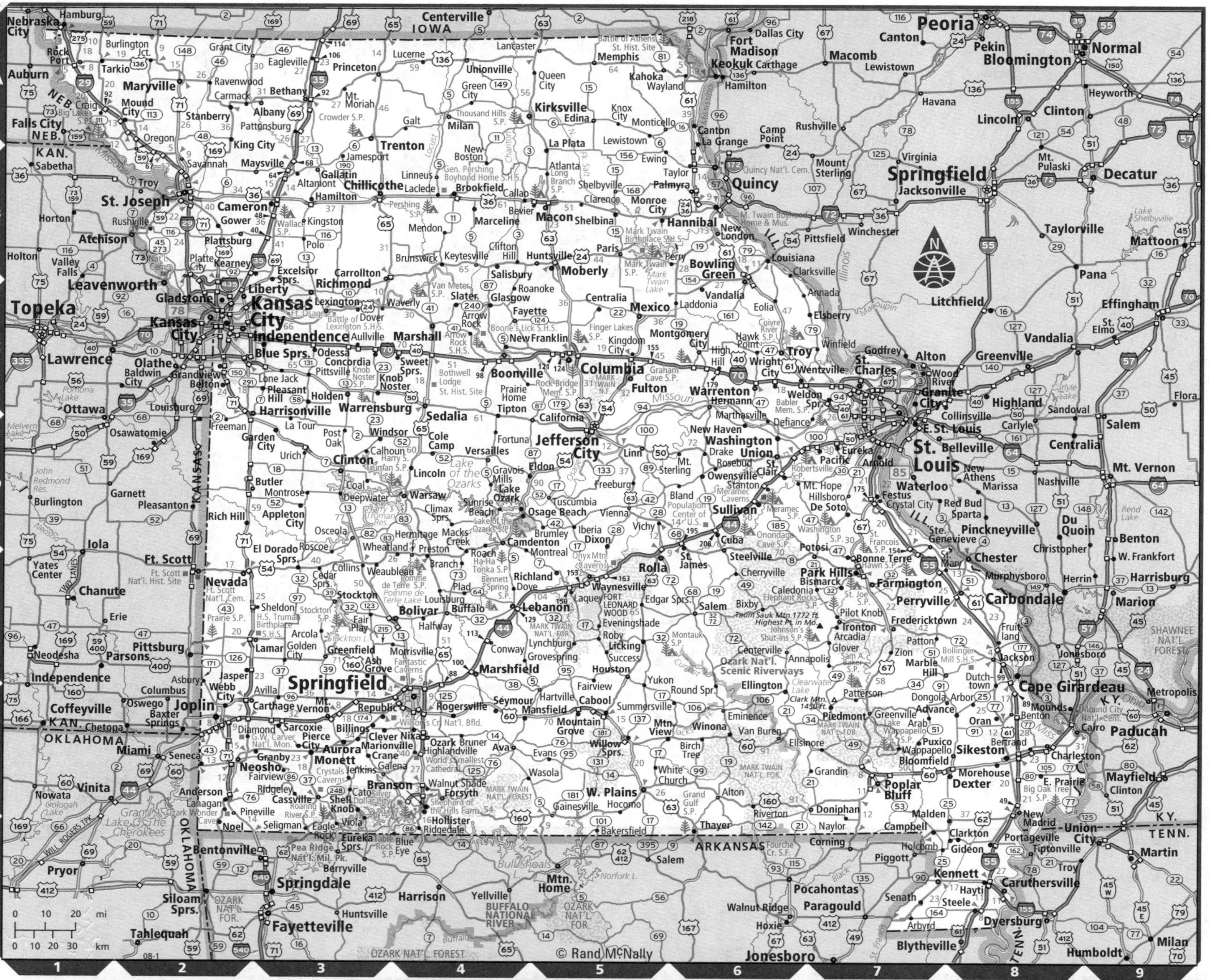

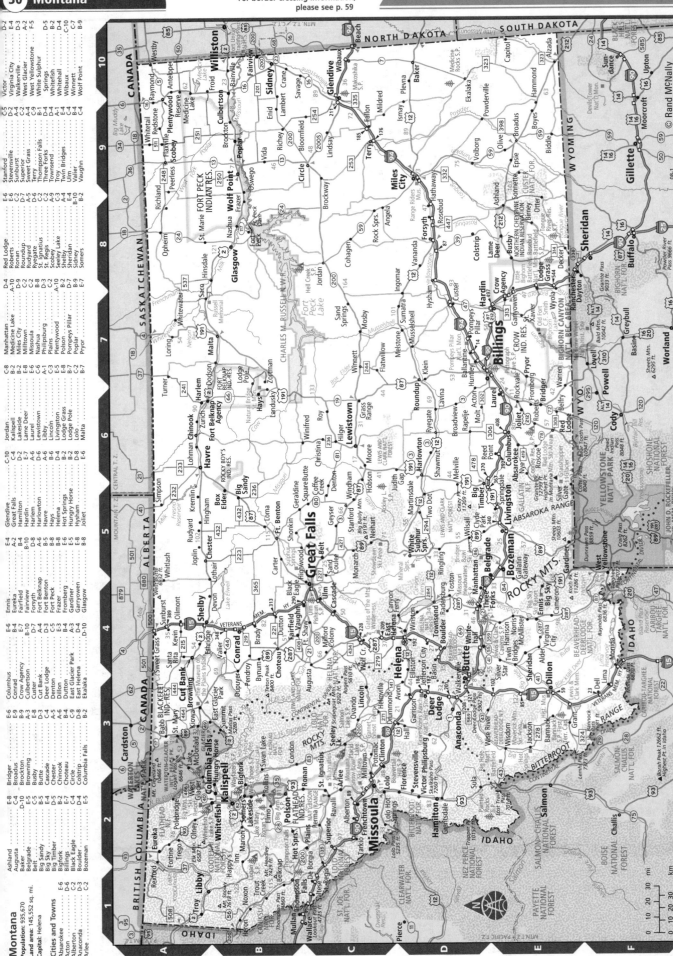

Montana
Population: 935,670
Land area: 145,552 sq. mi.
Capital: Helena

Cities and Towns

Absarokee	E-6
Acton	D-6
Anaconda	C-2
Arlee	C-2
Ashland	E-8
Augusta	C-4
Baker	D-10
Belgrade	D-5
Big Sky	D-5
Big Sandy	B-5
Big Timber	E-6
Bigfork	B-2
Billings	D-6
Black Eagle	C-2
Boulder	D-4
Bozeman	C-2
Bridger	E-6
Broadus	D-10
Brockton	A-2
Browning	B-2
Butte	D-3
Cardston	C-2
Cascade	D-3
Chester	B-5
Chinook	B-6
Choteau	C-4
Circle	C-9
Colstrip	D-8
Columbia Falls	B-2
Columbus	C-8
Conrad	B-2
Crow Agency	E-7
Cut Bank	B-8
Deer Lodge	C-8
Denton	A-4
Dillon	C-5
Dutton	B-4
East Glacier Park	B-4
East Helena	D-4
Ekalaka	D-10
Ennis	E-6
Eureka	A-2
Fairfield	B-4
Fairview	B-10
Forsyth	D-7
Fort Belknap	A-6
Fort Benton	B-5
Frazer	B-8
Fromberg	E-6
Gardiner	B-4
Garryowen	D-4
Glasgow	B-2
Glendive	E-4
Great Falls	A-2
Hamilton	B-4
Harlem	B-10
Harlowton	D-8
Havre	B-5
Hays	B-8
Helena	D-4
Hot Springs	E-6
Hungry Horse	B-4
Hysham	D-8
Joliet	E-8
Jordan	C-10
Kalispell	B-2
Lakeside	D-2
Lame Deer	E-7
Laurel	A-6
Lewistown	A-6
Libby	A-6
Lincoln	D-4
Livingston	B-6
Lodge Grass	E-7
Lodge Pole	A-8
Malta	E-6
Manhattan	C-8
Medicine Lake	A-10
Miles City	B-2
Milltown	B-2
Missoula	C-2
Nashua	B-8
Philipsburg	C-3
Plains	B-6
Plentywood	A-5
Polson	B-6
Poplar	D-4
Pompeys Pillar	C-2
Pryor	B-7
Red Lodge	D-4
Roberts	A-10
Ronan	D-9
Roundup	B-8
Rudyard	A-8
St. Ignatius	B-8
St. Regis	B-8
Scobey	D-3
Seeley Lake	A-9
Shelby	C-3
Sidney	E-4
Somers	B-2
Stanford	C-5
Stevensville	D-4
Sunburst	D-7
Sweet Grass	C-2
Terry	C-9
Thompson Falls	B-1
Three Forks	D-4
Townsend	D-4
Troy	A-1
Twin Bridges	C-3
Ulm	E-4
Valier	B-4
Vaughn	B-2
Victor	D-2
Virginia City	D-3
Walkerville	C-2
West Glacier	A-2
West Yellowstone	C-9
White Sulphur Springs	B-1
Whitefish	B-2
Whitehall	D-4
Winnett	B-8
Wolf Point	C-4

Nevada

Population: 2,414,807
Land area: 109,826 sq. mi.
Capital: Carson City

Cities and Towns

Alamo G-5
Amargosa Valley H-4
Austin E-3
Baker E-6
Battle Mountain C-4
Beowawe H-4
Boulder City I-6
Caliente G-6
Carlin C-4
Carson City E-1
Cherry Creek D-5
Coaldale F-3
Dayton E-1
Deeth C-5
Denio B-2
Duckwater E-5
Dunphy C-4
Elko C-5
Ely E-5
Empire C-1
Eureka E-4
Fallon E-2
Fernley D-2
Gabbs E-3
Gardnerville E-1
Gerlach C-1
Golconda C-3
Halleck C-5
Hawthorne F-2
Henderson I-5
Hiko G-5
Imlay C-2
Indian Springs H-5
Jackpot B-5
Jarbidge B-5
Jean I-5
Jiggs C-5
Las Vegas H-5
Laughlin J-6
Logandale H-6
Lovelock D-2
Lund E-5
Luning F-2
Manhattan F-3
McDermitt B-3
McGill E-5
Mesquite H-6
Mina F-3
Minden E-1
Montello C-6
Mountain City B-4
Nelson I-6
Oreana D-2
Orovada B-3
Overton H-6
Owyhee B-4
Pahrump H-4
Panaca G-6
Paradise Valley B-3
Pioche F-6
Reno E-1
Ruby Valley D-5
Ruth E-5
Schurz E-2
Scotty's Junction G-3
Searchlight I-5
Silver Peak G-3
Silver Springs E-2
Sparks D-1
Stateline E-1
Tonopah F-3
Tuscarora C-4
Valmy C-3
Verdi E-1
Virginia City E-1
Wadsworth D-1
Walker Lake F-2
Warm Springs F-4
Wellington E-1
Wells C-5
West Wendover C-6
Winnemucca C-3
Yerington E-2

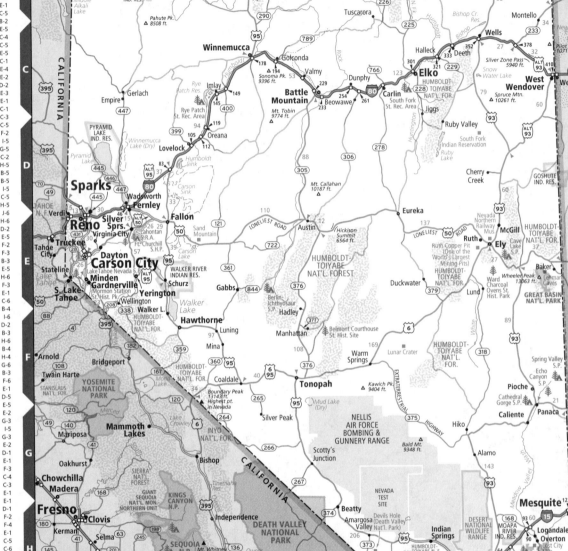

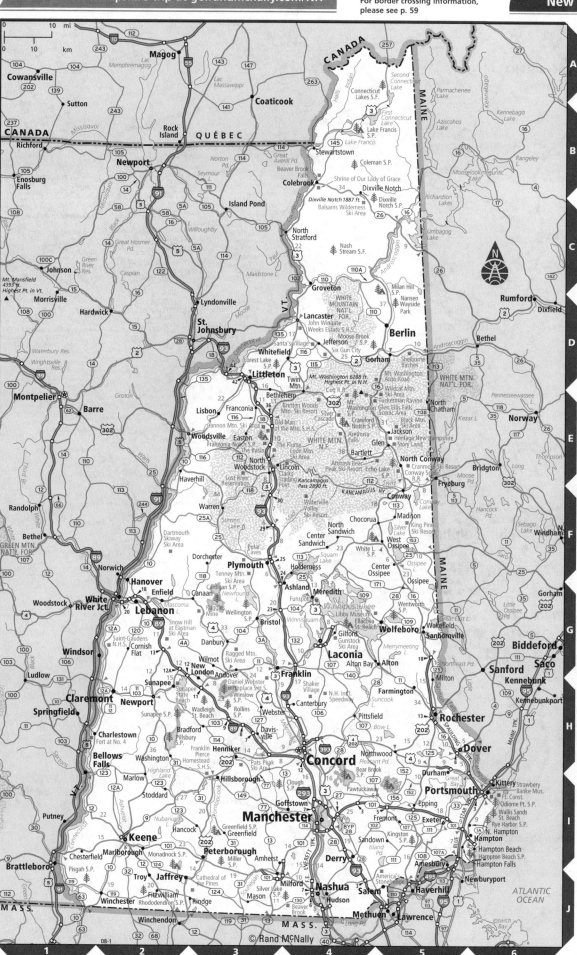

New Hampshire

Population: 1,309,940
Land area: 8,968 sq. mi.
Capital: Concord

Cities and Towns

Alton	G-
Alton Bay	G-
Amherst	I-
Andover	G-
Ashland	G-
Bartlett	E-
Berlin	D-
Bethlehem	E-
Bradford	H-
Bristol	G-
Canaan	G-
Canterbury	H-
Center Ossipee	F-
Center Sandwich	F-
Charlestown	H-
Chesterfield	I-
Chocorua	F-
Claremont	H-
Colebrook	B-
Concord	H-
Conway	F-
Cornish Flat	H-
Danbury	G-
Davisville	H-
Derry	I-
Dixville Notch	B-
Dorchester	F-
Dover	H-
Durham	H-
Easton	E-3
Enfield	G-2
Epping	I-5
Exeter	I-5
Farmington	H-5
Fitzwilliam	J-2
Franconia	E-3
Franklin	G-4
Fremont	I-5
Glen	E-5
Goffstown	I-4
Gorham	D-5
Greenfield	I-3
Groveton	C-4
Hampton	I-6
Hampton Beach	I-6
Hampton Falls	I-5
Hancock	I-3
Hanover	G-2
Haverhill	E-2
Henniker	H-3
Hillsborough	I-3
Holderness	F-4
Hudson	J-4
Jackson	E-5
Jaffrey	J-2
Jefferson	D-4
Keene	I-2
Laconia	G-4
Lancaster	D-4
Lebanon	G-2
Lincoln	E-3
Lison	E-3
Littleton	D-3
Madison	I-4
Manchester	I-4
Marlborough	I-2
Marlow	I-2
Mason	J-3
Meredith	G-4
Milford	I-3
Milton	H-5
Nashua	J-4
New London	H-3
North Chatham	E-5
North Conway	E-5
North Sandwich	F-4
North Stratford	C-4
North Woodstock	E-3
Northwood	H-5
Ossipee	G-5
Peterborough	I-3
Pittsfield	H-4
Plymouth	F-3
Portsmouth	I-6
Rindge	J-3
Rochester	H-5
Salem	J-5
Sanbornville	G-5
Sandown	I-5
Stewartstown	B-4
Stoddard	I-3
Sunapee	H-2
Troy	J-2
Twin Mountain	E-4
Wakefield	G-5
Warren	F-3
Washington	H-3
Webster	H-3
West Ossipee	F-5
Whitefield	D-4
Wilmot	G-3
Winchester	J-2
Wolfeboro	G-5
Woodsville	E-2

New Jersey

Population: 8,717,925
Land and area: 7,417 sq. mi.
Capital: Trenton

Cities and Towns

Absecon	H-4
Asbury Park	E-5
Atlantic City	I-4
Atlantic Highlands	E-5
Audubon	G-2
Barnegat Light	G-5
Bayonne	D-5
Beach Haven	H-5
Beachwood	F-5
Belleville	C-5
Belvidere	C-2
Berlin	G-3
Bernardsville	G-2
Blackwood	G-2
Bloomfield	C-5
Boonton	C-4
Bordentown	F-3
Bound Brook	D-4
Bridgeton	H-2
Bridgewater	D-4
Brigantine	H-4
Browns Mills	F-4
Budd Lake	C-3
Buena	H-3
Burlington	F-3
Butler	B-4
Caldwell	C-5
Camden	F-2
Cape May	J-3
Cape May Court	
House	J-3
Cherry Hill	F-3
Clark	D-5
Clifton	C-5
Cranford	D-4
Denville	C-4
Dover	C-4
Dumont	C-5
East Orange	C-5
Eatontown	D-4
Edison	D-4
Egg Harbor City	H-4
Elizabeth	D-5
Englewood	C-5
Ewing	E-3
Flemington	D-3
Franklin	B-4
Freehold	E-5
Glassboro	G-2
Gloucester City	G-2
Hackensack	C-5
Hackettstown	C-3
Hammonton	G-3
High Bridge	D-3
Highlands	E-5
Hightstown	E-4
Hopatcong	C-3
Irvington	C-5
Iselin	D-4
Jamesburg	E-4
Jersey City	C-5
Keansburg	D-5
Lakehurst	F-5
Lakewood	F-5
Lambertville	E-3
Lawrenceville	E-3
Linden	D-5
Little Silver	E-5
Long Branch	E-5
Madison	C-4
Mahwah	B-5
Manville	D-4
Margate City	I-4
Matawan	E-5
Mays Landing	H-3
Metuchen	D-4
Millville	H-2
Morris Plains	C-4
Morristown	C-4
Mount Holly	F-3
Neptune City	E-5
Netcong	C-3
New Brunswick	D-4
New Providence	C-4
Newark	C-5
Newfoundland	B-4
Newton	B-3
North Bergen	C-5
Oakland	B-5
Ocean City	I-4
Ocean Grove	E-5
Old Bridge	E-4
Palisades Park	C-5
Paramus	B-5
Passaic	C-5
Paterson	C-5
Paulsboro	G-2
Penns Grove	G-1
Pennsauken	F-2
Pennsville	G-1
Perth Amboy	D-5
Phillipsburg	D-2
Plainfield	D-4
Pleasantville	H-4
Point Pleasant	F-5
Princeton	E-3
Rahway	D-5
Ramsey	B-5
Raritan	D-4
Red Bank	E-5
Ridgewood	B-5
Salem	H-1
Sayreville	D-4
Scotch Plains	D-4
Sea Bright	E-5
Sea Isle City	I-3
Seaside Park	F-5
Ship Bottom	G-5
Somerdale	G-2
Somers Point	I-4
Somerville	D-4
South River	D-4
Sparta	B-4
Spring Lake	E-5
Stratford	G-2
Toms River	F-5
Trenton	E-3
Tuckerton	H-4
Union	C-5
Ventnor City	I-4
Villas	J-3
Vineland	H-2
Waldwick	B-5
Wanaque	B-5
Washington	C-3
West Orange	C-5
Wildwood	J-3
Williamstown	G-3
Willingboro	F-3
Woodbury	G-2
Woodstown	G-2
Wrightstown	F-4
Wyckoff	B-5

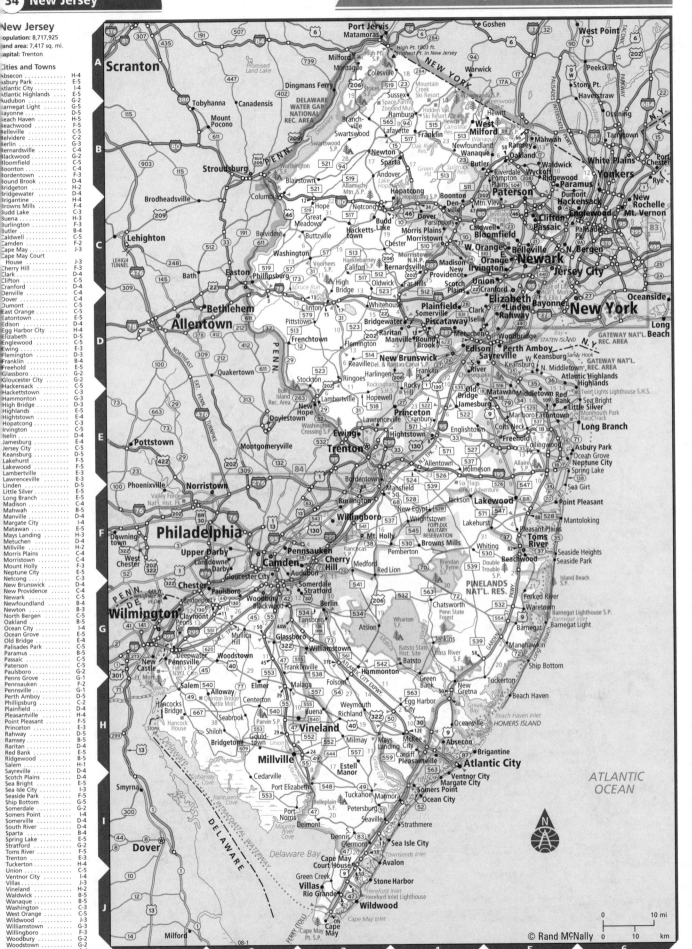

© Rand McNally

0   10 mi

0   10 km

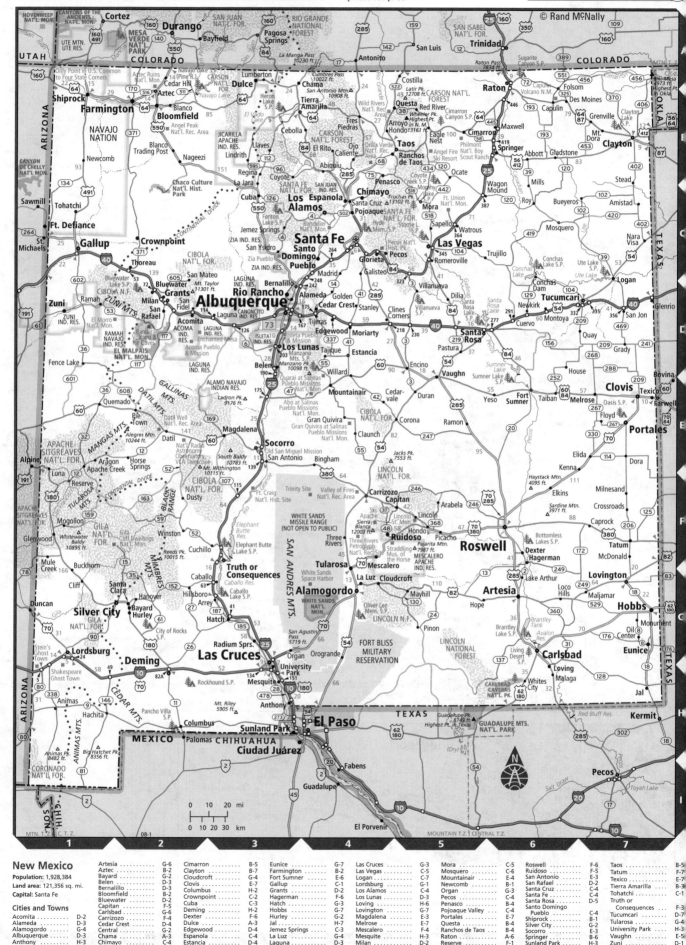

© Rand McNally

New Mexico

Population: 1,928,384
Land area: 121,356 sq. mi.
Capital: Santa Fe

Cities and Towns

Acomita	D-2
Alameda	D-3
Alamogordo	G-4
Albuquerque	D-3
Anthony	H-3
Artesia	G-6
Aztec	B-2
Bayard	G-2
Belen	D-3
Bernalillo	D-3
Bloomfield	B-2
Bluewater	D-2
Capitan	F-5
Carlsbad	G-6
Carrizozo	F-4
Cedar Crest	D-4
Central	G-2
Chama	A-3
Chimayo	C-4
Cimarron	B-5
Clayton	B-7
Cloudcroft	G-4
Clovis	E-7
Columbus	H-2
Crownpoint	C-2
Cuba	C-3
Deming	H-2
Dexter	F-6
Dulce	A-3
Edgewood	D-4
Espanola	C-4
Estancia	D-4
Eunice	G-7
Farmington	B-2
Fort Sumner	E-6
Gallup	C-1
Grants	D-2
Hagerman	F-6
Hatch	G-3
Hobbs	G-7
Hurley	G-2
Jal	H-7
Jemez Springs	C-3
La Luz	G-4
Laguna	D-3
Las Cruces	G-3
Las Vegas	C-5
Logan	C-7
Lordsburg	G-1
Los Alamos	C-4
Los Lunas	D-3
Loving	H-6
Lovington	G-7
Magdalena	E-3
Melrose	E-7
Mescalero	F-4
Mesquite	H-3
Milan	D-2
Mora	C-5
Mosquero	C-6
Mountainair	E-4
Newcomb	B-1
Organ	G-3
Pecos	C-4
Penasco	B-4
Pojoaque Valley	C-4
Portales	E-7
Questa	B-4
Ranchos de Taos	B-4
Raton	A-6
Reserve	F-1
Roswell	F-6
Ruidoso	F-5
San Antonio	E-3
San Rafael	D-2
Santa Cruz	C-4
Santa Fe	C-4
Santa Rosa	D-5
Santo Domingo Pueblo	C-4
Shiprock	B-1
Silver City	G-2
Socorro	E-3
Springer	B-6
Sunland Park	H-3
Taos	B-4
Tatum	F-7
Texico	E-7
Tierra Amarilla	B-3
Tohatchi	C-1
Truth or Consequences	F-3
Tucumcari	D-7
Tularosa	G-4
University Park	H-3
Vaughn	D-5
Zuni	D-1

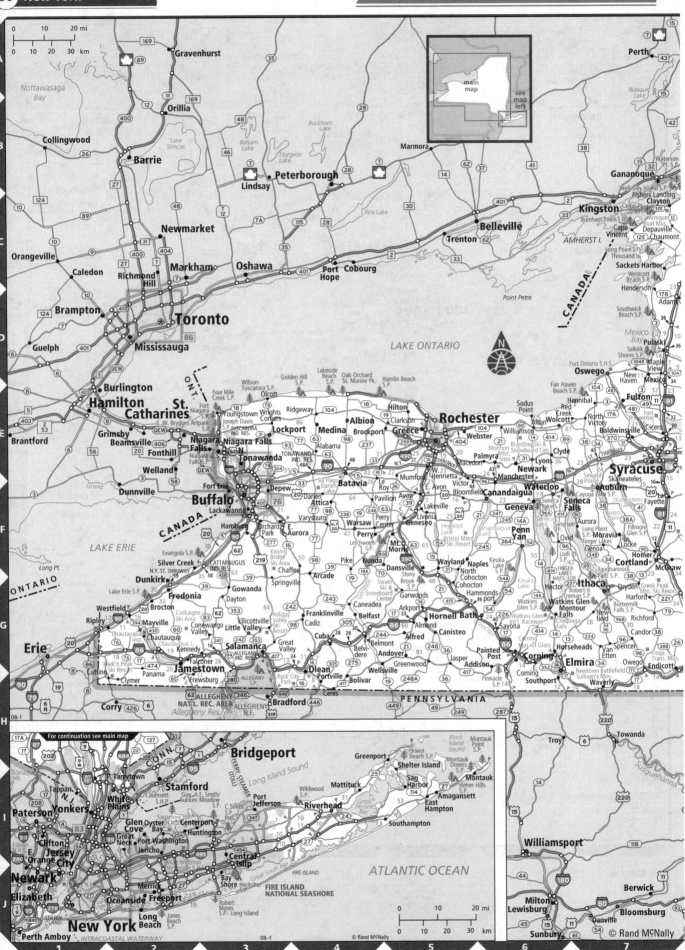

For border crossing information, please see p. 59

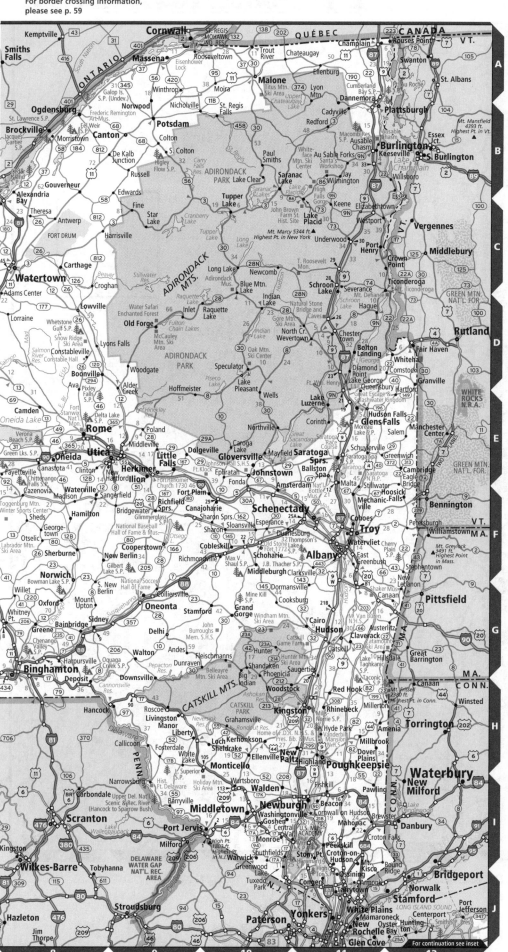

New York

Population: 19,254,630
Land area: 47,214 sq. mi.
Capital: Albany

Cities and Towns

Adams	D-7
Adams Center	D-8
Addison	G-6
Albany	F-11
Albion	E-4
Alexandria Bay	B-8
Alfred	G-5
Amagansett	I-5
Amenia	H-11
Amsterdam	F-10
Andover	G-5
Antwerp	C-8
Arcade	F-4
Attica	F-4
Au Sable Forks	B-11
Auburn	F-5
Avon	F-5
Bainbridge	G-8
Baldwinsville	E-7
Ballston Spa	E-11
Batavia	E-4
Bath	G-6
Bay Shore	J-3
Beacon	I-11
Belfast	G-5
Belmont	G-5
Binghamton	G-8
Blue Mountain Lake	C-10
Bolivar	H-4
Bolton Landing	D-11
Boonville	D-8
Brewster	I-11
Brockport	E-5
Brocton	G-2
Buffalo	F-3
Cadyville	B-11
Cairo	G-11
Cambridge	E-12
Camden	D-8
Canajoharie	F-10
Canandaigua	F-6
Canastota	E-8
Candor	G-7
Canisteo	G-5
Canton	B-9
Cape Vincent	C-7
Carthage	C-8
Catskill	G-11
Cazenovia	F-8
Centerport	J-12
Central Islip	J-3
Central Valley	I-10
Champlain	A-11
Chateaugay	A-10
Chaumont	C-7
Chautauqua	G-2
Cicero	E-7
Claverack	G-11
Clayton	C-7
Clinton	E-8
Clyde	E-6
Cobleskill	F-10
Cohocton	G-5
Cohoes	F-11
Congers	J-11
Cooperstown	F-9
Corinth	E-11
Corning	G-6
Cornwall on Hudson	I-11
Cortland	F-7
Croton Falls	I-11
Croton-on-Hudson	I-11
Crown Point	C-11
Cuba	G-4
Dannemora	B-11
Dansville	F-5
Delhi	G-9
Depew	F-3
Deposit	H-8
Dolgeville	E-9
Dover Plains	H-11
Downsville	H-9
Dryden	F-7
Dunkirk	G-2
East Aurora	F-3
East Greenbush	F-11
East Hampton	I-5
Elizabethtown	C-11
Ellenville	H-10
Elmira	H-6
Endicott	G-7
Falconer	G-2
Fayetteville	E-8
Fishkill	I-11
Fonda	F-10
Fort Plain	F-10
Franklinville	G-4
Fredonia	G-2
Freeport	J-2
Frewsburg	H-2
Fulton	E-7
Geneseo	F-5
Geneva	F-6
Glen Cove	J-11
Glens Falls	E-11
Gloversville	E-10
Goshen	I-10
Gouverneur	B-8
Gowanda	G-3
Grand Gorge	G-10
Granville	D-12
Great Neck	I-2
Greene	H-5
Greenport	I-5
Greenwich	E-11
Greenwood Lake	I-0
Hamburg	F-3
Hamilton	F-8
Hammondsport	G-6
Hancock	H-9
Herkimer	E-9
Highland	H-11
Hilton	E-5
Homer	F-7
Hoosick Falls	F-12
Hornell	G-5
Horseheads	G-6
Hudson	G-11
Hudson Falls	E-11
Huntington	J-12
Hyde Park	H-11
Ilion	E-9
Ithaca	G-7
Jamestown	G-2
Jericho	J-2
Johnstown	E-10
Keeseville	B-11
Kerhonkson	H-10
Kingston	H-11
Lackawanna	F-3
Lake George	D-11
Lake Luzerne	E-11

Lake Placid	C-11
Lake Pleasant	D-10
Lakeville	F-5
Le Roy	F-4
Liberty	H-10
Little Falls	E-9
Little Valley	G-3
Livingston Manor	H-9
Livonia	F-5
Loch Sheldrake	H-10
Lockport	E-3
Long Beach	J-
Lowville	D-8
Lyon Mountain	A-11
Lyons	E-6
Macedon	E-6
Mahopac	I-11
Malone	A-10
Mamaroneck	J-11
Manchester	F-6
Massena	A-10
Mattituck	I-5
Mayfield	E-10
Mayville	G-2
Mechanicville	F-11
Medina	E-4
Merrick	J-2
Mexico	D-7
Middleburgh	F-10
Middletown	I-10
Millbrook	H-11
Millerton	H-11
Monroe	I-10
Montauk	I-5
Monticello	H-10
Montour Falls	G-6
Moravia	F-7
Mount Kisco	I-11
Mount Morris	F-5
Naples	F-5
New Berlin	F-8
New Hartford	E-8
New Paltz	H-11
New Rochelle	J-11
Newark	E-6
Newburgh	I-10
Niagara Falls	E-3
North Tonawanda	E-3
Northville	E-10
Norwich	G-8
Norwood	A-9
Nunda	F-5
Oceanside	J-2
Ogdensburg	B-8
Olcott	E-4
Old Forge	D-9
Olean	H-4
Oneida	E-8
Oneonta	G-9
Orchard Park	F-3
Ossining	J-11
Oswego	D-7
Owego	G-7
Oxford	G-8
Oyster Bay	J-2
Painted Post	G-6
Palmyra	E-6
Paul Smiths	B-10
Pawling	I-11
Peekskill	I-11
Penn Yan	F-6
Perry	F-4
Plattsburgh	B-11
Port Henry	C-11
Port Jefferson	J-12
Port Jervis	I-2
Port Washington	I-2
Portville	H-4
Potsdam	B-9
Poughkeepsie	H-11
Pulaski	D-7
Red Hook	H-11
Rhinebeck	H-11
Richfield Springs	F-9
Ripley	G-2
Riverhead	I-4
Rochester	E-5
Rome	E-8
Roscoe	H-9
Rouses Point	A-12
Sackets Harbor	C-7
Sag Harbor	I-5
St. Regis Falls	B-10
Salamanca	G-3
Salem	E-12
Saranac Lake	B-10
Saratoga Springs	E-11
Saugerties	G-11
Schenectady	F-10
Schoharie	F-10
Schroon Lake	C-11
Schuylerville	E-11
Seneca Falls	F-6
Shelter Island	I-5
Sherburne	F-8
Sidney	G-8
Silver Creek	G-2
Skaneateles	F-7
Sodus Point	E-6
Southampton	I-5
Southport	H-6
Springville	G-3
Stamford	G-10
Star Lake	C-9
Stillwater	E-11
Stony Point	I-11
Syracuse	E-7
Tarrytown	J-11
Theresa	B-8
Ticonderoga	C-11
Troy	F-11
Tupper Lake	C-10
Utica	E-9
Victor	F-6
Walden	I-10
Walton	G-9
Warsaw	F-4
Warwick	I-10
Washingtonville	I-10
Waterloo	F-6
Watertown	C-8
Waterville	F-8
Watervliet	F-11
Watkins Glen	G-6
Waverly	H-7
Wayland	F-5
Webster	E-5
Wellsville	G-4
Westfield	G-2
White Plains	J-11
Whitehall	D-12
Whitney Point	G-8
Williamson	E-6
Wolcott	E-6
Woodstock	H-10
Wurtsboro	I-10
Yonkers	J-11
Youngstown	E-3

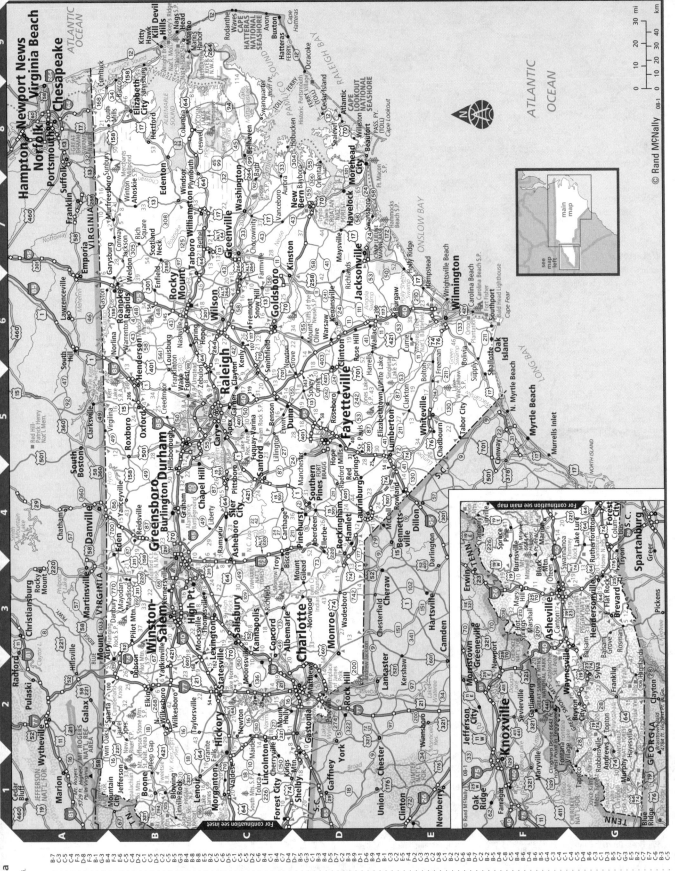

North Carolina

Population: 8,683,242
Land area: 48,711 sq. mi.
Capital: Raleigh

Cities and Towns

Ahoskie B-7
Albemarle C-4
Asheboro C-4
Asheville C-5
Beaufort D-8
Black Mountain F-3
Boone B-1
Brevard F-3
Burlington B-4
Carolina Beach D-7
Cary C-5
Chapel Hill C-4
Charlotte D-2
Cherryville C-2
Clayton C-5
Clinton D-6
Concord C-3
Dunn C-6
Durham B-5
Eden B-4
Edenton B-7
Elizabeth City B-8
Elizabethtown D-6
Elkin B-3
Erwin C-6
Farmville B-7
Fayetteville C-6
Forest City C-2
Fuquay-Varina C-5
Garner C-5
Gastonia C-2
Goldsboro C-6
Graham B-4
Granite Falls B-2
Greensboro B-4
Greenville B-7
Hamlet D-5
Havelock D-7
Henderson B-5
Hendersonville F-3
Hickory C-2
High Point B-4
Hillsborough B-4
Hope Mills C-6
Jacksonville D-7
Kannapolis C-3
Kernersville B-3
Kill Devil Hills B-9
Kings Mountain C-2
Kinston C-7
Kitty Hawk B-9
Laurinburg D-5
Lenoir B-2
Lexington C-3
Lincolnton C-2
Lumberton D-6
Marion C-1
Matthews C-3
Mocksville B-3
Monroe D-3
Mooresville C-3
Morehead City D-7
Morganton C-1
Mount Airy B-3
Mount Holly C-2
Mount Olive C-6
Nashville B-6
New Bern C-7
Newton C-2
North Wilkesboro B-2
Oxford B-5
Pinehurst C-5
Plymouth B-7
Raleigh C-5
Reidsville B-4
Roanoke Rapids B-6
Rocky Mount B-6
Roxboro B-5
Rutherfordton C-1
Salisbury C-3
Sanford C-5
Shelby C-2
Siler City C-4
Smithfield C-5
Southern Pines C-5
Tarboro B-7
Thomasville B-3
Valdese C-1
Wadesboro D-3
Wake Forest B-5
Washington B-7
Waynesville F-2
Whiteville D-6
Williamston B-7
Wilmington D-7
Wilson B-6
Winston-Salem B-3
Zebulon C-5

North Dakota

Population: 636,677
Land area: 68,976 sq. mi.
Capital: Bismarck

Cities and Towns

City	Coord.	City	Coord.
Abercrombie	E-10	Lidgerwood	E-9
Amidon	E-2	Lincoln	D-5
Anamoose	C-6	Linton	E-6
Arthur	D-9	Lisbon	D-9
Beach	D-1	Mandan	D-5
Belcourt	A-6	Manning	D-3
Belfield	D-2	Manvel	B-9
Berthold	B-4	Max	C-4
Beulah	D-4	Mayville	C-9
Bisbee	B-7	McClusky	C-5
Bismarck	D-5	McVille	C-8
Bottineau	A-5	Medora	D-2
Bowbells	A-3	Michigan	B-8
Bowman	F-2	Milnor	E-9
Burlington	B-4	Minnewaukan	B-6
Cando	B-7	Minot	B-4
Cannon Ball	E-5	Mohall	A-4
Carson	D-4	Mott	E-3
Casselton	D-9	Munich	B-7
Cavalier	A-8	Napoleon	D-6
Center	D-4	Neche	A-8
Cooperstown	C-8	New England	E-3
Crosby	A-2	New Rockford	C-7
Devils Lake	B-7	New Salem	D-4
Dickinson	D-3	New Town	C-3
Drake	C-6	Northwood	C-9
Drayton	A-9	Oakes	E-8
Dunseith	A-6	Park River	B-8
Edgeley	E-7	Parshall	C-4
Edmore	B-7	Powers Lake	B-3
Elgin	E-4	Ray	B-2
Ellendale	E-8	Richardton	D-3
Enderlin	D-9	Rolette	A-6
Fairmount	F-10	Rolla	A-6
Fargo	D-10	St. Thomas	B-9
Fessenden	C-6	Scranton	F-2
Finley	C-8	Sherwood	A-3
Flasher	E-5	Stanley	B-3
Forman	E-9	Stanton	D-4
Fort Totten	B-7	Strasburg	E-6
Fort Yates	E-5	Surrey	B-4
Garrison	C-4	Thompson	C-9
Gilby	B-9	Tioga	B-2
Glen Ullin	D-4	Towner	B-6
Grafton	B-9	Turtle Lake	C-5
Grand Forks	C-9	Valley City	D-8
Gwinner	D-9	Wahpeton	E-10
Halliday	D-3	Walhalla	A-8
Harvey	C-6	Washburn	D-5
Hatton	C-9	Watford City	C-2
Hazen	D-4	West Fargo	D-10
Hebron	E-4	Westhope	A-5
Hettinger	F-3	Williston	C-2
Hillsboro	C-9	Willow City	A-6
Hunter	D-9	Wilton	D-5
Jamestown	D-8	Wishek	D-6
Killdeer	C-3		
Kindred	E-9		
Kulm	D-8		
Lakota	B-8		
Langdon	A-7		
Larimore	C-8		
Leeds	B-7		

© Rand McNally

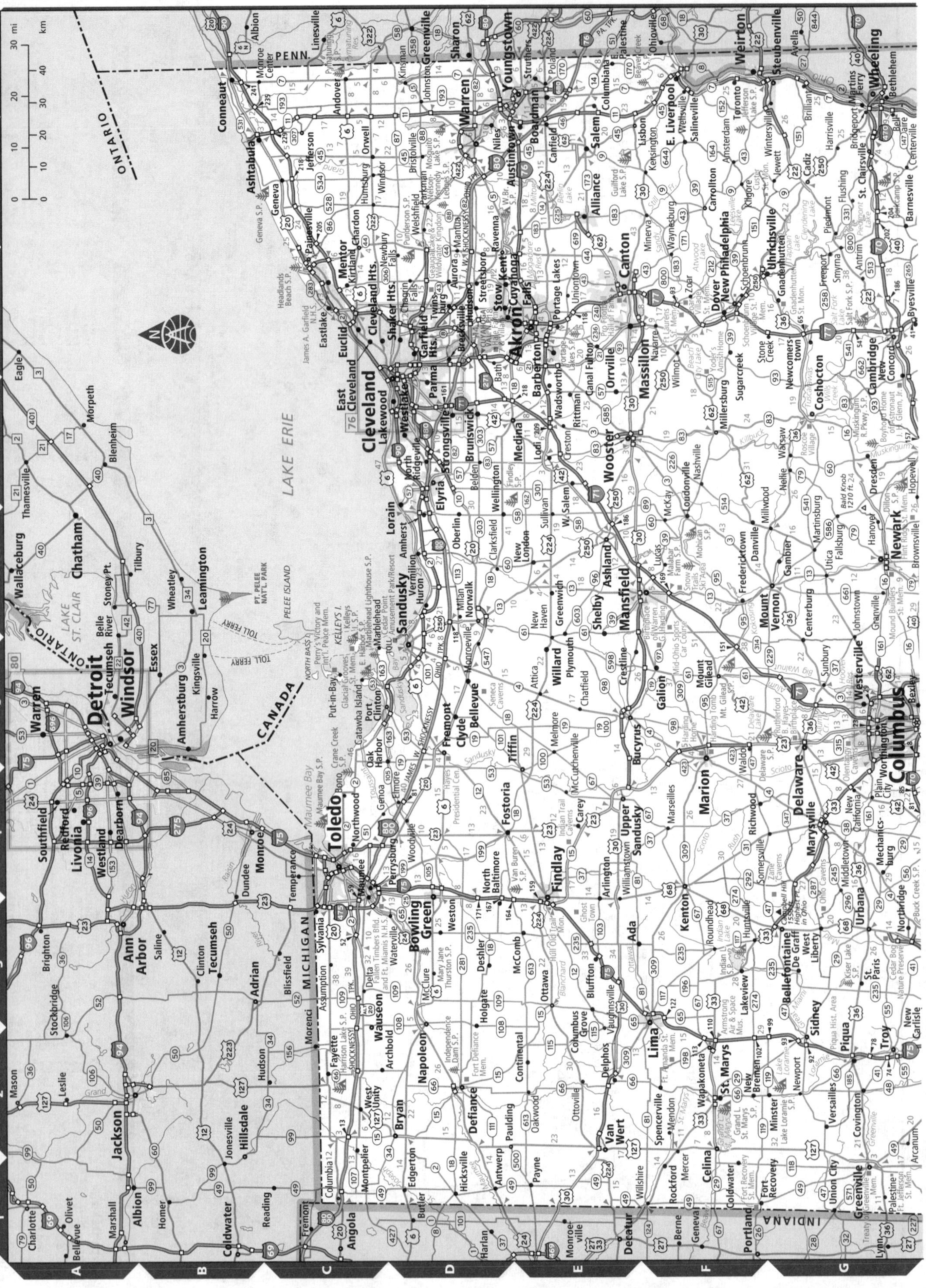
LAKE ERIE
LAKE ST. CLAIR
ONTARIO
CANADA
MICHIGAN
PENN.
INDIANA
Detroit
Windsor
Toledo
Cleveland
Akron
Canton
Youngstown
Columbus
Mansfield
Sandusky
Lima
Findlay
Marion
Delaware
Wooster
Warren
Ashtabula
Conneaut
Weirton
Steubenville
Wheeling
Ann Arbor
Jackson
Chatham
Leamington
PELEE ISLAND
TOLL FERRY

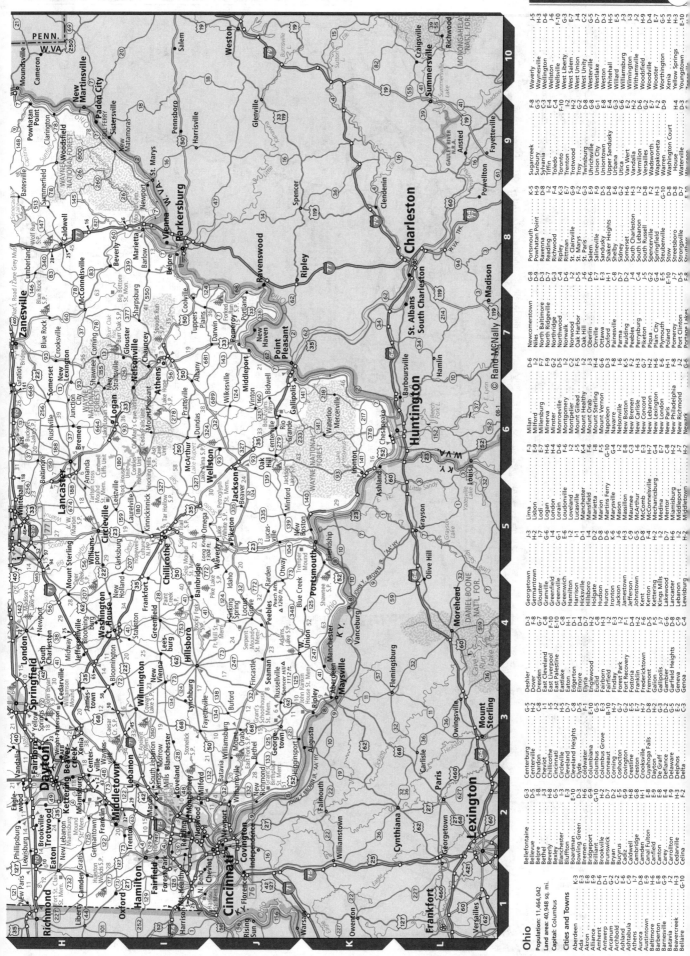

PENN.
W.VA.

© Rand McNally

Ohio

Population: 11,464,042
Land area: 40,948 sq. mi.
Capital: Columbus

Cities and Towns

Place	Grid	Place	Grid
Aberdeen	K-3	Bellefontaine	G-3
Ada	G-2	Bellevue	D-5
Akron	D-8	Belpre	I-8
Alliance	D-8	Beverly	H-8
Amherst	C-6	Bexley	G-5
Antwerp	D-1	Blanchester	I-3
Archbold	C-2	Bluffton	F-3
Ashland	E-6	Boardman	D-9
Ashtabula	B-9	Bowling Green	C-3
Aurora	D-8	Bremen	G-6
Austintown	D-9	Bridgeport	F-10
Baltimore	G-5	Brilliant	E-10
Barberton	D-8	Brookville	H-2
Barnesville	F-8	Brunswick	D-7
Batavia	J-2	Bryan	C-1
Beavercreek	H-3	Bucyrus	E-5
Bellaire	F-10	Cadiz	E-9
		Caldwell	G-8
		Cambridge	F-8
		Canal Fulton	D-8
		Canfield	D-9
		Canton	E-8
		Carey	E-4
		Carrollton	E-9
		Celina	F-2

Place	Grid	Place	Grid
Centerburg	G-3	Deshler	G-5
Centerville	D-5	Dover	H-2
Chardon	C-8	Dresden	C-8
Chillicothe	H-5	East Cleveland	G-7
Cincinnati	J-1	East Liverpool	E-10
Circleville	G-5	East Palestine	C-8
Cleveland	C-8	Eastlake	H-5
Cleveland Heights	C-8	Eaton	D-7
Coldwater	F-1	Edgerton	C-8
Columbiana	D-9	Elyria	F-5
Columbus	G-5	Englewood	E-10
Columbus Grove	E-2	Euclid	G-5
Conneaut	B-10	Fairborn	E-3
Coshocton	F-7	Fairfield	I-3
Covington	G-2	Fairport Harbor	H-2
Crestline	E-5	Forest Park	G-7
Creston	D-7	Fostoria	E-5
Cuyahoga Falls	D-8	Franklin	E-7
Dayton	H-2	Fredericktown	D-4
De Graff	G-2	Fremont	H-2
Defiance	D-2	Galion	F-5
Delaware	G-4	Gallipolis	J-7
Delta	F-2	Gambier	D-8

Place	Grid	Place	Grid
Garfield Heights	G-6	Lima	J-3
Genoa	C-3	Lisbon	I-7
Georgetown	D-3	Lodi	G-4
Germantown	F-8	London	G-4
Glouster	G-7	Lorain	G-1
Granville	F-6	Loudonville	C-8
Greenfield	E-10	Loveland	H-1
Greenville	C-8	Lucasville	I-1
Greenwich	H-1	Manchester	D-1
Hamilton	H-2	Mansfield	I-4
Harrison	D-1	Marietta	D-2
Hicksville	H-2	Marion	E-7
Hillsboro	C-8	Marysville	F-6
Holgate	E-3	Mason	K-6
Huron	E-3	Massillon	I-2
Ironton	H-3	Maumee	H-3
Jackson	I-2	McArthur	G-5
Jefferson	F-1	McComb	C-9
Johnstown	D-4	McConnelsville	E-3
Kenton	H-2	Mechanicsburg	G-4
Kettering	G-5	Medina	E-7
Kings Mills	J-7	Mentor	D-7
Lakewood	G-6	Miamisburg	H-6
Lancaster	D-8	Middleport	I-7
Lebanon	E-3	Middletown	H-2

Place	Grid	Place	Grid
Milan	F-3	Newcomerstown	D-6
Milford	E-7	Niles	F-7
Millersburg	H-6	North Baltimore	F-9
Minerva	G-4	North Ridgeville	D-5
Minster	D-6	Northridge	G-3
Monroeville	I-1	Norwalk	D-6
Montgomery	I-1	Norwood	E-7
Montpelier	J-4	Oak Harbor	F-5
Mount Gilead	F-6	Oak Hill	J-3
Mount Healthy	D-1	Oberlin	E-7
Mount Orab	I-4	Ottawa	F-9
Mount Sterling	D-2	Ottawa Hills	E-3
Mount Vernon	D-8	Oxford	H-1
Napoleon	K-6	Painesville	D-8
Nelsonville	I-6	Parma	D-7
New Boston	H-3	Paulding	K-5
New Bremen	C-9	Peebles	F-2
New Carlisle	C-3	Perrysburg	G-7
New Concord	E-3	Piketon	G-7
New Lebanon	G-4	Piqua	F-2
New London	E-7	Plain City	H-3
New Paris	G-6	Plymouth	E-5
New Philadelphia	D-8	Poland	G-10
New Richmond	J-7	Pomeroy	H-1
Newark	H-2	Port Clinton	F-8

Place	Grid	Place	Grid
Portsmouth	G-8	Sugarcreek	K-5
Powhatan Point	D-3	Sunbury	H-9
Reading	D-7	Sylvania	D-8
Ravenna	C-4	Tiffin	E-4
Richwood	G-3	Toledo	I-2
Ripley	D-6	Toronto	F-10
Ritman	E-7	Trenton	I-2
Rittman	H-2	Trotwood	H-2
St. Clairsville	F-5	Troy	T-4
St. Marys	J-6	Twinsburg	C-2
St. Paris	G-3	Uhrichsville	G-5
Salineville	F-9	Union City	D-8
Sandusky	D-5	Uniontown	D-7
Shaker Heights	D-8	Upper Sandusky	H-5
Sidney	D-7	Urbana	G-3
Solon	D-7	Van Wert	I-2
Somerset	J-4	Vandalia	D-6
South Lebanon	K-5	Vermilion	H-2
South Russell	F-2	Versailles	G-2
Spencerville	I-5	Wadsworth	E-7
Springfield	G-2	Wapakoneta	F-2
Steubenville	E-5	Warren	G-8
Stow	E-10	Washington Court House	H-4
Streetsboro	J-7	Waterville	H-3
Strongsville	D-8	Wauseon	H-3
		Waverly	E-10

Place	Grid
Waverly	J-5
Waynesville	H-3
Wellington	D-6
Wellston	H-6
Wellsville	C-4
West Liberty	G-3
West Salem	I-2
West Union	H-2
Westerville	G-3
Westlake	G-8
Weston	D-3
Whitehall	H-5
Willard	E-5
Williamsburg	I-3
Williamsport	J-2
Wilmington	H-2
Withamsville	D-6
Woodsfield	G-2
Woodstock	F-2
Wooster	E-7
Worthington	G-5
Xenia	H-4
Yellow Springs	H-3
Youngstown	H-3
Zanesville	E-10

Get more Oklahoma info at go.randmcnally.com/OK

Oklahoma

Population: 3,547,884
Land area: 68,667 sq. mi.
Capital: Oklahoma City

Cities and Towns

City	Grid
Ada	D-8
Altus	A-6
Alva	D-5
Anadarko	C-6
Antlers	E-9
Apache	D-6
Arapaho	E-5
Ardmore	B-4
Arnett	D-8
Atoka	A-4
Bartlesville	A-4
Beaver	A-3
Bixby	B-8
Blackwell	B-7
Blanchard	D-5
Boise City	A-1
Broken Arrow	B-9
Broken Bow	D-6
Buffalo	E-5
Carnegie	C-5
Chandler	D-8
Chelsea	A-8
Cherokee	A-6
Cheyenne	C-7
Chickasha	C-6
Chouteau	C-8
Cleveland	B-9
Clinton	C-5
Coalgate	B-9
Collinsville	B-9
Comanche	D-6
Commerce	C-7
Cordell	C-9
Coweta	B-8
Cushing	C-8
Davis	A-6
Dewey	C-4
Drumright	D-6
Durant	B-9
Edmond	C-5
El Reno	D-4
Elk City	B-9
Enid	E-6
Eufaula	C-7
Fairview	C-9
Frederick	B-8
Grove	B-8
Guthrie	D-5
Guymon	B-7
Haskell	E-8
Healdton	D-7
Heavener	B-6
Hennessey	C-5
Henryetta	C-6
Hobart	C-9
Holdenville	D-8
Hollis	B-6
Hugo	D-5
Idabel	E-9
Kingfisher	C-7
Konawa	D-8
Krebs	C-7
Lawton	D-10
Lexington	C-7
Lindsay	C-5
Lone Grove	C-8
Madill	C-9
Mangum	D-8
Marietta	D-5
Marlow	D-7
Medford	B-7
Miami	B-10
Midwest City	D-8
Muskogee	C-9
Newkirk	A-7
Norman	C-7
Nowata	A-8
Okemah	C-8
Oklahoma City	C-7
Okmulgee	C-8
Panama	D-10
Pawhuska	B-8
Pawnee	B-7
Perkins	C-7
Perry	B-7
Picher	A-10
Ponca City	A-7
Poteau	C-10
Prague	C-8
Pryor	B-9
Purcell	C-7
Sallisaw	C-10
Sand Springs	B-8
Sapulpa	B-8
Sayre	C-4
Seminole	C-8
Shattuck	B-4
Shawnee	B-7
Skiatook	B-8
Spiro	C-10
Stigler	C-9
Stilwell	B-10
Stillwater	B-7
Tahlequah	B-9
Taloga	C-5
Tecumseh	C-7
Tishomingo	B-4
Tonkawa	C-7
Vinita	A-9
Wagoner	B-9
Walters	E-6
Watonga	C-6
Waurika	E-6
Weatherford	C-5
Wewoka	C-8
Wilburton	D-9
Woodward	B-5
Wynnewood	D-7
Yukon	C-6

© Rand McNally

KANSAS • COLORADO • NEW MEXICO • TEXAS • ARKANSAS • MO.

© Rand McNally

Oregon

Population: 3,641,056
Land area: 95,997 sq. mi.
Capital: Salem

Cities and Towns

Albany	C-2
Aloha	C-2
Amity	C-2
Ashland	G-3
Astoria	A-2
Baker City	C-8
Bandon	F-1
Bay City	B-2
Beaverton	B-4
Bend	D-4
Boardman	B-6
Brookings	G-1
Bunker Hill	E-1
Burns	E-6
Cannon Beach	A-2
Canyon City	D-7
Canyonville	F-2
Cave Junction	G-2
Central Point	F-2
Clatskanie	A-3
Condon	C-6
Coos Bay	E-1
Coquille	F-1
Corvallis	C-2
Cottage Grove	D-2
Dallas	C-2
Depoe Bay	C-1
Drain	E-2
Elgin	B-8
Enterprise	B-8
Estacada	B-3
Eugene	D-2
Florence	D-1
Fossil	C-5
Gold Beach	F-1
Grants Pass	F-2
Heppner	C-6
Hermiston	B-6
Hillsboro	B-3
Hood River	B-4
Jacksonville	G-2
John Day	D-7
Joseph	B-8
Junction City	D-2
Klamath Falls	G-4
La Grande	C-8
Lakeview	G-5
Lebanon	C-2
Lincoln City	C-1
Madras	C-4
McMinnville	B-2
Medford	G-2
Mill City	C-3
Milton-Freewater	A-7
Molalla	B-3
Monmouth	C-2
Moro	C-5
Myrtle Creek	F-2
Myrtle Pt.	F-1
Newberg	B-3
Newport	C-1
North Bend	E-1
Nyssa	D-9
Oakridge	D-3
Ontario	D-9
Oregon City	B-3
Pendleton	B-7
Phoenix	G-2
Pilot Rock	C-7
Port Orford	F-1
Portland	B-3
Prospect	F-3
Rainier	A-3
Redmond	D-4
Reedsport	E-1
Roseburg	E-2
St. Helens	B-3
Salem	C-2
Sandy	B-3
Scappoose	B-3
Seaside	A-2
Silverton	C-3
Springfield	D-2
Sublimity	C-3
Sutherlin	E-2
Sweet Home	C-3
The Dalles	B-4
Tillamook	B-2
Toledo	C-1
Umatilla	B-6
Union	C-8
Vale	D-9
Veneta	D-2
Vernonia	B-2
Waldport	C-1
Warrenton	A-2
Winston	E-2
Woodburn	C-3

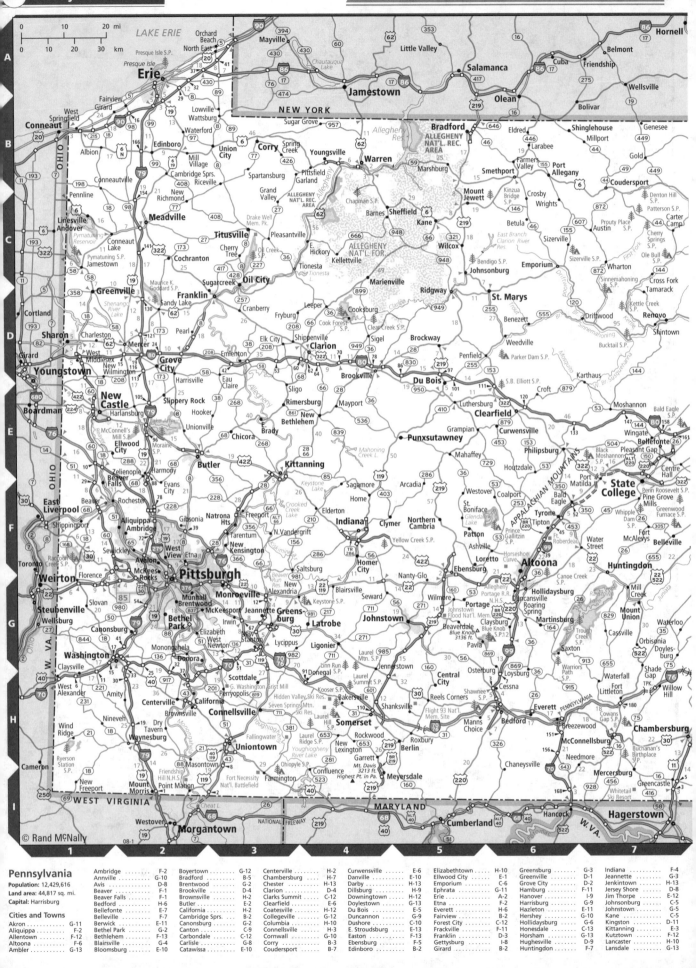

Pennsylvania

Population: 12,429,616
Land area: 44,817 sq. mi.
Capital: Harrisburg

Cities and Towns

Akron G-11
Aliquippa F-2
Allentown F-12
Altoona F-6
Ambler G-13

Ambridge F-2
Annville G-10
Avis D-8
Beaver F-1
Beaver Falls F-1
Bedford H-6
Bellefonte E-7
Belleville F-7
Berwick E-11
Bethel Park G-2
Bethlehem F-13
Blairsville G-4
Bloomsburg E-10

Boyertown G-12
Bradford B-5
Brentwood G-2
Brookville D-4
Brownsville H-2
Butler E-2
California H-2
Cambridge Sprs. ... B-2
Canonsburg G-2
Canton C-9
Carbondale C-12
Carlisle G-8
Catawissa E-10

Centerville H-2
Chambersburg H-7
Chester H-13
Clarion D-4
Clarks Summit C-12
Clearfield E-6
Coatesville G-12
Collegeville G-12
Columbia H-10
Connellsville H-3
Cornwall G-10
Corry B-3
Coudersport B-7

Curwensville E-6
Danville E-10
Darby H-13
Dillsburg H-9
Downingtown G-12
Doylestown G-13
Du Bois E-5
Duncannon G-9
Dushore C-10
E. Stroudsburg ... E-13
Easton F-13
Ebensburg F-5
Edinboro B-2

Elizabethtown H-10
Ellwood City E-1
Emporium C-6
Ephrata G-11
Erie A-2
Etna F-2
Everett H-6
Fairview B-2
Forest City C-12
Frackville F-11
Franklin D-3
Gettysburg I-8
Girard B-2

Greensburg G-3
Greenville D-1
Grove City D-2
Hamburg F-11
Hanover I-9
Harrisburg G-9
Hazleton F-11
Hershey G-10
Honesdale C-13
Horsham G-13
Hughesville D-9
Huntingdon F-7

Indiana F-4
Jeannette G-3
Jenkintown H-13
Jersey Shore D-8
Jim Thorpe E-12
Johnsonburg C-5
Johnstown G-5
Kane C-5
Kingston D-11
Kittanning E-3
Kutztown F-12
Lancaster H-10
Lansdale G-13

© Rand McNally   08-1

Laporte D-10	Marysville G-9	Milford D-14	Myerstown G-10	Palmerton E-12
Latrobe G-4	Masontown H-2	Millersburg F-9	Nanty-Glo G-5	Patton F-5
Lebanon G-10	McConnellsburg . . . H-7	Milton E-9	Nazareth F-13	Philadelphia H-13
Lehighton E-12	McKees Rocks F-2	Monongahela G-2	Nesquehoning E-12	Philipsburg F-6
Lewisburg E-9	McKeesport G-2	Monroeville G-2	New Bloomfield . . . F-9	Phoenixville H-12
Lewistown F-8	Meadville C-2	Montgomery D-9	New Castle E-1	Pittsburgh G-2
Ligonier G-4	Media H-13	Montgomeryville . . G-13	New Holland H-11	Pleasant Gap E-7
Lititz G-10	Mercer D-2	Montoursville D-9	New Kensington . . . F-3	Plymouth D-11
Lock Haven D-8	Meyersdale I-4	Montrose B-11	New Oxford H-9	Port Allegany B-6
Mahanoy City E-11	Middleburg F-9	Morrisville G-14	Newtown G-14	Portage G-5
Manheim G-10	Middletown G-9	Mount Carmel F-10	Norristown H-13	Pottstown G-12
Mansfield B-9	Mifflinburg E-9	Mount Joy H-10	Northern Cambria . . F-5	Pottsville F-11
Marienville C-4	Mifflintown F-8	Muncy D-9	Oil City C-3	Punxsutawney E-5
			Munhall G-2	Oxford I-11	Quakertown G-13

Reading G-11	Shenandoah E-11	Tower City F-10
Red Lion H-10	Sinking Spring G-11	Tunkhannock C-11
Renovo D-7	Smethport B-6	Tyrone F-6
Ridgway D-5	Somerset H-4	Union City B-3
Roaring Spring G-6	Souderton G-13	Uniontown H-3
Rochester F-1	State College F-7	Upper Darby H-13
St. Clair F-11	Stroudsburg E-13	Warminster G-13
St. Marys D-6	Sugarcreek D-3	Wilkes-Barre D-11
Sayre B-10	Sunbury E-9	Williamsport D-9
Scottdale H-3	Susquehanna B-12	Yeadon H-13
Scranton D-12	Tamaqua F-11	York H-9
Selinsgrove E-9	Tionesta C-3	Zelienople E-2
Shamokin F-10	Titusville C-3	
Sharon D-1	Towanda C-10	

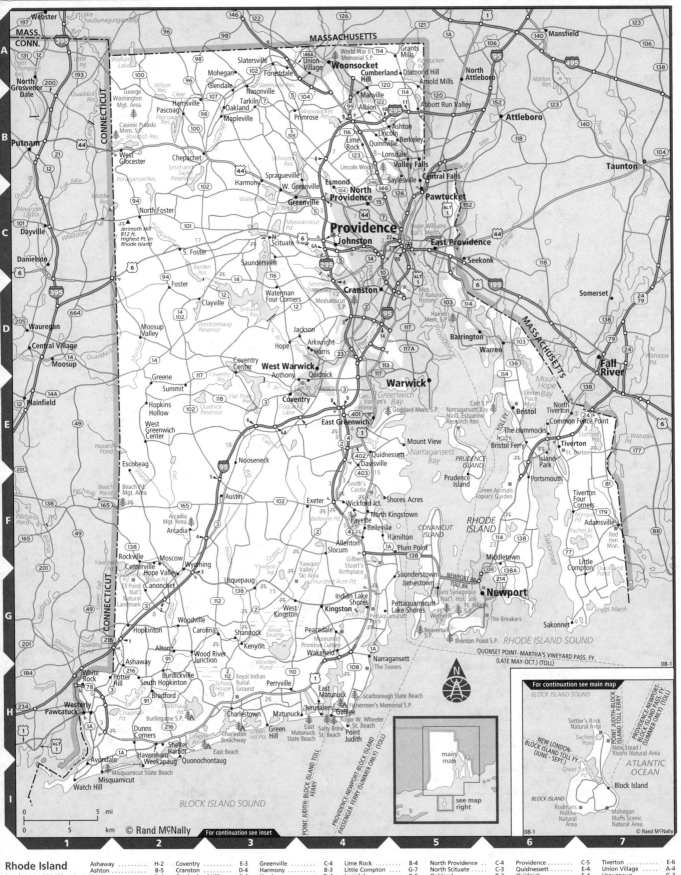

© Rand McNally

For continuation see inset

For continuation see main map

08-1

Rhode Island

Population: 1,076,189
Land area: 1,045 sq. mi.
Capital: Providence

Cities and Towns

Abbott Run Valley .	B-5
Adamsville .	F-7
Allenton .	F-4
Anthony .	E-4
Arnold Mills .	A-5

Ashaway .	H-2
Ashton .	B-5
Barrington .	D-6
Berkeley .	B-5
Bradford .	H-2
Bristol .	E-6
Burdickville .	H-2
Carolina .	G-3
Central Falls .	B-5
Charlestown .	H-3
Chepachet .	B-3
Common Fence Point .	E-6

Coventry .	E-3
Cranston .	D-4
Cumberland Hill .	B-4
Davisville .	E-4
Diamond Hill .	A-5
East Greenwich .	E-4
East Matunuck .	H-4
East Providence .	C-5
Exeter .	F-4
Forestdale .	A-3
Galilee .	H-4
Glendale .	B-3
Green Hill .	H-3

Greenville .	C-4
Harmony .	B-3
Harris .	D-4
Harrisville .	B-3
Hope .	D-3
Hope Valley .	G-2
Hopkinton .	G-2
Island Park .	E-6
Jamestown .	G-5
Johnston .	C-4
Kenyon .	G-3
Kingston .	G-4
LaFayette .	F-4

Lime Rock .	B-4
Little Compton .	G-7
Lonsdale .	B-5
Manville .	B-4
Mapleville .	B-3
Matunuck .	H-4
Middletown .	F-6
Mohegan .	A-3
Mount View .	E-5
Narragansett .	G-4
Nasonville .	A-3
Newport .	G-6
North Kingstown .	F-4

North Providence .	C-4
North Scituate .	C-3
Oakland .	B-3
Pascoag .	B-2
Pawtucket .	C-5
Peace Dale .	G-4
Pettaquamscutt Lake Shores .	F-5
Plum Point .	F-5
Point Judith .	H-4
Portsmouth .	F-6
Potter Hill .	H-1
Primrose .	B-4

Providence .	C-5
Quidnessett .	E-4
Quidnick .	E-3
Quinnville .	B-5
Quonochontaug .	H-2
Rockville .	G-2
Saunderstown .	G-5
Saylesville .	B-5
Shannock .	G-3
Shores Acres .	F-4
Slatersville .	A-3
South Hopkinton .	H-2
Tarkiln .	B-3

Tiverton .	E-6
Union Village .	A-4
Usquepaug .	G-3
Valley Falls .	B-5
Warren .	D-6
Warwick .	E-5
WatchHill .	I-1
West Warwick .	E-4
Westerly .	H-1
White Rock .	H-1
Woonsocket .	B-3
Wyoming .	G-2

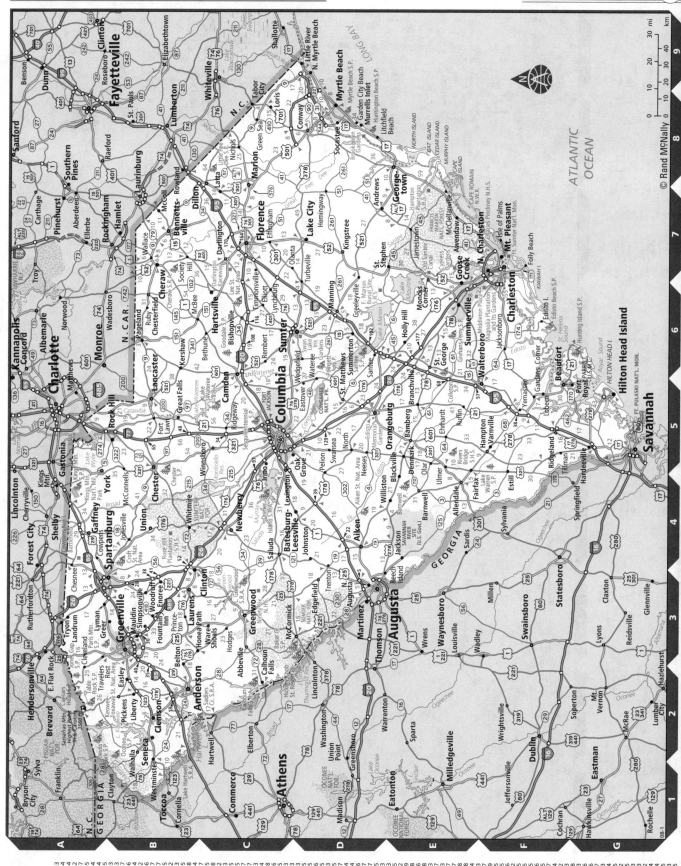

© Rand McNally

South Carolina

Population: 4,255,083
Land area: 30,109 sq. mi.
Capital: Columbia

Cities and Towns

Abbeville C-3
Aiken D-4
Allendale E-4
Anderson B-2
Andrews D-7
Bamberg E-5
Barnwell E-4
Batesburg-Leesville D-4
Beaufort F-5
Belton B-3
Bennettsville B-7
Bishopville C-6
Blackville E-4
Blacksburg C-6
Calhoun Falls C-2
Camden C-5
Charleston F-7
Cheraw B-7
Chester B-5
Chesterfield B-6
Clemson B-2
Clinton C-3
Columbia D-5
Conway C-8
Cowpens A-4
Darlington C-7
Denmark E-5
Dillon B-8
Easley B-3
Edgefield D-3
Estill E-4
Fairfax E-4
Florence C-7
Folly Beach F-7
Fountain Inn B-3
Gaffney A-4
Georgetown D-8
Great Falls B-5
Greenville B-3
Greenwood C-3
Greer B-3
Hampton E-4
Hardeeville F-4
Hartsville C-6
Hilton Head Island G-5
Honea Path B-3
Irmo C-5
Isle of Palms F-7
Jackson E-4
Johnston D-4
Kershaw C-6
Kingstree D-7
Lake City C-7
Lancaster B-6
Landrum A-3
Laurens C-3
Lexington C-5
Liberty B-2
Loris C-8
Manning D-6
Marion C-7
McColl B-7
McCormick D-3
Moncks Corner E-7
Mount Pleasant F-7
Murrells Inlet D-8
Myrtle Beach C-9
Newberry C-4
North Augusta D-3
North Charleston F-7
North Myrtle Beach C-9
Oak Grove D-5
Orangeburg D-5
Pageland B-6
Port Royal F-5
Ridgeland F-4
Rock Hill B-5
St. George E-6
St. Matthews D-5
St. Stephen E-7
Saluda D-4
Seneca B-2
Simpsonville B-3
Socastee C-9
Spartanburg B-3
Sumter D-6
Timmonsville C-7
Travelers Rest B-3
Union B-4
Varnville E-4
Walhalla B-2
Walterboro E-6
Ware Shoals C-3
Wellford B-3
Westminster B-2
Whitmire C-4
Williston D-4
Woodruff B-3
York B-5

08-1

South Dakota

Population: 775,933
Land area: 75,885 sq. mi.
Capital: Pierre

Cities and Towns

Aberdeen B-8
Alexandria D-8
Arlington C-9
Armour E-8
Avon F-8

Belle Fourche ... C-1
Beresford E-10
Big Stone City ... B-10
Bison A-3
Blunt C-6
Bowdle B-6
Bridgewater D-9
Bristol B-8
Britton A-8
Bryant C-9
Buffalo A-2

Burke E-7
Canton E-10
Castlewood C-9
Chamberlain D-7
Cherry Creek C-4
Clark C-8
Clear Lake C-9
Colman D-10
Colome E-6
Custer D-2
De Smet C-9
Dell Rapids D-10

Doland C-8
Dupree B-4
Eagle Butte B-4
Edgemont E-1
Elk Point F-10
Elkton C-10
Estelline C-9
Ethan D-8
Eureka A-6
Faith B-4
Faulkton C-7
Flandreau C-10
Fort Pierre C-6

Fort Thompson ... D-6
Gannvalley D-7
Gregory E-7
Groton B-8
Hecla A-8
Herreid A-6
Highmore C-7
Hill City D-2
Hoven B-7
Howard C-9
Huron C-8
Ipswich B-7

Iroquois C-8
Isabel B-4
Kadoka D-4
Kennebec D-6
Kimball D-7
Kyle D-3
Lake Andes E-7
Lake Preston C-9
Langford A-8
Lead D-2
Lemmon A-3
Lennox D-10
Leola B-7

Madison D-9
Martin E-4
McIntosh A-5
McLaughlin A-5
Menno D-8
Milbank B-10
Miller C-7
Mission E-5
Mitchell D-8
Mobridge B-5
Mound City A-6
Mount Vernon ... D-8
Murdo D-5

New Underwood ... D-2
Newell C-2
Oglala E-3
Olivet D-8
Onida C-6
Parkston D-8
Parmelee E-5
Philip D-4
Piedmont D-2
Pierre C-6
Pine Ridge E-3
Plankinton D-8

Platte D-7
Presho D-6
Rapid City D-2
Redfield C-8
Roscoe B-7
Rosebud E-6
Roslyn B-8
St. Francis E-5
Salem D-9
Scotland D-8
Selby B-6
Sioux Falls D-10
Sisseton A-9

Spearfish D-1
Sturgis D-2
Summit B-9
Timber Lake B-4
Tripp D-8
Tyndall E-8
Veblen A-9
Vermillion E-10
Viborg D-9
Wall D-3
Watertown B-9

Waubay B-9
Webster B-8
Wessington Sprs. .. D-7
White Lake D-7
White River E-5
Willow Lake C-8
Wilmot A-9
Winner E-6
Wolsey C-7
Woonsocket D-7
Yankton E-9

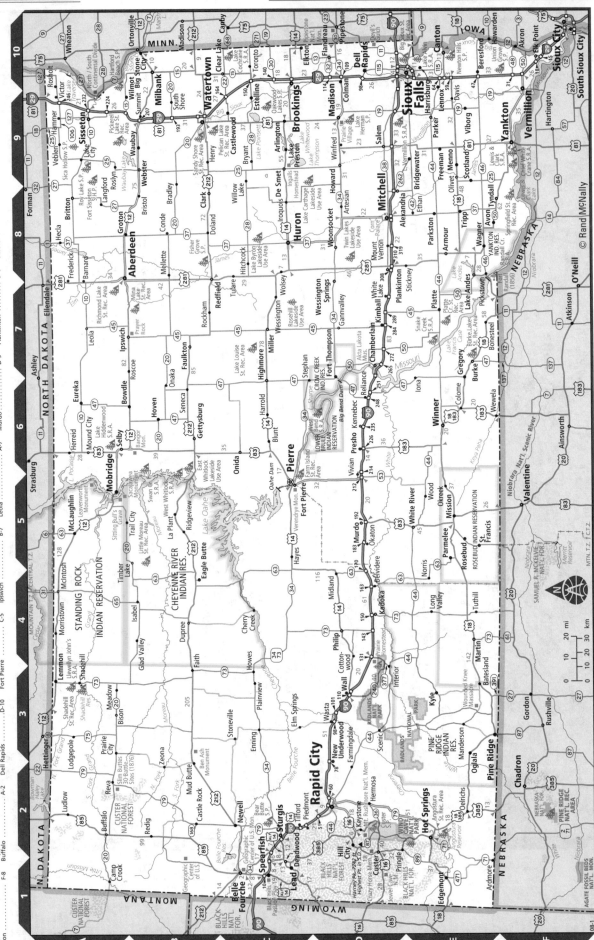

© Rand McNally

I-40 will be completely closed between exits 388 and 389 in downtown Knoxville from May 2008 until late 2009. Visit www.tdot.state.tn.us/smartfix for more info.

Western Tennessee | Eastern Tennessee

Tennessee

Population: 5,962,959
Land area: 41,217 sq. mi.
Capital: Nashville

Cities and Towns

City	Ref	City	Ref	City	Ref
Alcoa	G-4	Greeneville	G-6	Oneida	F-3
Ashland City	B-6	Harriman	G-3	Paris	B-4
Athens	H-3	Henderson	C-3	Pigeon Forge	G-5
Bartlett	D-1	Hohenwald	C-5	Portland	A-7
Bolivar	D-3	Humboldt	C-3	Pulaski	D-6
Bristol	F-7	Huntingdon	C-4	Ripley	C-2
Brownsville	C-2	Jackson	C-3	Rockwood	G-3
Camden	B-4	Jamestown	F-2	Rogersville	F-5
Carthage	G-1	Jasper	I-1	Savannah	D-4
Centerville	C-5	Jefferson City	G-5	Selmer	D-3
Chattanooga	I-2	Jellico	F-4	Sevierville	G-5
Clarksville	B-5	Johnson City	F-6	Shelbyville	D-7
Cleveland	I-2	Jonesborough	F-6	Signal Mountain	I-2
Clinton	G-4	Kingsport	F-6	Smithville	G-2
Columbia	C-6	Kingston	G-3	Smyrna	C-7
Cookeville	G-1	Knoxville	G-4	Soddy-Daisy	H-2
Covington	C-2	La Follette	F-4	South Fulton	B-3
Crossville	G-2	La Vergne	C-6	South Pittsburg	I-1
Dayton	H-2	Lafayette	B-7	Sparta	G-2
Dickson	B-5	Lake City	G-4	Springfield	B-6
Dresden	B-3	Lawrenceburg	D-5	Sweetwater	H-3
Dunlap	H-2	Lebanon	B-7	Trenton	C-3
Dyersburg	B-2	Lenoir City	G-3	Tullahoma	D-7
Elizabethton	F-7	Lewisburg	D-6	Union City	B-3
Erwin	G-6	Lexington	C-4	Waverly	B-5
Etowah	H-3	Livingston	F-2	Winchester	D-7
Farragut	G-4	Loudon	G-3	Woodbury	C-7
Fayetteville	D-6	Madisonville	H-3		
Franklin	C-6	Manchester	D-7		
Gallatin	B-7	Martin	B-3		
Gatlinburg	G-5	Maryville	G-4		
Goodlettsville	B-6	McKenzie	B-4		
		McMinnville	H-1		
		Memphis	D-1		
		Milan	C-3		
		Millington	D-1		
		Monterey	G-2		
		Morristown	G-5		
		Mount Pleasant	C-7		
		Murfreesboro	C-7		
		Nashville	B-6		
		Newport	G-5		
		Oak Ridge	G-4		

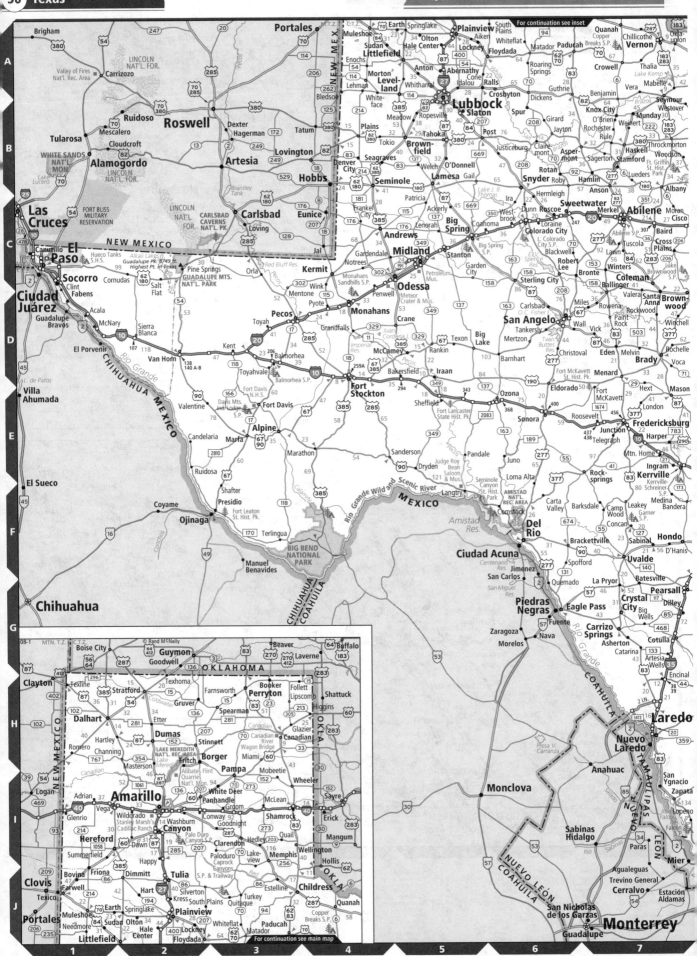

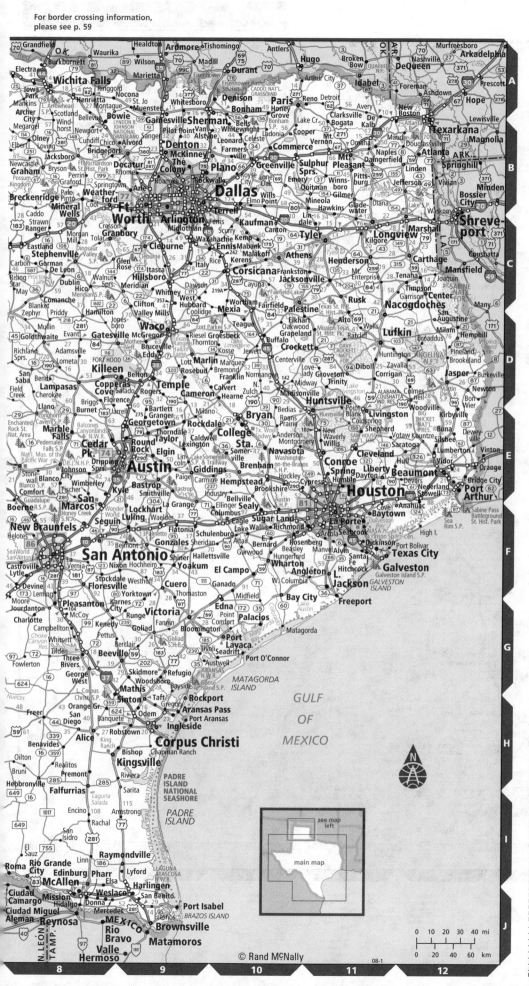

For border crossing information, please see p. 59

© Rand McNally

08-1

Texas

Population: 22,859,968
Land area: 261,797 sq. mi.
Capital: Austin

Cities and Towns

Abilene	C-7
Albany	B-7
Alice	H-8
Alpine	E-3
Alvin	F-11
Amarillo	I-2
Anahuac	F-11
Andrews	C-4
Angleton	F-11
Anson	B-7
Archer City	B-8
Arlington	B-9
Aspermont	B-7
Athens	C-10
Austin	E-9
Baird	C-7
Ballinger	D-7
Bandera	F-7
Bastrop	E-9
Baytown	F-11
Bay City	F-10
Beaumont	E-12
Beeville	G-9
Belton	E-10
Big Lake	D-5
Big Spring	C-5
Boerne	F-8
Bonham	A-10
Borger	H-2
Bracketville	F-6
Brady	D-7
Breckenridge	B-8
Brenham	E-10
Brownfield	B-5
Brownsville	J-9
Brownwood	D-8
Bryan	E-10
Burkburnett	A-8
Burnet	E-8
Caldwell	E-9
Cameron	D-9
Canadian	H-3
Canton	C-10
Canyon	I-2
Carrizo Springs	G-7
Carthage	C-12
Cedar Park	E-8
Center	C-12
Centerville	D-10
Childress	I-3
Clarendon	I-2
Clarksville	A-11
Cleburne	B-9
Coldspring	E-11
Coleman	C-7
College Station	E-10
Colorado City	C-6
Columbus	F-10
Comanche	C-8
Conroe	E-11
Cooper	B-10
Copperas Cove	D-8
Corpus Christi	H-9
Corsicana	C-10
Cotulla	G-7
Crane	D-5
Crockett	D-11
Crosbyton	A-6
Crowell	A-7
Crystal City	G-7
Cuero	F-9
Daingerfield	B-11
Dalhart	H-1
Dallas	B-9
Decatur	A-9
Del Rio	E-6
Denison	A-9
Denton	B-4
Denver City	B-4
Dimmitt	J-8
Donna	J-8
Dumas	H-2
Eagle Pass	F-6
Eastland	C-8
Edinburg	I-8
Edna	G-10
El Campo	F-10
El Paso	C-1
Eldorado	D-6
Emory	B-10
Ennis	C-9
Fairfield	C-10
Falfurrias	H-8
Farwell	J-1
Floresville	F-8
Floydada	A-6
Fort Davis	E-3
Fort Stockton	D-4
Fort Worth	B-9
Franklin	D-10
Fredericksburg	E-8
Freeport	F-11
Friona	J-1
Gainesville	A-9
Galveston	F-11
Garden City	C-5
Gatesville	D-9
George West	G-8
Georgetown	E-9
Gilmer	B-11
Glen Rose	C-8
Goldthwaite	D-8
Goliad	F-9
Gonzales	F-9
Graham	B-8
Granbury	C-8
Greenville	B-10
Groesbeck	D-10
Groveton	D-11
Hallettsville	F-9
Hamilton	D-8
Harlingen	J-9
Haskell	B-7
Hebbronville	H-8
Hemphill	D-12
Hempstead	E-10
Henderson	C-11
Henrietta	A-8
Hereford	I-1
Hillsboro	C-9
Hondo	F-7
Houston	F-11
Humble	E-11
Huntsville	E-11
Jacksboro	B-8
Jacksonville	C-11
Jasper	D-12
Jayton	B-6
Jefferson	B-12
Johnson City	E-8
Jourdanton	G-8
Junction	E-7
Karnes City	G-8
Kaufman	C-10
Kermit	C-4
Kerrville	E-7
Kilgore	C-11
Killeen	D-9
Kingsville	H-8
Kountze	E-12
La Grange	E-9
La Porte	F-11
Lake Jackson	F-11
Lamesa	B-5
Lampasas	D-8
Laredo	H-7
Leakey	F-7
Levelland	A-5
Liberty	E-11
Linden	B-12
Littlefield	A-5
Livingston	E-11
Llano	E-8
Lockhart	E-9
Longview	C-11
Lubbock	B-5
Lufkin	D-11
Madisonville	A-1
Marfa	E-3
Marlin	D-9
Marshall	B-11
Mason	E-7
Matador	A-6
McAllen	J-8
McKinney	B-9
Memphis	I-3
Menard	E-7
Mercedes	J-8
Meridian	C-9
Mertzon	D-6
Miami	H-3
Midland	C-5
Mineral Wells	B-8
Mission	J-8
Monahans	D-4
Montague	A-8
Morton	A-4
Mount Pleasant	B-11
Mount Vernon	B-11
Muleshoe	A-4
Nacogdoches	D-11
Nederland	E-12
New Braunfels	F-8
Newton	D-12
Odessa	C-5
Orange	E-12
Ozona	D-6
Paducah	A-6
Paint Rock	D-7
Palestine	C-10
Palo Pinto	B-8
Pampa	I-3
Panhandle	I-2
Paris	A-10
Pearsall	G-7
Pecos	D-3
Perryton	H-3
Pharr	J-8
Pittsburg	B-11
Plains	A-5
Plainview	A-5
Plano	B-9
Pleasanton	G-8
Port Lavaca	G-10
Post	B-6
Quanah	A-7
Quitman	B-11
Rankin	D-5
Raymondville	I-9
Refugio	G-9
Richmond	F-11
Rio Grande City	I-8
Robert Lee	C-6
Robstown	H-9
Roby	B-6
Rockport	G-9
Rocksprings	E-7
Rockwall	B-10
Rosenberg	F-10
Round Rock	E-9
Rusk	C-11
San Angelo	D-6
San Antonio	F-8
San Augustine	D-12
San Benito	J-9
San Diego	H-8
San Marcos	F-8
San Saba	D-8
Sanderson	E-4
Seguin	F-8
Seminole	B-4
Seymour	A-7
Sherman	A-9
Sierra Blanca	D-2
Silverton	J-2
Sinton	H-9
Snyder	B-6
Socorro	C-1
Sonora	E-6
Spearman	H-3
Stamford	B-7
Stanton	C-5
Stephenville	C-8
Sterling City	C-6
Stinnett	H-2
Stratford	H-1
Sugar Land	F-11
Sulphur Springs	B-10
Sweetwater	C-6
Tahoka	B-5
Taylor	E-9
Temple	D-9
Terrell	B-10
Texarkana	B-12
Texas City	F-11
The Colony	B-9
Three Rivers	G-8
Throckmorton	B-7
Tilden	G-8
Tulia	J-2
Tyler	C-11
Uvalde	F-7
Van Horn	D-2
Vega	I-1
Vernon	A-7
Victoria	G-9
Vidor	E-12
Waco	D-9
Waxahachie	C-9
Weatherford	B-9
Wellington	I-3
Weslaco	J-8
Wharton	F-10
Wheeler	I-3
Wichita Falls	A-8
Woodville	D-12
Zapata	I-7

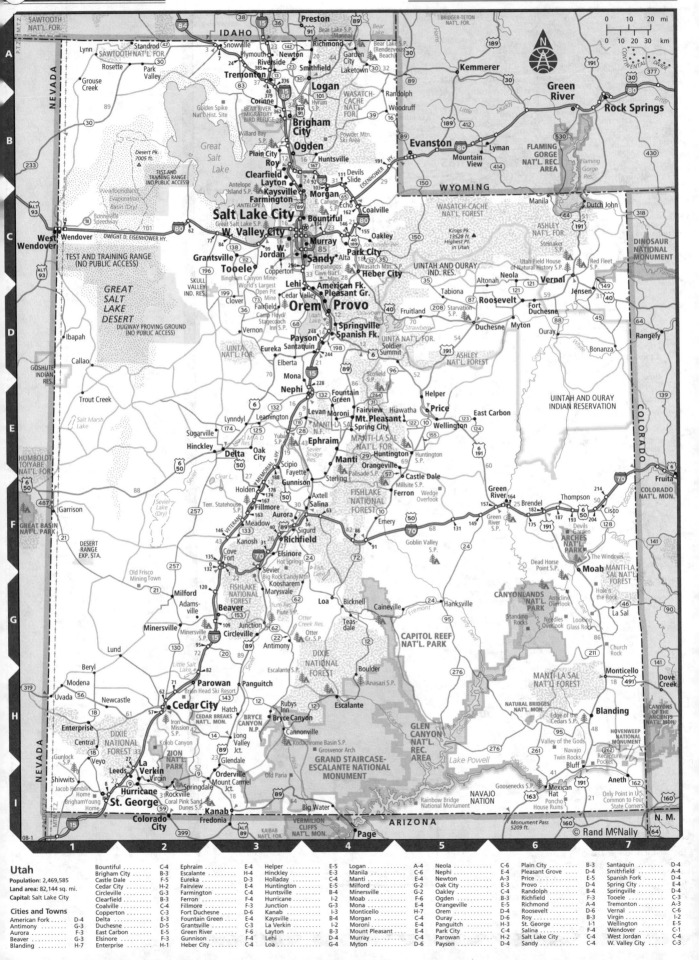

Plan a Utah trip at go.randmcnally.com/UT

Utah

Population: 2,469,585
Land area: 82,144 sq. mi.
Capital: Salt Lake City

Cities and Towns

American Fork D-4
Antimony G-3
Aurora F-3
Beaver G-3
Blanding H-7
Bountiful C-4
Brigham City B-3
Castle Dale F-5
Cedar City H-2
Circleville G-3
Clearfield B-3
Coalville C-4
Copperton C-3
Delta E-3
Duchesne D-5
East Carbon E-5
Elsinore F-3
Enterprise H-1
Ephraim E-4
Escalante H-4
Eureka D-3
Fairview E-4
Farmington C-4
Ferron F-4
Fillmore F-3
Fort Duchesne D-6
Fountain Green ... E-4
Grantsville C-3
Green River F-6
Gunnison F-4
Heber City C-4
Helper E-5
Hinckley E-3
Holladay C-4
Huntington E-5
Huntsville B-4
Hurricane I-2
Junction G-3
Kanab I-3
Kaysville C-4
La Verkin I-2
Layton C-4
Lehi D-4
Loa G-4
Logan A-4
Manila C-6
Manti E-4
Milford G-2
Minersville G-2
Moab F-6
Mona E-4
Monticello H-7
Morgan C-4
Moroni E-4
Mount Pleasant ... E-4
Murray C-4
Myton D-6
Neola C-6
Nephi E-4
Newton A-3
Oak City E-3
Oakley C-4
Ogden B-3
Orangeville E-4
Orem D-4
Ouray D-6
Panguitch H-3
Park City C-4
Parowan H-2
Payson D-4
Plain City B-3
Pleasant Grove ... D-4
Price E-5
Provo D-4
Randolph B-4
Richfield F-3
Richmond A-4
Roosevelt D-6
Roy B-3
St. George I-1
Salina F-4
Salt Lake City ... C-4
Sandy C-4
Santaquin D-4
Smithfield A-4
Spanish Fork D-4
Spring City E-4
Springville D-4
Tooele C-3
Tremonton A-3
Vernal C-6
Virgin I-2
Wellington E-5
Wendover C-1
West Jordan C-4
W. Valley City ... C-4

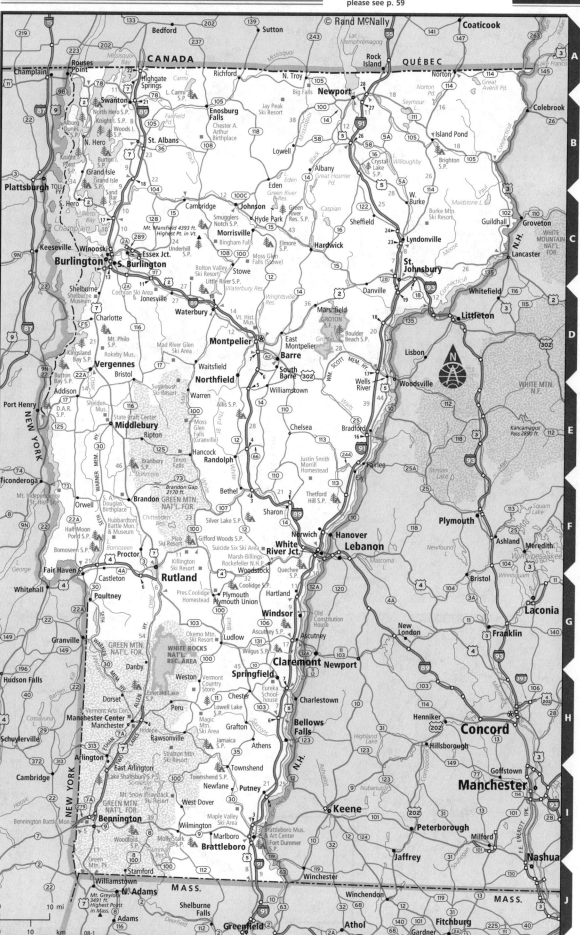

Cities and Towns

Addison	E-1
Albany	B-3
Arlington	H-1
Ascutney	G-4
Athens	H-3
Barre	D-3
Bellows Falls	H-3
Bennington	I-1
Bethel	F-3
Bradford	E-4
Brandon	F-2
Brattleboro	I-3
Bristol	D-2
Burlington	C-1
Cambridge	C-2
Castleton	F-2
Charlotte	D-1
Chelsea	E-4
Chester	H-3
Danby	G-2
Danville	C-5
Dorset	H-1
East Arlington	H-1
East Montpelier	D-3
Eden	B-3
Ely	E-4
Enosburg Falls	B-3
Essex Junction	C-1
Fair Haven	G-1
Fairlee	E-4
Grafton	H-3
Grand Isle	B-1
Guildhall	C-6
Hancock	E-3
Hardwick	C-4
Hartland	G-4
Highgate Springs	A-2
Hyde Park	C-3
Island Pond	B-5
Johnson	C-3
Jonesville	D-2
Lowell	B-4
Ludlow	G-3
Lyndonville	C-5
Manchester	H-2
Manchester Center	H-1
Marlboro	I-3
Marshfield	D-4
Middlebury	E-2
Montpelier	D-3
Morrisville	C-3
Newfane	I-3
Newport	B-4
North Hero	B-1
North Troy	A-4
Northfield	D-3
Norton	A-5
Norwich	F-4
Orwell	F-1
Peru	H-2
Plymouth	G-3
Plymouth Union	G-3
Poultney	G-1
Proctor	F-2
Putney	I-3
Randolph	E-3
Rawsonville	H-2
Richford	A-3
Ripton	E-2
Rutland	F-2
St. Albans	B-2
St. Johnsbury	C-5
Sharon	F-4
Sheffield	C-4
Shelburne	D-1
South Barre	D-3
South Burlington	C-1
South Hero	B-1
Springfield	H-3
Stamford	J-2
Stowe	C-3
Swanton	B-2
Townshend	I-3
Vergennes	D-1
Waitsfield	D-3
Warren	E-2
Waterbury	D-3
Wells River	D-5
West Burke	C-5
West Dover	I-2
Weston	H-3
White River Junction	F-4
Williamstown	E-3
Wilmington	I-2
Windsor	G-4
Winooski	C-2
Woodstock	F-3

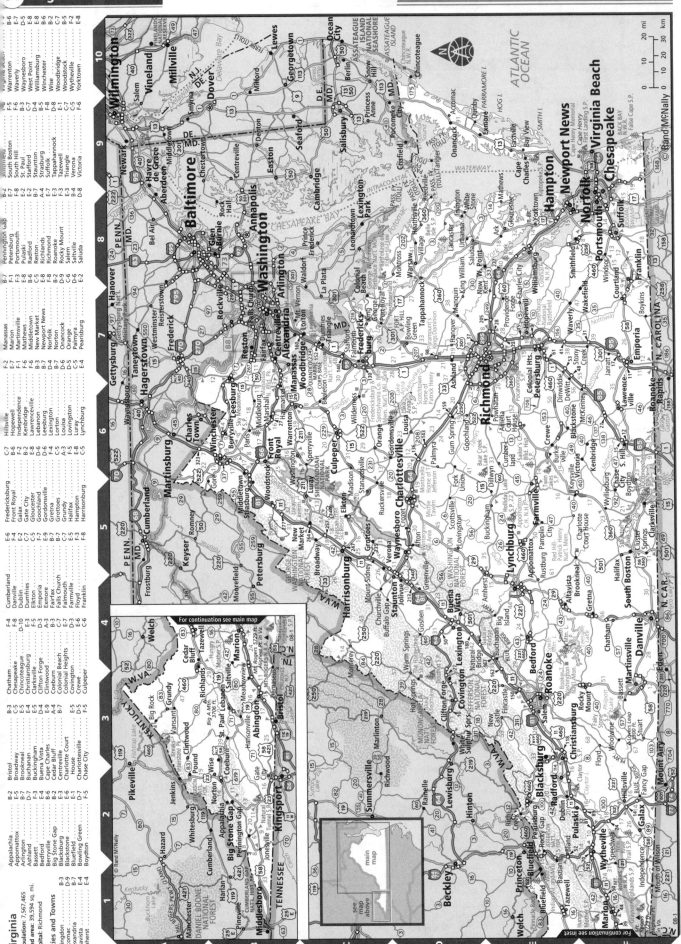

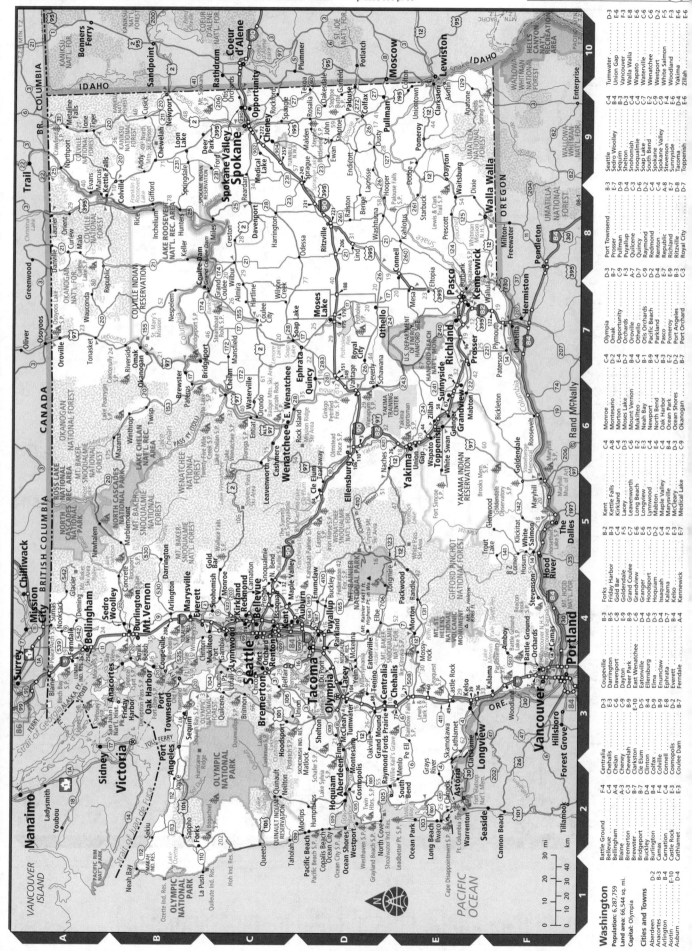

Turnwater	C-4	Seattle	B-3
Union Gap	B-4	Sedro Woolley	E-7
Vancouver	D-3	Selah	B-3
Walla Walla	D-3	Shelton	C-3
Wapato	C-6	Snohomish	D-6
Waterville	C-7	Snoqualmie	C-6
Wenatchee	C-6	Soap Lake	C-7
Westport	C-9	South Bend	B-2
White Salmon	D-2	Spokane	C-9
Woodland	F-5	Spokane Valley	A-8
Yakima	F-3	Stevenson	E-8
Zillah	D-4	Sunnyside	B-7
		Tacoma	D-4
		Toppenish	D-7

Olympia	C-4	Port Townsend	D-3
Omak	D-2	Prosser	B-7
Opportunity	E-4	Pullman	C-3
Orchards	D-7	Puyallup	A-7
Oroville	B-4	Quilcene	F-3
Othello	B-1	Quincy	D-7
Othello Orchards	B-9	Raymond	E-2
Pacific Beach	C-4	Redmond	D-2
Parkland	B-3	Renton	D-4
Pasco	C-4	Republic	E-2
Paterson	C-4	Richland	E-3
Pomeroy	E-2	Ritzville	B-9
Port Angeles	B-4	Rosalia	C-9
Port Orchard	C-3	Okanogan	C-9

Monroe	C-4	Kent	B-2
Montesano	A-8	Kettle Falls	B-3
Morton	C-4	Lacey	C-9
Moses Lake	D-3	Kirkland	D-6
Mount Vernon	E-2	Long Beach	E-6
Mukilteo	E-3	Longview	C-3
Naches	C-4	Lynnwood	D-2
Neah Bay	C-4	Mabton	C-4
Newport	C-3	Maple Valley	D-7
North Bend	D-4	Marysville	E-3
Oak Harbor	B-3	McCleary	E-7
Ocean Park	B-4	Medical Lake	C-9
Ocean Shores	D-3		

Forks	B-3	Coupeville	D-3
Friday Harbor	B-5	Darrington	B-9
Goldendale	C-9	Davenport	C-9
Grand Coulee	B-9	Dayton	D-7
Grandview	C-6	Deer Park	E-9
Granger	D-6	East Wenatchee	C-6
Hoodsport	C-3	Eatonville	E-3
Hoquiam	D-3	Ellensburg	D-5
Issaquah	D-2	Elma	B-9
Kalama	D-7	Enumclaw	D-4
Kelso	D-7	Ephrata	C-3
Kennewick	E-7	Everett	B-4
		Ferndale	B-7

Washington
Population: 6,287,759
Land area: 66,544 sq. mi.
Capital: Olympia

Cities and Towns
Aberdeen	D-2
Anacortes	B-3
Arlington	B-4
Asotin	E-10
Auburn	D-4

Battle Ground		Centralia	F-4
Bellevue		Chehalis	A-4
Bellingham		Chelan	A-3
Blaine		Cheney	C-3
Bremerton		Chewelah	B-7
Brewster		Clarkston	E-10
Bridgeport		Cle Elum	D-5
Buckley		Clinton	B-7
Burlington		Colfax	B-4
Camas		Colville	C-4
Carnation		Connell	B-4
Castle Rock		Cosmopolis	E-3
Cathlamet		Coulee City	E-3

West Virginia

Population: 1,816,856
Land area: 24,078 sq. mi.
Capital: Charleston

Cities and Towns

Alderson F-4
Ansted E-4
Barboursville E-2
Beckley F-3
Belington D-5
Belle E-3
Berkeley Springs C-8
Bethlehem C-7
Bluefield G-3
Bridgeport D-5
Buckhannon D-5
Buffalo E-2
Cameron C-6
Chapmanville F-2
Cedar Grove E-3
Charleston E-3
Charles Town C-9
Clarksburg D-5
Clay E-4
Clendenin E-3
Craigsville E-4
Davis D-6
Dunbar E-3
Elizabeth D-3
Elkins D-5
Fairmont D-5
Fayetteville F-3
Fort Ashby C-8
Fort Gay E-1
Franklin E-6
Gauley Bridge E-3
Glenville D-4
Grafton D-5
Grantsville D-4
Green Bank E-5
Hamlin E-2
Harpers Ferry C-9
Harrisville D-4
Hinton F-4
Huntington E-2
Keyser C-7
Kingwood C-6
Lewisburg F-4
Logan F-2
Madison E-3
Man F-2
Mannington C-5
Marlinton E-5
Marmet E-3
Martinsburg C-8
Middlebourne C-4
Montgomery E-3
Moorefield D-7
Moundsville C-6
Mullens F-3
New Martinsville C-4
New Cumberland B-6
Nutter Fort D-5
Oak Hill F-3
Parkersburg D-3
Pennsboro D-4
Petersburg D-6
Philippi D-5
Piedmont C-7
Pineville F-3
Point Pleasant D-2
Princeton G-3
Rainelle F-4
Rand E-3
Ravenswood D-3
Richwood E-4
Ripley D-3
Romney C-7
Ronceverte F-4
St. Albans E-3
St. Marys C-3
Salem D-4
Shepherdstown C-9
Shinnston D-5
Sistersville C-4
Sophia F-3
South Charleston E-3
Spencer D-4
Summersville E-4
Sutton E-4
Union F-4
Vienna D-3
War G-3
Wayne E-2
Webster Springs E-5
Weirton B-6
Welch G-3
Wellsburg B-6
West Hamlin E-2
West Union D-4
Weston D-4
Wheeling C-6
White Sulphur Springs . F-5
Whitesville F-3
Williamson F-2
Winfield E-3

© Rand McNally

Wisconsin

Population: 5,536,201
Land area: 54,310 sq. mi.
Capital: Madison

Cities and Towns

Antigo	D-5	Beloit	H-5	Elkhorn	H-5	Kenosha	H-6	Menomonee Falls	G-6	Onalaska	F-2	River Falls	D-1	Washburn	B-3
Appleton	E-5	Berlin	F-5	Fond du Lac	F-5	Kewaunee	E-6	Menomonie	D-2	Oshkosh	F-5	Shawano	E-5	Watertown	G-5
Ashland	B-3	Black River Falls	E-3	Fort Atkinson	G-5	La Crosse	F-2	Mequon	G-6	Phillips	C-3	Sheboygan	F-6	Waukesha	G-6
Baraboo	G-4	Burlington	H-6	Grafton	G-6	Ladysmith	D-3	Merrill	D-4	Platteville	H-3	South Milwaukee	G-6	Waupaca	E-5
Beaver Dam	G-5	Chilton	F-6	Green Bay	E-6	Lake Geneva	H-6	Middleton	G-4	Plover	E-4	Sparta	F-3	Waupun	F-5
		Chippewa Falls	D-2	Hartford	G-5	Lancaster	H-3	Milwaukee	G-6	Port Washington	G-6	Stevens Point	E-4	Wausau	D-4
		Crandon	C-5	Hayward	C-2	Madison	G-4	Monroe	H-4	Portage	G-5	Stoughton	G-5	Wautoma	F-5
		Darlington	H-4	Hudson	D-1	Manitowoc	F-6	Mount Horeb	G-4	Prairie du Chien	G-2	Sturgeon Bay	D-7	West Bend	G-6
		Delavan	H-5	Hurley	B-4	Marinette	E-6	Muskego	G-6	Racine	H-6	Sun Prairie	G-5	Whitefish Bay	G-6
		De Pere	E-6	Janesville	H-5	Marshfield	E-4	Neenah	F-5	Rhinelander	C-4	Superior	B-2	Whitewater	H-5
		Dodgeville	G-4	Jefferson	G-5	Mauston	F-4	New Glarus	H-4	Rice Lake	D-2	Tomah	F-3	Wisconsin Dells	F-4
		Eagle River	C-5	Juneau	G-5	Medford	D-3	Oconomowoc	G-6	Richland Cen.	G-3	Tomahawk	D-4	Wisconsin Rapids	E-4
		Eau Claire	E-2	Kaukauna	E-6	Menasha	E-5	Oconto	D-6	Ripon	F-5	Two Rivers	F-6	Viroqua	F-3

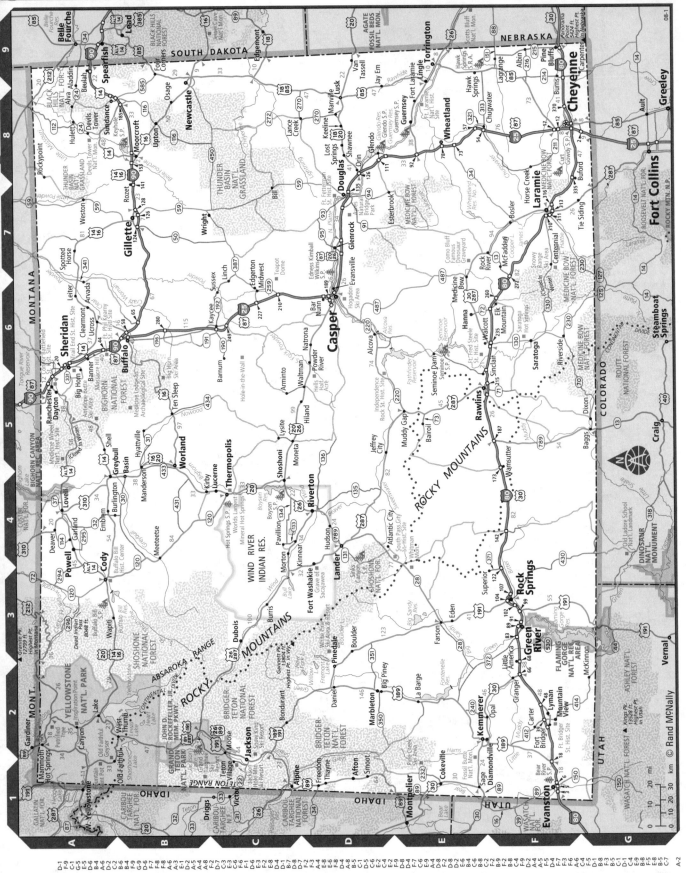

Border Crossing
Information

With advance planning, crossing the border to Mexico or Canada can be easier than you think.

Citizenship Documents

A U.S. passport or proof of citizenship, such as an original or certified birth certificate and photo identification (such as a driver's license) is required for entry into Mexico or Canada. Naturalized U.S. citizens should carry citizenship papers; permanent residents of the United States must bring proof of residency and photo identification.

Traveling with Kids

For children under the age of 18, parents should be prepared to provide evidence, such as a birth certificate or adoption decree, to prove they are indeed the parents. Single or divorced parents and parents traveling without spouses should carry a letter of consent from the absent parent or guardian to bring a child across either border. Mexico requires the letter to be original and notarized. Divorced parents should also bring copies of their custody decree. Adults who are not the parents or guardians of the children they are traveling with must have written permission from the parents or guardians to supervise the children.

Traveling with Pets

U.S. visitors may bring a dog or cat to Mexico with a pet health certificate signed by a registered veterinarian and issued within 72 hours of entry and a vaccination certificate for rabies, distemper, hepatitis, pip, and leptospirosis. A permit fee is charged at the time of entry. All dogs and cats three months and older are required to have a current rabies vaccination certificate that should identify the pet and indicate the trade name of the licensed rabies vaccine, serial number and duration of validity in order to enter Canada. Pit bulls are not permitted to enter Ontario.

Re-entry to the U.S.

Proof of both citizenship and identity is required for entry into the United States. Be able to provide proof of U.S. citizenship via a U.S. passport, or a certified copy of your birth certificate, a Certificate of Naturalization, a Certificate of Citizenship, or a Report of Birth Abroad of a U.S. citizen. To prove your identity, present either a valid driver's license, or a government identification card that includes a photo or physical description.

By January 1, 2008, the Western Hemisphere Travel Initiative will require all U.S. citizens to carry a passport or other secure document in order to enter or re-enter the United States. This initiative will be rolled out in two phases:

● December 31, 2006: Requirement applied to all air and sea travel to or from Canada, Mexico, Central and South America, the Caribbean, and Bermuda.

● December 31, 2007: Requirement extended to all land border crossings.

In 2006, the government began producing a secure, alternative passport card for U.S. citizens in border communities who frequently cross to Mexico or Canada. The biometric card will meet the requirement for this initiative and help expedite travel through ports of entry.

Border Crossing Waits

Allow plenty of time. The average time for customs clearance is 30 minutes, but this varies greatly depending on traffic flow and security issues.

Mexico Only
Driving in Mexico

According to U.S. Department of State, tourists traveling beyond the border zone must obtain a temporary import permit or risk having their car confiscated by Mexican customs officials. To acquire a permit, you must submit evidence of citizenship, title for the car, a car registration certificate, driver's license, and a processing fee to either a Banjercito (Mexican Army Bank) branch located at a Mexican Customs office at the port of entry, or at one of the Mexican consulates in the U.S. Mexican law also requires posting a bond at a Banjercito office to guarantee departure of the car from Mexico within a period determined at the time of application. Carry proof of car ownership (the current registration card or a letter of authorization from the finance or leasing company). Auto insurance policies, other than Mexican, are not valid in Mexico. A short-term liability policy is obtainable at the border.

Tourist Cards

Tourist cards are valid up to six months, require a fee, and are required for all persons, regardless of age, to visit the interior of Mexico. Cards may be obtained from Mexican border authorities, Consuls of Mexico, or Federal Delegates in major cities. Cards are also distributed to passengers en route to Mexico by air.

For additional information on traveling in Mexico, contact the Mexican Embassy in Washington, D.C.: (202) 736-1000; www.embassy ofmexico.org or go to the U.S. Department of State website, www.travel.state.gov/travel/tips/regional/regional_1174.html.

Canada Only
Driving in Canada

Drivers need proof of ownership of the vehicle or documentation of its rental, a valid U.S. driver's license, and automobile insurance.

Fast Pass for Frequent Travelers

For frequent travelers, the United States and Canada have instituted the NEXUS program, which allows pre-screened, low-risk travelers to be processed with little or no delay by U.S. and Canadian border officials. Approved applicants are issued photo identification and a proximity card, and they can quickly cross the border in a dedicated traffic lane without routine customs and immigration questioning (unless they are randomly selected).

For additional information on traveling in Canada, contact the Canadian Embassy in Washington, D.C.: (202) 682-1740; www.canadianembassy.org or go to the U.S. Department of State website, travel.state.gov/travel/tips/regional/regional_1170.html.

Duty-free Defined

Duty-free shops are shops where taxes on commercial goods are neither collected by a government, nor paid by an importer. For example, a Swiss watch purchased in a jewelry store in Mexico may cost you $250, a price that includes the duty and taxes that the importer paid to import it. The same watch purchased in a duty-free shop may only cost $175. That's because as long as the item stays in the duty-free shop, or exits the country with the purchaser, it has not been formally imported into the country. There has been no duty charged on it, and the duty-free shop owner has been able to pass on that savings. Its price is free of duty.

If you exceed your personal exemption, when you bring purchases home to the U.S from any shops, including those called duty-free, you will have to pay duty.

Source: U.S. Customs and Border Protection

Food Police

To protect community health and preserve domestic plant and animal life, many kinds of foods either are prohibited from entering the United States or require an import permit.

1. Every fruit or vegetable must be declared and presented for inspection, no matter how free of pests it appears to be. Failure to declare all food products can result in civil penalties.

2. Bakery goods and cured cheeses are generally admissible.

3. Permission to bring meats, livestock, poultry, and their by-products into the United States depends on the animal disease condition in the country of origin.

● Fresh meat is generally prohibited from most countries.

● Canned, cured, or dried meat is severely restricted from some countries.

Contact the U.S. Department of Agriculture, Animal Plant Health Inspection Services for more detailed information.

Source: U.S. Customs and Border Protection

Insider's Tips

1. Get the U.S. Customs and Border Protection booklet "Know Before You Go" before your next trip. (202) 354-1000 or (877) 227-5511; or download it at www.customs.ustreas.gov/xp/cgov/travel/vacation/kbyg/.

2. Currency: Exchange rates are often more favorable at ATMs and banks than at hotels and stores.

3. Duty-free: The duty-free personal exemption is $800, but there are some exceptions, depending on the country visited, how long you were there and whether the items are gifts or for personal use. See www.cbp.gov/xp/cgov/travel/vacation/kbyg/duty_free.xml for more information.

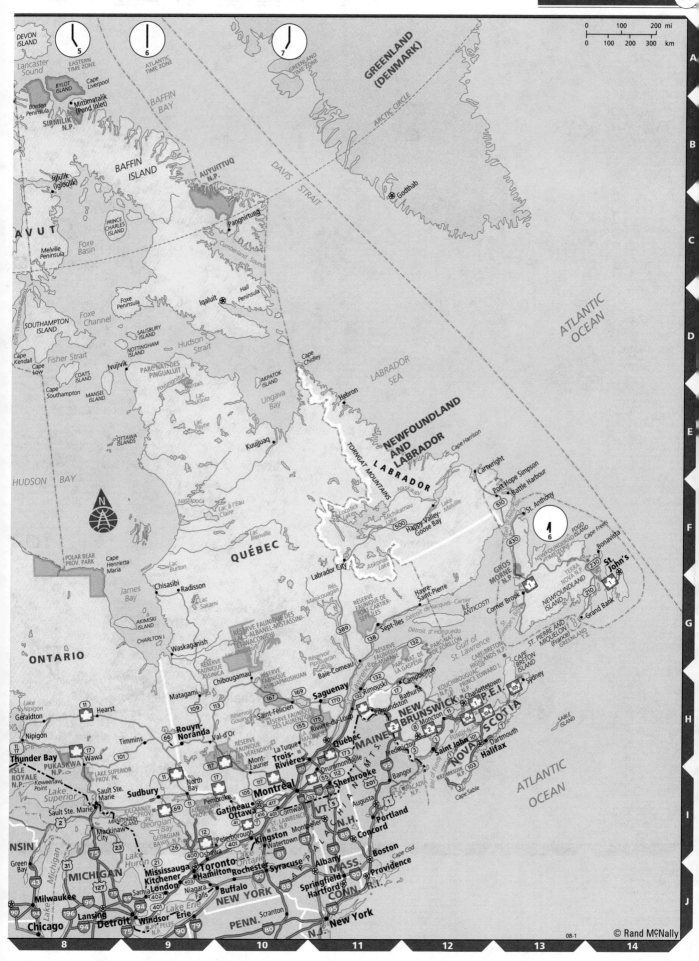

08-1

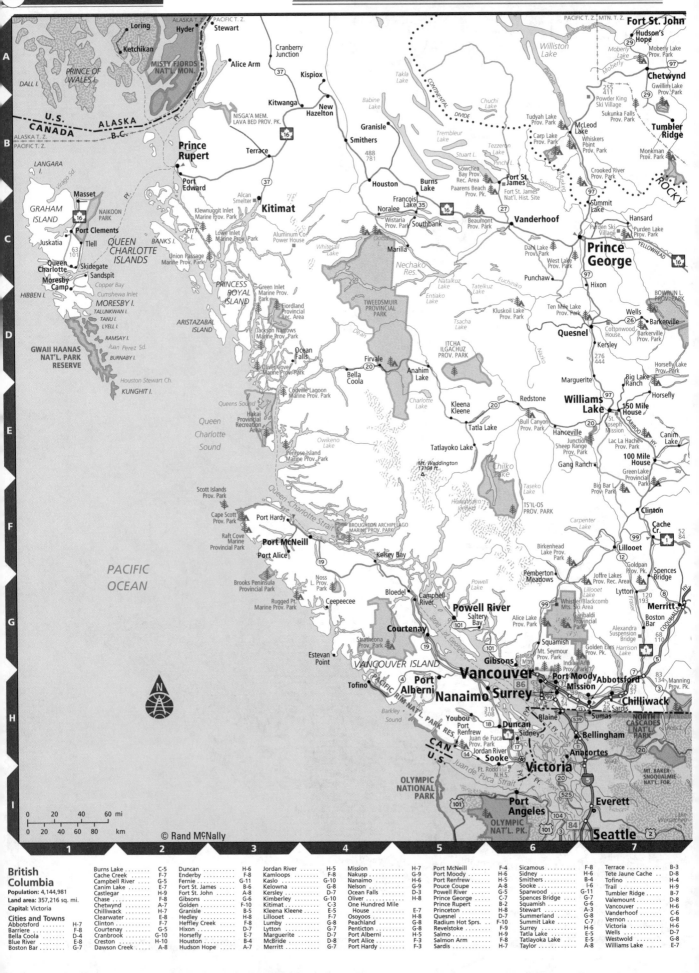

British Columbia

Population: 4,144,981
Land area: 357,216 sq. mi.
Capital: Victoria

Cities and Towns

Abbotsford	H-7	Burns Lake	C-5	Duncan	H-6	Jordan River	H-5
Barriere	F-8	Cache Creek	F-7	Enderby	F-8	Kamloops	F-8
Bella Coola	D-4	Campbell River	G-5	Fernie	G-11	Kaslo	G-10
Blue River	E-8	Canim Lake	E-7	Fort St. James	B-6	Kelowna	G-8
Boston Bar	G-7	Castlegar	E-7	Fort St. John	A-8	Kersley	D-7
		Chase	F-8	Gibsons	G-6	Kimberley	G-10
		Chetwynd	A-7	Golden	F-10	Kitimat	C-3
		Chilliwack	H-7	Granisle	B-5	Kleena Kleene	E-5
		Clearwater	E-8	Hedley	G-8	Lillooet	F-7
		Clinton	F-7	Heffley Creek	D-7	Lumby	G-8
		Courtenay	G-5	Hixon	D-7	Lytton	G-7
		Cranbrook	G-10	Horsefly	E-7	Marguerite	D-7
		Creston	H-10	Houston	B-4	McBride	D-8
		Dawson Creek	A-8	Hudson Hope	A-7	Merritt	G-7

Mission	H-7	Port McNeill	F-4	Sicamous	F-8	Terrace	B-3
Nakusp	G-9	Port Moody	H-6	Sidney	H-6	Tete Jaune Cache	D-8
Nanaimo	H-6	Port Renfrew	H-5	Smithers	B-4	Tofino	H-4
Nelson	H-9	Pouce Coupe	A-8	Sooke	I-6	Trail	H-9
Ocean Falls	D-3	Powell River	G-6	Sparwood	G-11	Tumbler Ridge	B-7
Oliver	H-8	Prince George	C-7	Spences Bridge	G-7	Valemount	D-8
One Hundred Mile		Prince Rupert	B-2	Squamish	G-6	Vancouver	H-6
House	E-7	Princeton	H-8	Stewart	A-3	Vanderhoof	C-6
Osoyoos	H-8	Quesnel	D-7	Summerland	G-8	Vernon	G-8
Peachland	G-8	Radium Hot Sprs.	F-10	Summit Lake	C-7	Victoria	H-6
Penticton	G-8	Revelstoke	F-9	Surrey	H-6	Wells	D-7
Port Alberni	H-5	Salmo	H-9	Tatla Lake	E-5	Westwold	E-7
Port Alice	F-3	Salmon Arm	F-8	Tatlayoka Lake	E-5	Williams Lake	E-7
Port Hardy	F-3	Sardis	H-7	Taylor	A-8		

Alberta

Population: 3,114,390
Land area: 248,000 sq. mi.
Capital: Edmonton

Cities and Towns

Airdrie	F-11	
Alix	D-12	
Athabasca	B-12	
Banff	F-10	
Barrhead	C-11	
Bashaw	D-12	
Bassano	F-12	
Bentley	D-11	
Black Diamond	F-11	
Bonnyville	B-13	
Bow Island	G-13	
Boyle	B-12	
Brooks	F-13	
Calgary	F-11	
Calmar	C-11	
Camrose	D-12	
Cardston	H-11	
Castor	E-13	
Claresholm	G-11	
Coaldale	G-12	
Cold Lake	B-13	
Coronation	E-13	
Crossfield	E-11	
Crowsnest Pass	G-11	
Drayton Valley	D-11	
Drumheller	E-12	
Edmonton	C-12	
Edson	C-10	
Elk Point	C-13	
Fairview	A-9	
Falher	A-9	
Foremost	G-13	
Forestburg	D-13	
Fox Creek	C-10	
Fort Macleod	G-12	
Fort Saskatchewan	C-12	
Grand Centre	B-13	
Grande Cache	C-8	
Grande Prairie	B-9	
Grimshaw	A-9	
Hanna	E-13	
Hardisty	D-13	
High Prairie	B-10	
High River	F-11	
Hinton	D-9	
Innisfail	E-11	
Jasper	D-9	
Killam	D-13	
Lac la Biche	B-12	
Lacombe	D-12	
Lake Louise	F-10	
Lamont	C-12	
Leduc	D-12	
Lethbridge	G-12	
Lloydminster	C-14	
Magrath	G-12	
McLennan	A-10	
Medicine Hat	F-13	
Milk River	H-13	
Morinville	C-11	
Nanton	F-11	
Okotoks	F-11	
Olds	E-11	
Oyen	E-14	
Peace River	A-9	
Penhold	E-11	
Pincher Creek	G-11	
Ponoka	D-12	
Provost	D-14	
Raymond	G-12	
Red Deer	E-11	
Redcliff	F-13	
Rimbey	D-11	
Rocky Mountain House	E-11	
Rycroft	A-8	
St. Albert	C-11	
St. Paul	C-13	
Sedgewick	D-13	
Slave Lake	B-11	
Smoky Lake	C-12	
Spirit River	A-8	
Stettler	D-12	
Stirling	G-13	
Stony Plain	C-11	
Sundre	E-11	
Swan Hills	B-10	
Sylvan Lake	E-11	
Taber	G-12	
Three Hills	E-12	
Tofield	C-12	
Trochu	E-12	
Turner Valley	F-11	
Two Hills	C-13	
Valleyview	B-9	
Vegreville	C-12	
Vermilion	C-13	
Viking	D-13	
Vulcan	F-12	
Wabasca-Desmarais	A-11	
Wainwright	D-13	
Westlock	C-11	
Wetaskiwin	D-12	
Whitecourt	C-10	

Manitoba

Population: 1,155,492
Land area: 213,729 sq. mi.
Capital: Winnipeg

Cities and Towns

Amaranth	H-9
Angusville	H-7
Arborg	G-10
Ashern	G-10
Austin	I-9
Baldur	I-9
Beausejour	H-11
Belmont	I-9
Benito	F-7
Binscarth	H-7
Birch River	F-7
Birtle	H-7
Boissevain	I-8
Bowsman	F-7
Brandon	I-8
Camperville	F-8
Carberry	I-9
Carman	I-10
Cartwright	J-9
Clearwater	J-9
Cormorant	C-8
Cranberry Portage	C-7
Cross Lake	C-10
Crystal City	J-9
Darlingford	J-10
Dauphin	G-8
Deloraine	J-8
Douglas	I-9
Duck Bay	F-8
Easterville	E-8
Elkhorn	I-7
Elm Creek	I-10
Elphinstone	H-8
Emerson	J-11
Erickson	H-8
Eriksdale	G-10
Ethelbert	G-8
Fisher Branch	G-10
Flin Flon	C-7
Gilbert Plains	G-8
Gimli	H-11
Gladstone	H-9
Glenboro	I-9
Grand Rapids	E-9
Grandview	G-8
Gretna	J-10
Gypsumville	F-9
Hamiota	H-8
Hartney	I-8
Hodgson	G-10
Holland	I-9
Inglis	G-7
Kenville	F-7
Killarney	J-9
La Broquerie	I-11
Lac du Bonnet	H-11
Langruth	H-9
Letellier	J-10
Lockport	H-11
Lowe Farm	I-10
Lundar	H-10
MacGregor	I-9
Mafeking	E-7
Manigotagan	G-11
Manitou	I-9
McCreary	H-9
Melita	J-8
Miniota	H-7
Minitonas	F-7
Minnedosa	H-8
Minto	I-8
Moose Lake	D-8
Moosehorn	G-9
Morden	I-10
Morris	I-10
Neepawa	H-9
Newdale	H-8
Ninette	I-9
Niverville	I-11
Norway House	D-10
Oak River	H-8
Oakville	I-10
Ochre River	G-8
Petersfield	H-11
Pierson	J-7
Pilot Mound	J-9
Pine Falls	H-11
Pine River	H-8
Pipestone	I-8
Plum Coulee	J-10
Portage la Prairie	H-10
Rathwell	I-9
Rennie	I-12
Reston	I-7
Rivers	H-8
Riverton	G-11
Roblin	G-7
Roland	I-10
Rorketon	G-9
Rosenfeld	J-10
Rossburn	H-8
Russell	H-7
St. Georges	H-11
St. Jean Baptiste	J-10
St. Laurent	H-10
St. Malo	J-11
St. Pierre	I-11
Ste. Ann	I-11
Ste. Rose du Lac	G-9
Sanford	I-10
Selkirk	H-11
Shoal Lake	H-8
Snow Lake	B-8
Somerset	I-9
Souris	I-8
Sperling	I-10
Sprague	J-12
Steinbach	I-11
Swan River	F-7
Teulon	H-10
The Pas	D-7
Thompson	A-10
Tolstoi	J-11
Treherne	I-9
Tyndall	H-11
Virden	I-7
Vita	J-11
Wabowden	B-9
Wawanesa	I-8
Whitemouth	H-11
Winkler	J-10
Winnipeg	I-11
Winnipeg Beach	H-11
Winnipegosis	F-8
Woodlands	H-10
Woodridge	I-11

Saskatchewan

Population: 995,490
Land area: 228,445 sq. mi.
Capital: Regina

Cities and Towns

Alsask	F-1
Arborfield	E-6
Arcola	I-6
Asquith	F-3
Assiniboia	I-4
Avonlea	H-5
Balcarres	G-6
Battleford	E-2
Beauval	B-3
Bengough	I-5
Bienfait	J-6
Big River	D-3
Biggar	F-3
Blaine Lake	E-3
Bredenbury	G-7
Broadview	H-6
Buffalo Narrows	A-3
Burstall	G-1
Cabri	G-2
Canora	F-6
Carlyle	I-6
Carnduff	J-7
Carrot River	D-6
Central Butte	G-4
Choiceland	D-5
Coronach	J-4
Craik	G-4
Creighton	C-7
Cudworth	E-4
Cumberland House	D-7
Cupar	G-5
Cut Knife	E-2
Davidson	G-4
Delisle	F-3
Duck Lake	E-4
Dundurn	F-4
Eastend	I-2
Eatonia	G-1
Elrose	G-2
Esterhazy	G-7
Eston	G-2
Foam Lake	F-6
Fort Qu'Appelle	H-5
Glaslyn	D-2
Gravelbourg	I-3
Green Lake	C-3
Grenfell	H-6
Gull Lake	H-2
Hafford	E-3
Hague	E-4
Herbert	H-3
Hudson Bay	E-6
Humboldt	F-5
Indian Head	H-6
Ituna	G-6
Kamsack	G-7
Kelvington	F-6
Kerrobert	F-2
Kindersley	F-2
Kinistino	E-5
Kyle	G-2
La Ronge	B-5
Lafleche	I-3
Langenburg	G-7
Lanigan	F-5
Lashburn	D-1
Leader	G-1
Lloydminster	D-1
Lumsden	H-5
Luseland	F-1
Macklin	E-1
Maidstone	D-2
Maple Creek	H-1
Martensville	F-4
Meadow Lake	C-2
Melfort	E-5
Melville	G-6
Midale	I-6
Milestone	H-5
Montmartre	H-6
Moose Jaw	H-4
Moosomin	H-7
Mossbank	H-4
Naicam	E-5
Nipawin	D-5
Nokomis	G-5
Norquay	F-7
Outlook	G-3
Oxbow	I-7
Pelican Narrows	B-6
Pense	H-5
Pierceland	C-2
Ponteix	I-3
Porcupine Plain	E-6
Preeceville	F-6
Prince Albert	D-4
Qu'Appelle	H-5
Quill Lake	F-5
Radisson	E-3
Raymore	G-5
Redvers	I-7
Regina	H-5
Regina Beach	G-5
Rocanville	H-7
Rockglen	I-4
Rose Valley	F-6
Rosthern	E-4
St. Louis	E-4
St. Walburg	D-2
Saskatoon	F-4
Shaunavon	I-2
Shellbrook	D-4
Southey	G-5
Spiritwood	D-3
Star City	E-5
Stoughton	I-6
Strasbourg	G-5
Sturgis	F-6
Swift Current	H-2
Theodore	G-6
Tisdale	E-5
Turtleford	D-2
Unity	E-2
Wadena	F-6
Wakaw	E-4
Waldheim	E-4
Watrous	F-5
Watson	F-5
Weyburn	I-5
Whitewood	H-6
Wilkie	E-2
Willow Bunch	I-4
Wolseley	H-6
Wynyard	F-5
Yellow Grass	H-5
Yorkton	G-6

© Rand McNally

0 20 40 mi
0 20 40 60 km

SASKATCHEWAN
MANITOBA
ONTARIO

Thompson
Paint Lake Provincial Park
Sandy Bay
Pelican Narrows
Flin Flon
Creighton
Channing
Cranberry Portage
Wanless
Cumberland House
The Pas
Westray
Prospector
Finger
Moose Lake
Snow Lake
Herb Lake
Herb Lake Landing
Wekusko
Tyrrell
Ponton
Dunlop
Wabowden
Pipun
Cross Lake
Norway House
Warren Landing
Grass River Prov. Park
Cormorant Provincial Forest
Cormorant
Clearwater Lake Prov. Park
Cumberland House Prov. Hist. Park
Wildcat Hill 2565 ft.
Carrot River
Arborfield
Crooked River
Bjorkdale
Porcupine Plain
Somme
Bertwell
Hudson Bay
Westgate
Powell
Mafeking
Novra
Birch River
Spirit Mtn. 2585 ft.
Porcupine Provincial Forest
Overflowing River
Easterville
Grand Rapids
HORSE ISLAND
LAKE WINNIPEG
Long Pt.
ROSS ISLAND
REINDEER ISLAND
BERENS ISLAND
Berens River
Rose Valley
Kelvington
Wadena
Okla
Preeceville
Margo
Sturgis
Usherville
Swan River
Bowsman
Minitonas
Lenswood
Duck Bay
Camperville
Skownan
Cowan
Kenville
Durban
Benito
Pelly
Pine River
SWAN-PELICAN PROV. FOREST
Lake Winnipegosis
BIRCH ISLAND
Chitek Lake
Inland Lake
PELICAN ISLAND
Norquay
Amsterdam
Canora
Kamsack
Gorlitz
San Clara
Baldy Mtn. 2729 ft. Highest Pt. in Manitoba
Ketchum Hill 2500 ft.
Roblin
Grandview
Gilbert Plains
Dauphin
Winnipegosis
Meadow Portage
Garland
Ethelbert
Fork River
Sifton
Ashville
Rorketon
Cayer
Ste. Rose du Lac
Sher- grove
Toutes Aides
Steep Rock
Gypsumville
Hilbre
Grahamdale
Lake St. Martin
Moosehorn
Hodgson
Dallas
Fisher River
Pine Dock
Matheson Island
Jackhead
Dauphin River
Lake St. George
Theodore
Willowbrook
Yorkton
Kelliher
Jasmin
Ituna
Melville
Bredenbury
Langenburg
Russell
Inglis
Angusville
Rossburn
Oakburn
RIDING MOUNTAIN NATIONAL PARK
Elphinstone
Shoal Lake
Birtle
Newdale
Minnedosa
Hamiota
Neepawa
Gladstone
Macdonald
Delta Beach
Warren
Poplar Point
Grosse Isle
Stonewall
Selkirk
Lockport
Beausejour
Whitemouth
Anola
Ashern
Camper
Poplarfield
Fisher Branch
Arborg
Riverton
Hnausa
Gimli
Fraserwood
Narcisse
Inwood
Teulon
Petersfield
Matlock
Winnipeg Beach
Grand Beach
Victoria Beach
Pine Falls
St. Georges
Great Falls
Lac du Bonnet
Seven Sisters Falls
Broken- head
Tyndall
Lundar
Eriksdale
Deerhorn
Chatfield
Fisher Bay
Reykjavik
Moosehorn
Woodlands
St. Laurent
St. Francis
Woodside
Ogilvie
Plumas
Glenella
Langruth
Amaranth
Clarkleigh
Portage la Prairie
Brandon
Carberry
Austin
MacGregor
Oakville
Headingley
WINNIPEG
Sanford
Oak Bluff
Grande Pointe
Ile des Chênes
Ste. Anne- des-Chênes
Richer
La Broquerie
Steinbach
St-Pierre-Jolys
Niverville
St. Adolphe
Ste. Agathe
Morris
St. Malo
Woodridge
Sprague
Piney
Sundown
Vita
Tolstoi
Gretna
Emerson
Pembina
Altona
Winkler
Morden
Manitou
Carman
Roseisle
Somerset
Glenboro
Baldur
Killarney
Boissevain
Deloraine
Melita
Waskada
Pierson
Reston
Virden
Elkhorn
Hargrave
Griswold
Oak Lake
Souris
Wawanesa
Treherne
Holland
St. Claude
Notre Dame de Lourdes
Rathwell
Treesbank
Douglas
Rivers
Crandall
Manson
Miniota
Beulah
Binscarth
Rocanville
Esterhazy
Whitewood
Grenfell
Broadview
Wolseley
Moosomin
Virden
Kennedy
Fairlight
Stoughton
Carlyle
Arcola
Redvers
Storthoaks
Alameda
Hitchcock
Oxbow
Carnduff
Estevan
Bienfait
Crosby
Bowbells
Mohall
Westhope
Bottineau
Dunseith
Rolla
Langdon
Cavalier
Walhalla
St. Thomas
Hallock
Karlstad
Greenbrush
Roseau
Warroad

UNITED STATES
N. DAK.
MINN.

ONTARIO
ATIKAKI PROVINCIAL PARK
Werner Lake
Falcon Lake
Rennie
Hadashville
WHITESHELL PROVINCIAL PARK
Bissett
Manigotagan

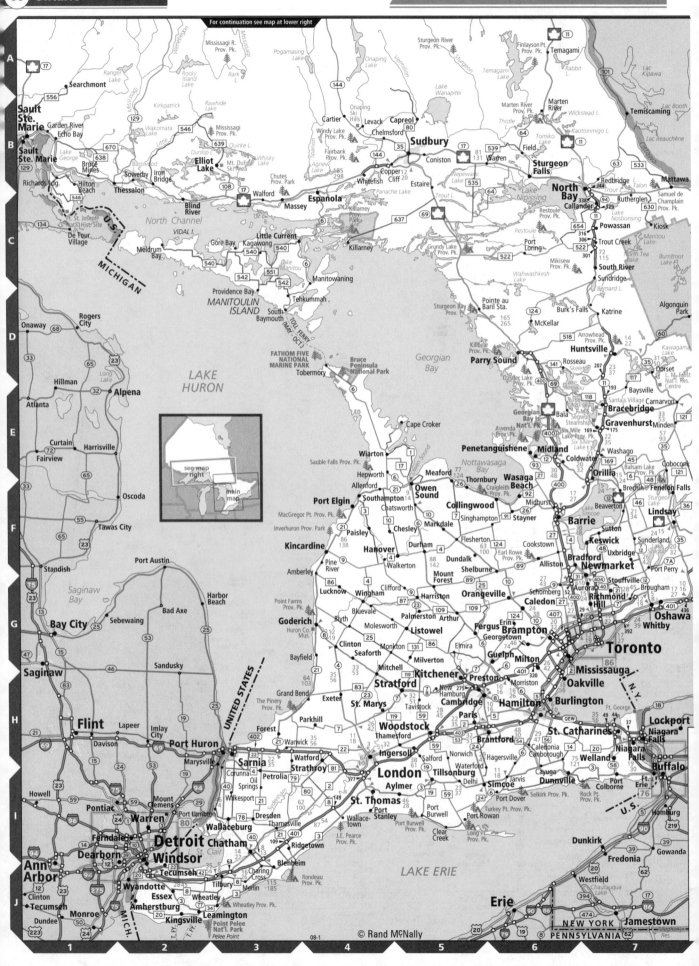

For border crossing information, please see p. 59

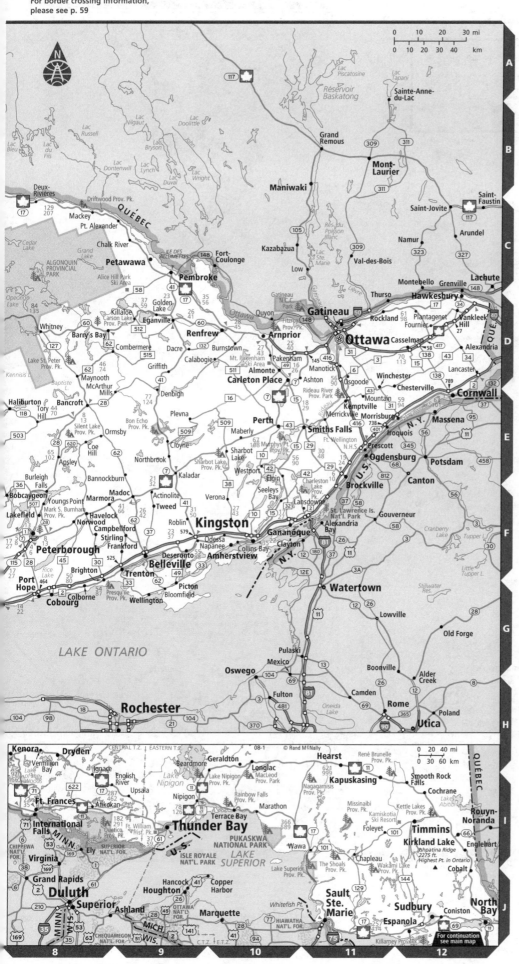

Ontario
Population: 12,096,627
Land area: 354,342 sq. mi.
Capital: Toronto

Cities and Towns

Actinolite	F-9
Alexandria	D-12
Algonquin Park	D-7
Allenford	F-4
Alliston	F-6
Almonte	D-10
Amherstburg	J-2
Apsley	E-8
Arnprior	D-10
Arthur	G-5
Atikokan	I-8
Aurora	G-7
Aylmer	I-4
Bala	E-6
Bancroft	E-8
Barrie	F-6
Barry's Bay	D-8
Bayfield	G-4
Baysville	E-7
Beardmore	H-10
Beaverton	F-7
Belleville	F-9
Blenheim	J-3
Blind River	G-2
Bloomfield	G-9
Bluevale	G-4
Blyth	G-4
Bobcaygeon	F-8
Bracebridge	E-7
Bradford	F-6
Brampton	G-6
Brantford	H-6
Brechin	F-7
Brighton	F-8
Brockville	E-11
Bruce Mines	B-1
Burk's Falls	D-7
Burlington	H-6
Caledonia	H-6
Callander	C-7
Cambridge	H-5
Campbellford	F-8
Cape Croker	E-5
Capreol	B-5
Carleton Place	D-10
Cartier	B-4
Casselman	D-12
Cayuga	H-6
Chalk River	C-9
Chapleau	I-11
Charing Cross	J-3
Chatham	J-3
Chatsworth	F-5
Chelmsford	B-5
Chesley	F-4
Chesterville	D-11
Clifford	G-5
Clinton	G-4
Cobalt	J-12
Cobocunk	E-7
Coburg	G-8
Cochrane	I-12
Colborne	G-8
Coldwater	E-6
Collingwood	F-6
Collins Bay	F-10
Coniston	B-5
Cookstown	F-6
Cornwall	E-12
Coruna	I-3
Delhi	I-5
Deseronto	F-9
Dresden	I-3
Dryden	H-9
Dundalk	F-5
Dunnville	I-6
Durham	F-5
Echo Bay	B-1
Eganville	D-9
Elgin	E-10
Elliot Lake	B-3
Elmira	G-5
Englehart	I-12
Erin	G-6
Espanola	C-4
Essex	J-2
Estaire	B-5
Exeter	H-4
Fenelon Falls	F-7
Fergus	G-5
Flesherton	F-5
Foleyet	I-11
Forest	H-3
Fort Erie	I-7
Fort Frances	I-8
Fournier	D-12
Frankford	F-9
Gananoque	F-10
Garden River	B-1
Georgetown	G-6
Geraldton	H-10
Goderich	G-4
Golden Lake	D-9
Gore Bay	C-3
Grand Bend	H-4
Granvenhurst	E-7
Guelph	G-6
Hagersville	H-6
Haliburton	E-8
Hamilton	H-6
Hanover	G-5
Harriston	G-5
Havelock	F-8
Hawkesbury	D-12
Hearst	H-11
Hepworth	E-4
Huntsville	D-7
Ignace	I-8
Ingersoll	H-5
Iron Bridge	B-2
Iroquois	E-11
Kagawong	C-3
Kaladar	E-9
Kapuskasing	I-11
Kemptville	E-11
Kenora	H-8
Keswick	F-6
Killaloe	D-9
Killarney	C-4
Kincardine	F-4
Kingston	F-10
Kingsville	J-2
Kirkland Lake	I-12
Kitchener	H-5
Lakefield	F-8
Lancaster	D-12
Lansdowne	F-11
Leamington	J-2
Levack	B-4
Lindsay	F-7
Listowel	G-5
Little Current	C-3

London	H-4
Longlac	H-10
Lucknow	G-4
Madoc	F-9
Manotick	D-11
Marathon	I-10
Markdale	F-5
Marmora	F-8
Marten River	B-6
Massey	C-3
Mattawa	B-7
Maynooth	D-8
McKellar	D-6
Meaford	F-5
Merlin	J-3
Merrickville	E-11
Midland	E-6
Milton	G-6
Milverton	G-5
Minden	E-7
Mississauga	G-6
Mitchell	H-4
Monkton	G-4
Morrisburg	E-11
Mount Forest	G-5
Mountain	E-11
Napanee	F-9
New Hamburg	H-5
Newmarket	F-7
Niagara Falls	H-7
Nipigon	I-9
North Bay	B-7
Northbrook	E-9
Norwich	H-5
Norwood	F-8
Oakville	H-6
Odessa	F-9
Oil Springs	I-3
Orangeville	G-6
Orillia	F-6
Ormsby	E-8
Osgoode	D-11
Oshawa	G-7
Ottawa	D-11
Owen Sound	F-5
Paisley	F-4
Pakenham	D-10
Palmerston	G-5
Paris	H-5
Parkhill	H-4
Parry Sound	D-6
Pembroke	C-9
Penetanguishene	E-6
Perth	E-10
Petawawa	C-9
Peterborough	F-8
Petrolia	I-3
Plantagenet	D-12
Plevna	E-9
Pointe au Baril Station	D-5
Port Burwell	I-5
Port Colborne	I-7
Port Elgin	F-4
Port Hope	G-8
Port Perry	F-7
Port Rowan	I-5
Port Stanley	I-4
Powassan	C-7
Prescott	E-11
Renfrew	D-10
Richards Landing	B-1
Richmond Hill	G-7
Ridgetown	I-3
Rockland	D-11
Rosseau	D-6
St. Catharines	H-7
St. Mary's	H-4
St. Thomas	I-4
Sarnia	H-3
Sault Ste. Marie	B-1
Schomberg	G-6
Seaforth	G-4
Searchmont	A-1
Seeleys Bay	F-10
Sharbot Lake	E-10
Shelburne	F-6
Simcoe	I-5
Smiths Falls	E-11
Smooth Rock Falls	I-12
South River	C-7
Southampton	F-4
Stayner	F-6
Stirling	F-9
Stouffville	G-7
Stratford	H-5
Strathroy	H-4
Sturgeon Falls	B-6
Sudbury	B-5
Sunderland	F-7
Sundridge	C-7
Sutton	F-7
Tavistock	H-5
Tecumseh	J-2
Terrace Bay	I-10
Thamesville	I-3
Thessalon	B-2
Thornbury	F-5
Thunder Bay	I-9
Tilbury	J-3
Tillsonburg	I-5
Timmins	I-12
Tobermory	D-4
Toronto	G-7
Trenton	F-9
Trout Creek	C-7
Tweed	F-9
Upsala	I-9
Uxbridge	F-7
Vankleek Hill	D-12
Verona	F-10
Walkerton	G-4
Wallaceburg	I-3
Wallaceton	I-3
Warren	B-6
Wasaga Beach	F-6
Washago	E-7
Watford	H-3
Wawa	I-11
Welland	H-7
Wellington	G-9
Wheatley	J-3
Whitby	G-7
Whitney	D-8
Wiarton	E-4
Winchester	D-11
Windsor	J-2
Wingham	H-5
Woodstock	H-5
Youngs Point	F-8

Plan a Québec trip at go.randmcnally.com/QC

Québec

Population: 7,443,491
Land area: 527,079 sq. mi.
Capital: Québec City

Cities and Towns

Acton Vale H-7	Baie-Saint-Paul ... F-9	Cap-Saint-Ignace ... F-9	Dégelis E-10
Alma D-8	Barraute D-3	Causapscal D-11	Delisle E-8
Amos D-2	Beauceville G-14	Chambly H-11	Disraëli H-8
Amqui D-11	Bécancour G-12	Chandler D-14	Donnacona G-8
Asbestos H-7	Bedford I-7	Châteauguay H-6	Drummondville ... H-7
Baie-Comeau C-11	Berthierville G-11	Chibougamau ... B-6	East Angus H-8
	Black Lake G-8	Chicoutimi D-8	East Broughton ... G-7
	Blainville H-6	Chute-aux-	Ferme-Neuve F-4
	Bromptonville ... H-13	Outardes C-10	Forestville D-10
	Cabano E-10	Coaticook I-7	Fort-Coulonge ... H-3
	Cap-Chat C-12	Contrecoeur H-6	Gaspé D-14
	Cap-de-la-	Cookshire H-8	Gatineau H-4
	Madeleine G-12	Cowansville I-7	Granby H-7
Grand-Mère G-7	La Malbaie E-9	Lévis F-8	Montmagny F-8
Grande-Rivière ... D-14	La Pocatière F-9	Longueuil H-6	Montréal H-6
Hébertville D-8	La Sarre C-1	Louiseville G-7	Morin-Heights G-10
Huntingdon I-5	La Tuque F-7	Lyster G-8	Napierville I-11
Iberville H-6	Lac-Etchemin G-8	Macamic C-1	New Richmond ... E-13
Joliette G-6	Lac-Mégantic H-8	Magog I-7	Nicolet G-7
Jonquière D-8	Lachute H-5	Malartic D-2	Normandin D-7
Kingsey Falls H-12	Lacolle I-11	Maniwaki G-4	Notre-Dame-
L'Assomption H-11	Laval H-6	Mascouche H-10	du-Lac E-10
L'Isle-Verte E-10	Le Gardeur H-11	Matagami B-3	Ormstown I-6
La Baie D-8	Lebel-sur-	Matane D-11	Papineauville H-5
La Doré D-7	Québillon C-3	Mont-Joli D-11	Percé D-14
La Guadeloupe ... H-8	Les Escoumins ... D-9	Mont-Laurier G-4	Plessisville G-8

For border crossing information, please see p. 59

© Rand McNally

Pohénégamook	F-10	Rimouski	D-10	Saint-Casimir	G-7	Saint-Léonard-		Sainte-Agathe-des-		Salaberry-de-		Thetford Mines	G-8
Pointe-du-Lac	G-12	Rivière-Bleue	F-10	Saint-Côme-		d'Aston	G-12	Monts	G-5	Valleyfield	H-6	Thurso	H-4
Pont-Rouge	F-13	Rivière-du-		Linière	G-14	Saint-Lin-		Sainte-Anne-de-		Sayabec	D-11	Trois-Pistoles	E-10
Port-Cartier	B-12	Loup	E-9	Saint-Constant	H-10	Laurentides	H-10	Beaupré	F-8	Senneterre	D-3	Trois-Rivières	G-7
Portneuf	G-7	Rivière-Rouge	G-5	Saint-Eustache	H-10	Saint-Pacôme	F-9	Sainte-Anne-des-		Sept-Îles	B-12	Val-d'Or	D-2
Price	D-11	Robertsonville	G-14	Saint-Félicien	D-7	Saint-Pamphile	F-9	Monts	C-12	Shawinigan	G-7	Vallée-Jonction	G-8
Princeville	G-13	Roberval	D-7	Saint-Félix-de-		Saint-Pascal	F-9	Sainte-Blandine	D-10	Shawinigan-		Varennes	H-6
Québec	F-8	Rock Forest	I-13	Valois	G-11	Saint-Prime	D-7	Sainte-Marie	G-8	Sud	F-12	Victoriaville	G-7
Rawdon	G-10	Roxton Falls	H-12	Saint-Ferréol-les-		Saint-Raphaël	F-8	Sainte-Perpétue	F-9	Sherbrooke	H-7	Ville-Marie	E-1
Repentigny	H-6	Rouyn-Noranda	D-1	Neiges	F-8	Saint-Raymond	F-7	Sainte-Sophie	H-10	Sorel-Tracy	G-7	Warwick	G-13
Richmond	H-7	Saguenay	D-8	Saint-François-du-		Saint-Rémi	I-10	Sainte-Thècle	F-12	Sutton	I-12	Weedon	H-8
Rigaud	H-9	Saint-Ambroise	D-8	Lac	G-11	Saint-Tite	G-7			Terrebonne	H-10	Windsor	H-8
		Saint-Anselme	F-14	Saint-Gabriel	G-6	Saint-Gédéon-de-		Saint-Georges	G-8				

08-1   NEW YORK   U.S.   VT.

New Brunswick

Population: 750,183
Land area: 27,587 sq. mi.
Capital: Fredericton

Cities and Towns

Acadie Siding E-5
Adamsville E-5
Alma G-6
Anagance F-5
Bathurst C-5
Belledune C-5
Big Cove E-6
Blackville E-5
Blissfield E-5
Boiestown E-4
Bouctouche E-6
Campbellton C-4
Canaan F-6
Cap-Pele F-6
Cape Tormentine ... F-7
Caraquet C-6
Chatham D-5
Chipman F-5
Coles Island F-5
Cross Creek F-4
Dalhousie C-4
Doaktown E-5
Eastport H-4
Edmundston D-2
Escuminac D-6
Florenceville E-3
Fredericton F-4
Grand Falls (Grand
 Sault) D-3
Hammondvale G-5
Hampton G-5
Harcourt E-5
Hartland E-3
Harvey F-4
Hillsborough F-5
Jemseg F-5
Juniper E-3
Kedgwick C-3
Keswick Ridge F-4
Kouchibouguac ... C-6
Lameque C-6
Lawrence Station .. G-3
Long Creek F-4
Lutes Mountain ... F-6
Memramcook F-6
Millville F-3
Minto F-5
Miramichi D-5
Moncton F-6
Nashwaak Bridge .. F-4
Neguac D-5
Newcastle D-5
Nictau D-3
North Head H-4
Oromocto F-4
Perth-Andover E-3
Plaster Rock E-3
Pointe-Sapin E-6
Pointe-Verte C-5
Port Elgin F-6
Renous E-5
Rexton E-6
Richibucto E-6
Riverside-Albert ... F-6
Rogersville E-5
Sackville F-6
St. Andrews G-3
St. Croix G-3
St. George G-4
Saint John G-5
St. Martins G-5
St-Quentin D-3
St. Stephen G-3
Salisbury F-6
Shediac F-6
Shippagan C-6
Sussex G-5
Sussex Corner G-5
Thomaston Corner . G-3
Tracy F-4
Upper Hainesville . F-4
Welsford G-4
Woodstock F-3
Youngs Cove F-5

Newfoundland and Labrador

Population: 519,270
Land area: 144,353 sq. mi.
Capital: St. John's

Cities and Towns

Baie Verte B-11
Bay de Verde C-12
Bishop's Falls C-11
Bonavista C-12
Brig Bay A-10
Buchans C-10
Burgeo C-10
Channel-Port aux
 Basques C-9
Corner Brook C-10
Daniel's Harbour .. B-10
Deer Lake B-11
Englee B-11
Gander C-11
Goobies C-12
Grand Bank D-11
Grand Falls-Windsor . C-11
Harbour Breton ... D-11
Lark Harbour C-10
Marystown D-11
Placentia D-12
Port Blandford ... C-11
Roddickton B-11
Rose-Blanche-Harbour
 le Cou C-10
St. Alban's C-11
St. Anthony A-11
St. John's C-12
St. Lawrence D-11
Torbay C-12
Trout River B-10

Nova Scotia

Population: 934,392
Land area: 20,594 sq. mi.
Capital: Halifax

Cities and Towns

Advocate Harbour . G-6
Albany Cross H-6
Amherst F-6
Annapolis Royal ... H-5
Antigonish G-9
Apple River G-6
Baddeck F-10
Barrington Passage . J-5
Bass River G-7
Big Pond F-10
Bridgetown H-5
Bridgewater I-6
Brookfield G-7
Brooklyn H-7
Canso G-10
Carleton I-5
Centreville H-5
Chester H-6
Cheticamp E-10
Clementsport H-5
Clyde River J-5
Corberrie I-5
Dartmouth H-7
Digby H-5
East Bay F-11
Earltown G-7
Elmsdale H-7
Glace Bay F-11
Glenholme G-7
Goldboro G-9
Goldenville G-9
Grand River F-10
Greywood H-5
Guysborough G-9
Halifax H-7
Halls Harbour G-6
Hebron I-5
Indian Brook E-10
Ingonish E-11
Ingonish Beach ... E-10
Inverness F-10
Joggins G-6
Kentville H-6
Larrys River G-9
Liverpool I-6
Lockeport J-5
Louisbourg F-11
Lunenburg I-6
Maccan F-6
Mahone Bay I-6
Margaree Forks ... E-10
Margaree Harbour . E-10
Mavilette I-4
Middle
 Musquodoboit ... H-7
Middlefield I-6
Middleton H-6
Mill Village I-6
Moser River H-8
Mulgrave G-9
Musquodoboit
 Harbour H-7
Neil's Harbour ... E-11
New Germany H-6
New Glasgow G-8
New Ross H-6
New Waterford ... E-11
Newport Station .. H-6
North Sydney F-11
Nyanza F-10
Oxford F-7
Parrsboro G-6
Peggys Cove H-7
Picton G-8
Pleasant Bay E-10
Port Hastings F-9
Port Hawkesbury . G-10
Port Hood F-9
Pubnico J-5
Sable River I-6
St. Peters G-10
Salmon River I-5
Sand Point G-10
Shag Harbour ... J-5
Sheet Harbour ... H-8
Shelburne J-5
South Brookfield .. I-6
Southampton G-6
Springhill G-6
Stewiacke G-7
Sunnybrae G-8
Sydney F-11
Sydney Mines E-11
Tatamagouche ... G-7
Tiverton I-4
Truro G-7
Upper
 Musquodoboit ... G-8
Upper Rawdon ... H-7
Vaughan H-6
Wedgeport J-5
Westport I-4
Weymouth I-5
Whycocomagh ... F-10
Windsor H-6
Wolfville G-6
Yarmouth I-5

Prince Edward Island

Population: 136,998
Land area: 2,185 sq. mi.
Capital: Charlottetown

Cities and Towns

Alberton E-6
Belle River F-8
Borden-Carleton .. F-7
Campbellton E-6
Cavendish E-7
Charlottetown ... F-7
Georgetown F-8
Kensington E-7
Montague F-8
Murray Harbour .. F-8
Portage E-6
Rocky Point F-7
St. Peters E-8
Souris E-8
South Lake E-9
Summerside F-7
Tignish D-6
West Point E-6

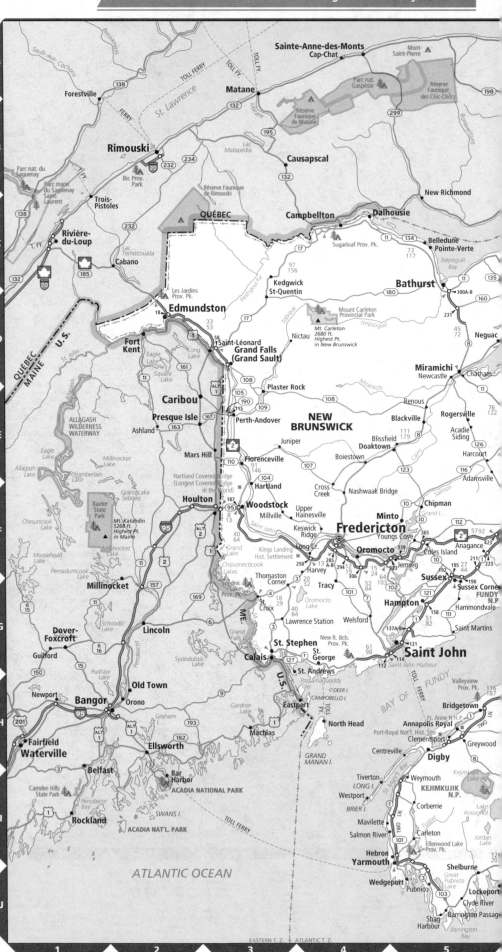

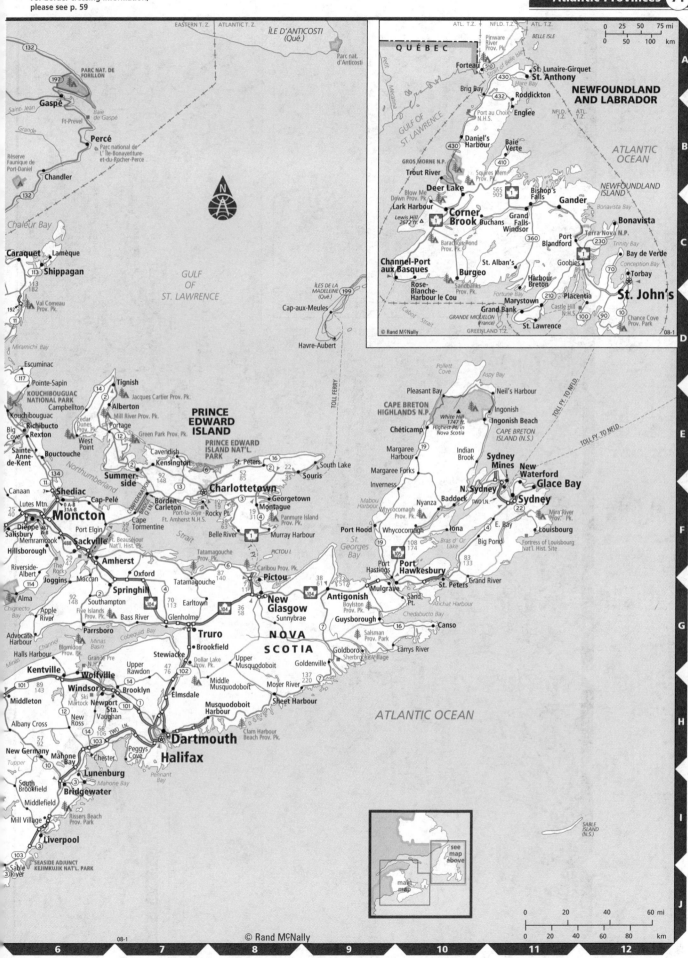

For border crossing information, please see p. 59

Mexico

Population: 97,483,412
Land area: 758,450 sq. mi.
Capital: Mexico City

Cities and Towns

Acaponeta	D-5	Pitiquito	A-3
Acapulco	F-8	Poza Rica	E-6
Acayucan	E-7	Puebla	E-7
Aguascalientes	D-5	Puerto Ángel	F-7
Arriaga	E-7	Puerto Escondido	F-7
Atlixco	E-7	Puerto Morelos	D-10
Autlán de Navarro	E-5	Puerto Peñasco	A-2
Bahía Kino	B-3	Puerto Vallarta	E-5
Bermejillo	B-5	Punta Prieta	B-2
Buenaventura	B-4	Querétaro	E-6
Campeche	D-10	Reynosa	C-7
Cancún	D-10	Río Lagartos	D-10
Champotón	E-10	Rosario	B-6
Chetumal	F-6	Sabinas	B-6
Chihuahua	B-4	Sabinas Hidalgo	C-6
Chilpancingo	F-8	Sahuaripa	B-4
Choix	C-4	Salamanca	E-6
Cholula	E-7	Saltillo	C-5
Cintalapa	F-7	San Blas	C-4
Ciudad Camargo	B-3	San Carlos	B-3
Ciudad del Carmen	B-5	San Felipe	A-2
Ciudad de México	E-7	San Fernando	C-7
Ciudad Juárez	A-4	San Francisco del Orco	C-6
Ciudad Madero	D-7	San José del Cabo	C-4
Ciudad Mante	D-6	San Luis Potosí	D-6
Ciudad Obregón	B-3	Santa Ana	A-3
Ciudad Valles	D-6	Santa Bárbara	C-3
Ciudad Victoria	D-6	Santa Rosalía	B-3
Coatzacoalcos	E-8	Santo Domingo	E-6
Colima	E-5	Tehuantepec	F-8
Cozumel	C-4	Tamazunchale	D-6
Cuajinicuilapa	F-8	Tampico	D-7
Cuauhtémoc	B-4	Tapachula	F-8
Culiacán	C-4	Taxco	E-6
Durango	C-5	Tehuacán	E-7
El Fuerte	B-4	Tepic	D-5
El Sueco	B-4	Tijuana	A-1
Ensenada	A-2	Tlaxcala	D-6
Escárcega	E-9	Toluca	E-6
Fresnillo	D-5	Tonichi	B-3
Gómez Palacio	C-5	Topolobampo	C-3
Guadalajara	E-5	Torreón	C-5
Guamúchil	C-4	Tuxtla Gutiérrez	F-8
Guanajuato	D-6	Uruapan del Progreso	E-5
Guaymas	B-3	Veracruz	E-7
Guerrero	C-3	Villahermosa	E-8
Guzmán	C-4	Xalapa	E-6
Hermosillo	B-3	Xilagráh	E-6
Hidalgo del Parral	C-4	Zacatecas	A-1
Huajuapan de León	E-7	Zihuatanejo	F-6
Iguala	E-6		
Irapuato	E-6		
Jalpa	D-5		
Jiménez	C-5		
Juan Aldama	C-5		
La Paz	C-4		
La Pesca	D-7		
León	D-6		
Linares	C-6		
Loreto	C-3		
Los Mochis	B-3		
Manzanillo	E-5		
Matamoros	C-7		
Matehuala	D-6		
Mérida	D-9		
Mexicali	A-2		
Mexico City	E-7		
Mondova	C-6		
Monterrey	C-6		
Morelia	E-6		
Navojoa	B-3		
Nogales	A-3		
Nueva Rosita	B-6		
Nuevo Casas Grandes	A-4		
Oaxaca	E-7		
Ojinaga	B-5		
Orizaba	E-7		
Pachuca	E-7		
Parras	C-5		
Piedras Negras	B-6		

Mexico City

Atizapán	B-8
Coacalco	B-8
Ciudad Netzahualcóyotl	C-9
Chimalhuacán	C-9
Ecatepec	B-9
Naucalpan	B-8
San Mateo Tecoloapan	A-8
Tlalnepantla	B-8

Ciudad de México (Mexico City)

Puerto Rico (U.S.)

© Rand McNally

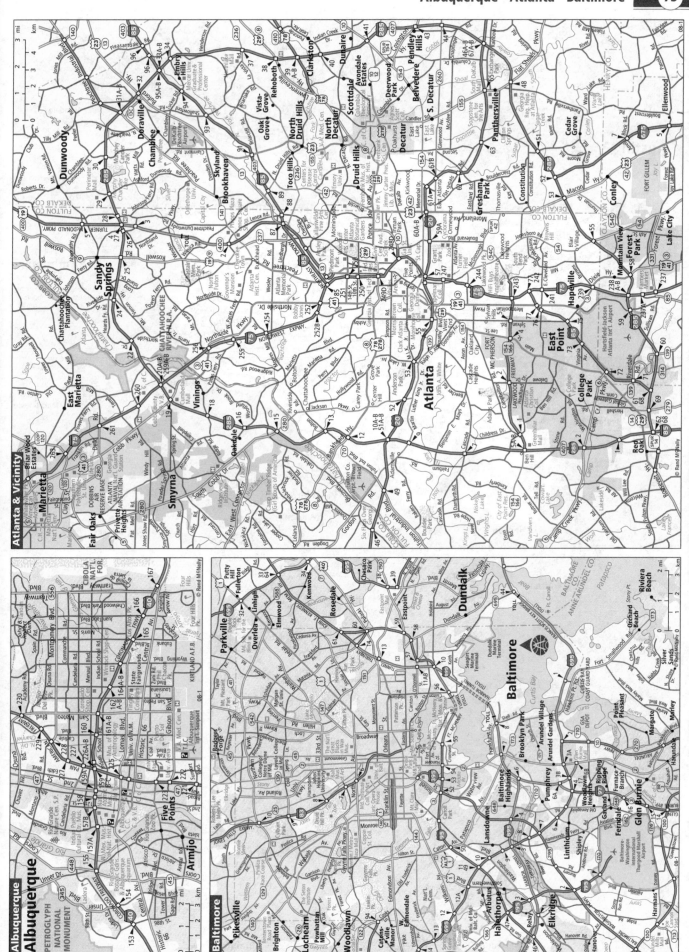

Atlanta & Vicinity

Albuquerque

Baltimore

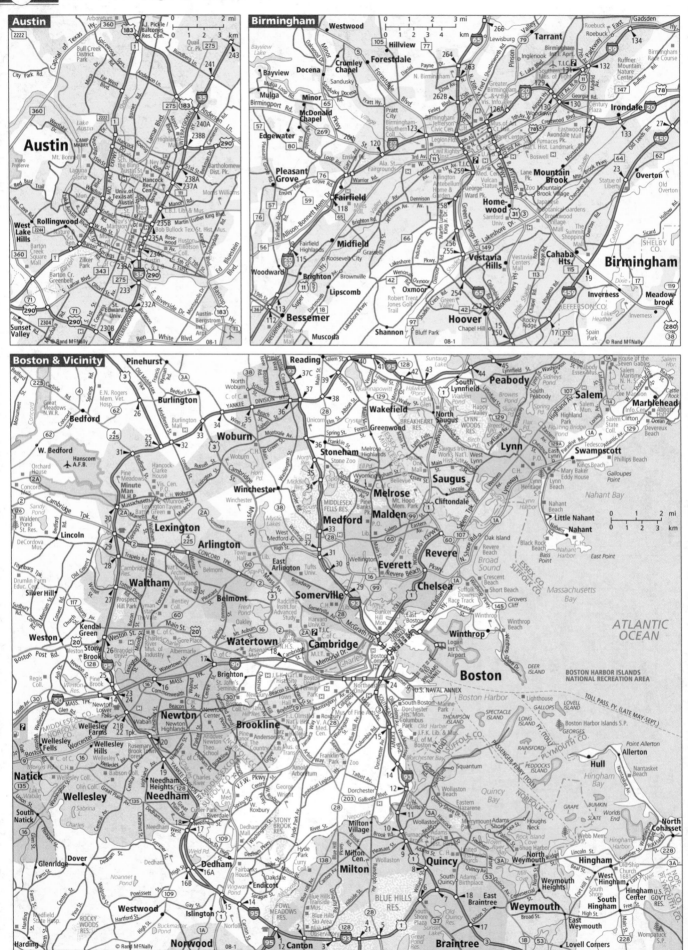

Chicago & Vicinity

© Rand McNally

0 1 2 3 4 mi
0 1 2 3 4 5 6 km

LAKE MICHIGAN
El. 579 ft. above sea level

Chicago

Lake Zurich, Long Grove, Deer Park, Kildeer, Barrington, Barrington Hills, Inverness, Palatine, South Barrington, Hoffman Estates, Streamwood, Schaumburg, Hanover Park, Ontarioville, Bartlett, Roselle, Keeneyville, Medinah, Bloomingdale, Itasca, Carol Stream, Glendale Heights, Addison, Wood Dale, Bensenville, Wheeling, Buffalo Grove, Northbrook, Prospect Heights, Arlington Heights, Rolling Meadows, Mount Prospect, Des Plaines, Park Ridge, Elk Grove Village, Schiller Park, Norridge, Harwood Heights, Franklin Park, Northlake, Melrose Park, River Grove, Elmwood Park, Villa Park, Lombard, Glen Ellyn, Wheaton, Winfield, Glen Ellyn Countryside, Carol Stream

Highwood, Half Day, Lincolnshire, Bannockburn, Deerfield, Riverwoods, Highland Park, Ravinia Park, Ravinia Festival Music Center, Botanic Garden, Glencoe, Northfield, Winnetka, Kenilworth, Golf, Glenview, Morton Grove, Niles, Skokie, Wilmette, Evanston, Lincolnwood, Rogers Park, Loyola Univ. of Chicago, Northwestern Univ.

O'Hare, Chicago O'Hare Int'l. Arpt., Rosemont, Norridge, Dunning, Cragin, River Forest, Oak Park, Berkeley, Bellwood, Maywood, Hillside, Elmhurst, York Center, Oakbrook Terrace, Broadview, Westchester, Riverside, Berwyn, Cicero, Forest Park, Brookfield, La Grange Park, Western Springs, La Grange, Stickney, Lyons, McCook, Summit, Countryside, Hodgkins, Indian Head Park, Justice, Bridgeview, Burbank, Hometown, Evergreen Park, Bedford Park, Oak Brook, Oak Brook Terrace, Brandywine, Butterfield, Lisle, Downers Grove, Clarendon Hills, Hinsdale, Westmont, Burr Ridge, La Grange Highlands, Willowbrook, Woodridge, Darien, Tri-State Village, Willow Springs, Hickory Hills, Palos Hills, Worth, Oak Lawn, Chicago Ridge, Alsip

Naperville, Bolingbrook, Romeoville, Lemont, Homer Glen, Orland Park, Lockport, Crest Hill, Fairmont, Joliet, Rockdale, Ingalls Park, New Lenox, Preston Heights, Mokena, Arbury Hills, Marley, Frankfort, Orland Hills, Tinley Park, Country Club Hills, Hazel Crest, Homewood, Flossmoor, Olympia Fields, Chicago Heights, Ford Heights, Park Forest, South Chicago Heights, Richton Park, Matteson, Markham, Harvey, Phoenix, Robbins, Dixmoor, Posen, Midlothian, Crestwood, Palos Heights, Palos Park, Blue Island, Calumet Park, Riverdale, Dolton, Calumet City, South Holland, Thornton, Glenwood, Lansing, Munster, Lynwood, Sauk Village, Dyer, Schererville, Highland, Hammond, Whiting, Burnham

Navy Pier, Grant Park, Lincoln Park, Lincoln Park Zoo, Wrigley Field, Children's Memorial Hosp., Chicago Historical Society, Mus. of Science & Industry, Jackson Pk., Hyde Park, U.S. Cellular Field, United Center, DePaul Univ., Univ. of Illinois at Chicago, Ill. Inst. of Tech., Chicago Midway Int'l. Arpt., Chicago Lawn, Englewood, Marquette Pk., Gage Park, Ford City Shop. Cen., Pullman, Roseland, South Deering, Calumet Park, Lake Calumet, South Chicago, Hegewisch, Wolf Lake

ILLINOIS / INDIANA

DU PAGE CO. / WILL CO. / COOK CO.

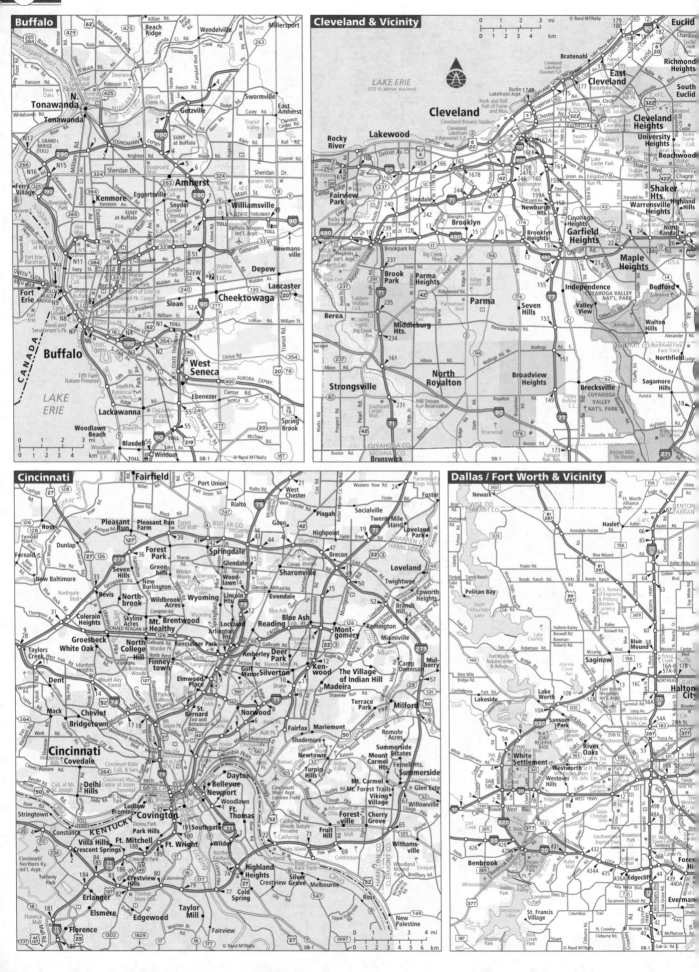

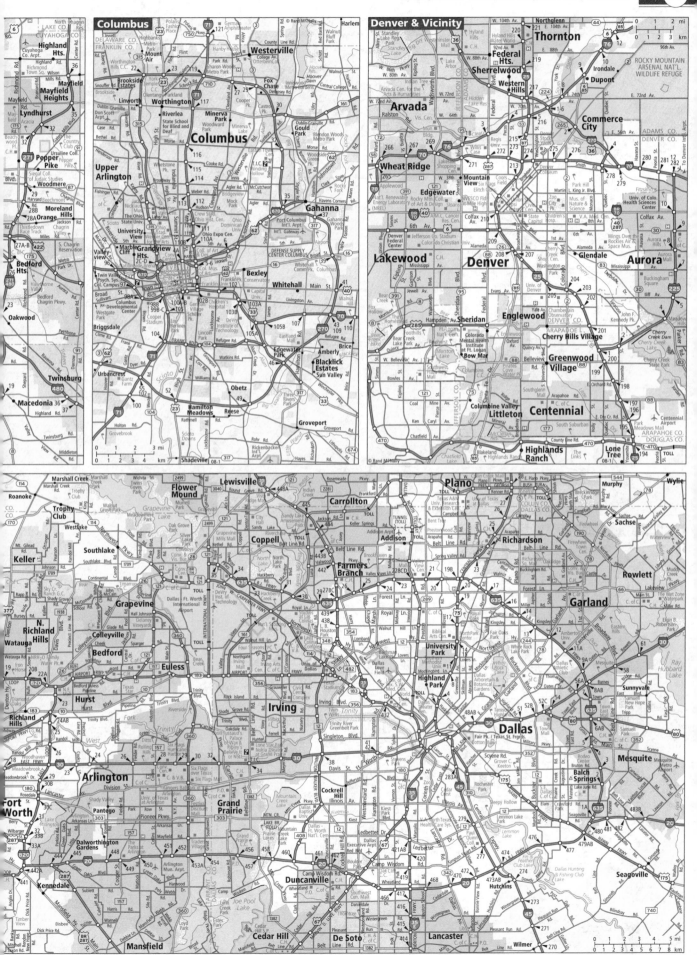

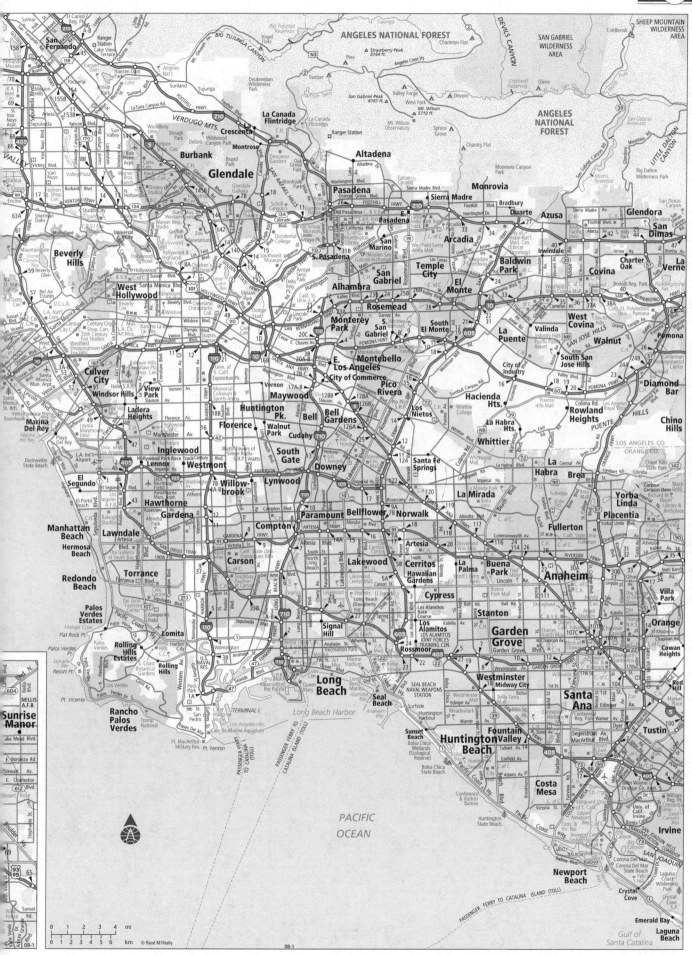

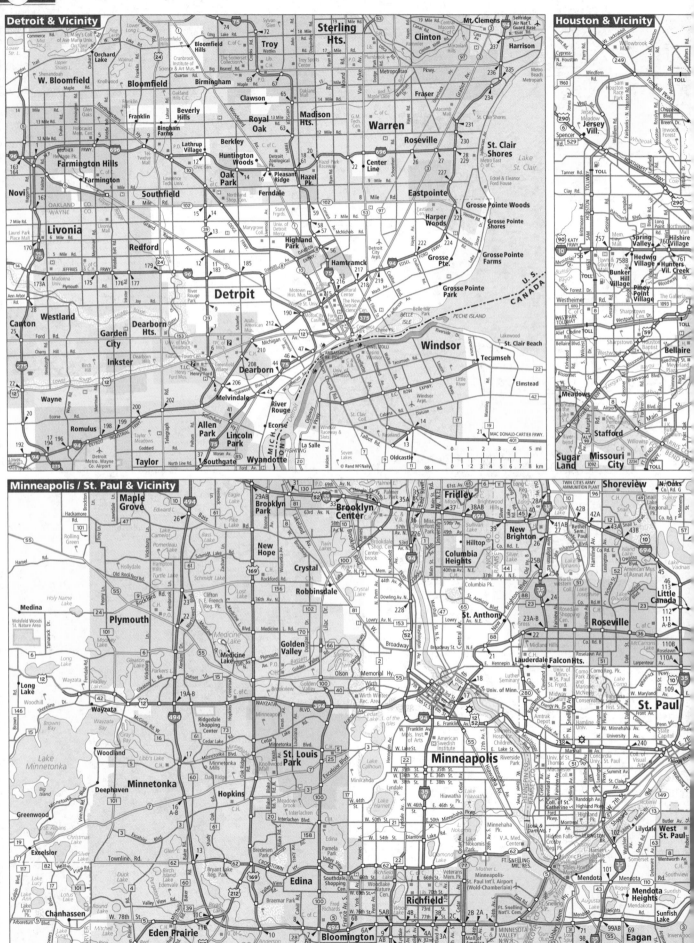

Detroit & Vicinity

Houston & Vicinity

Minneapolis / St. Paul & Vicinity

© Rand McNally

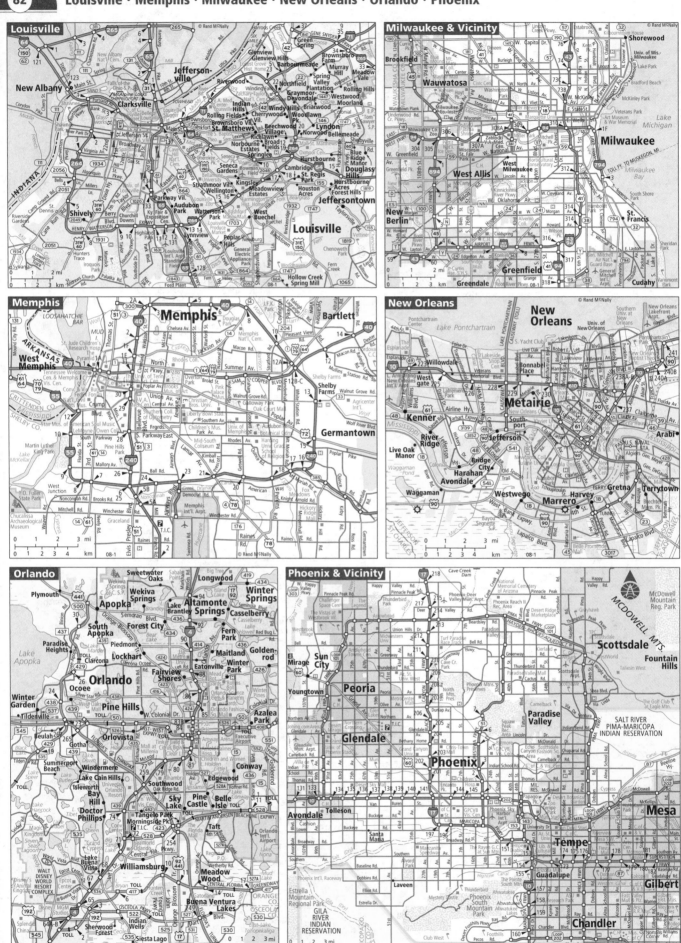

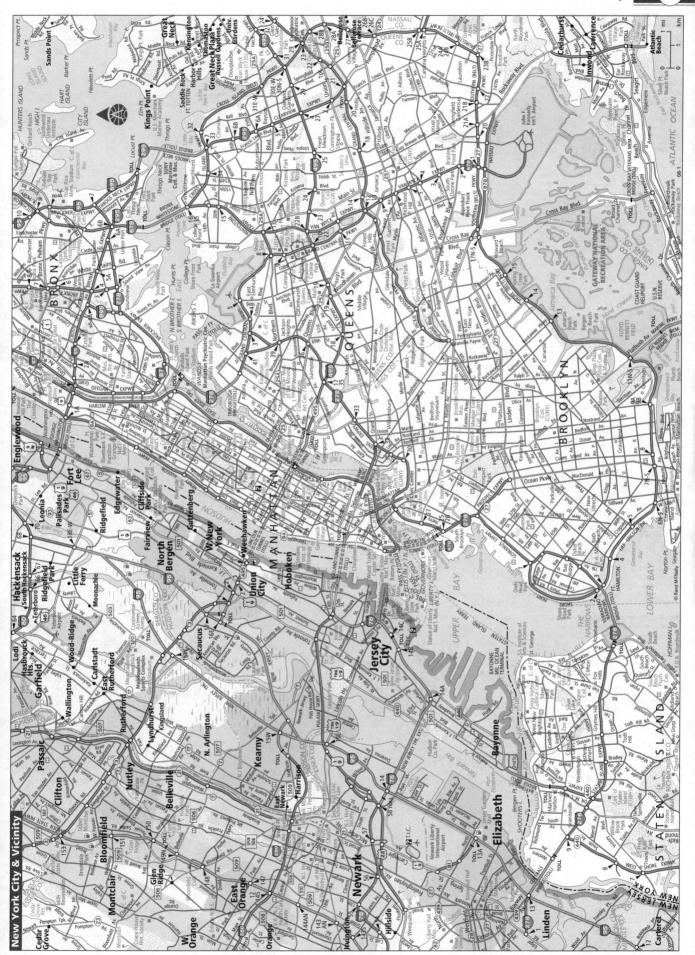

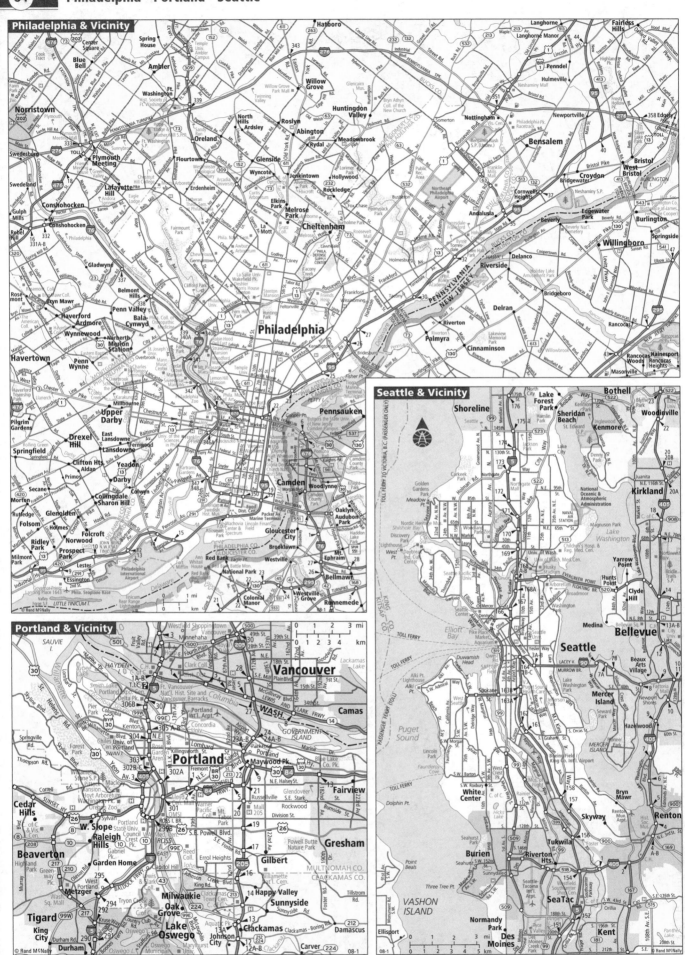

Philadelphia & Vicinity

Portland & Vicinity

Seattle & Vicinity

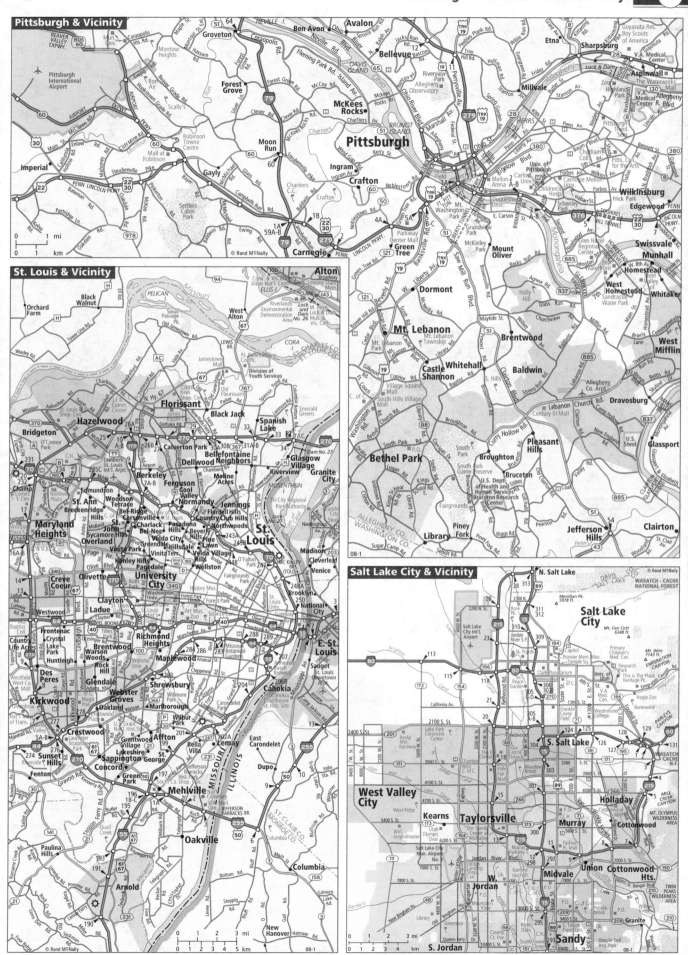

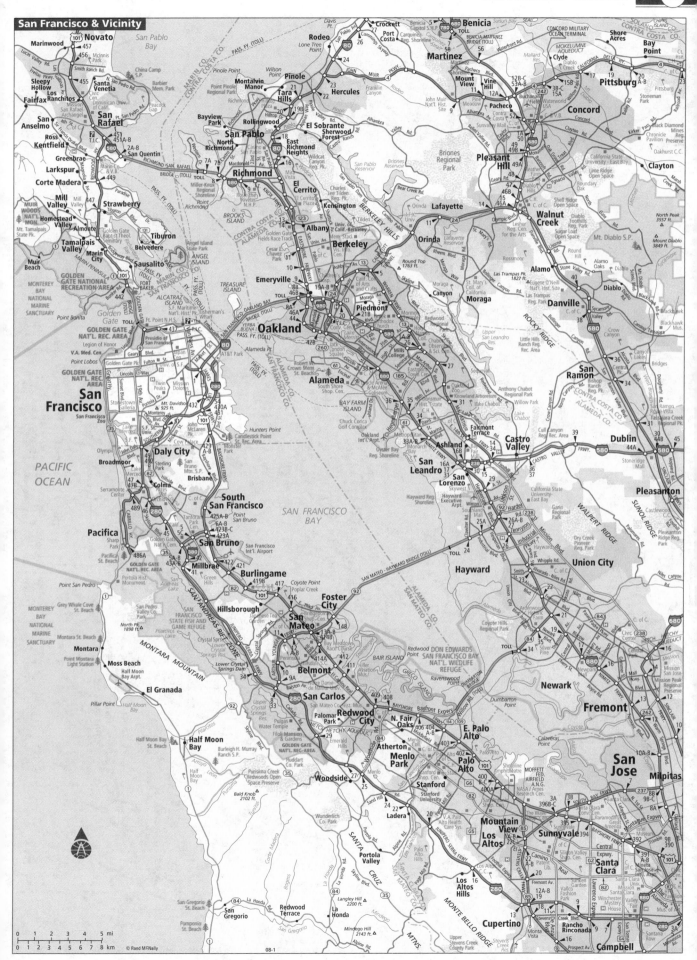

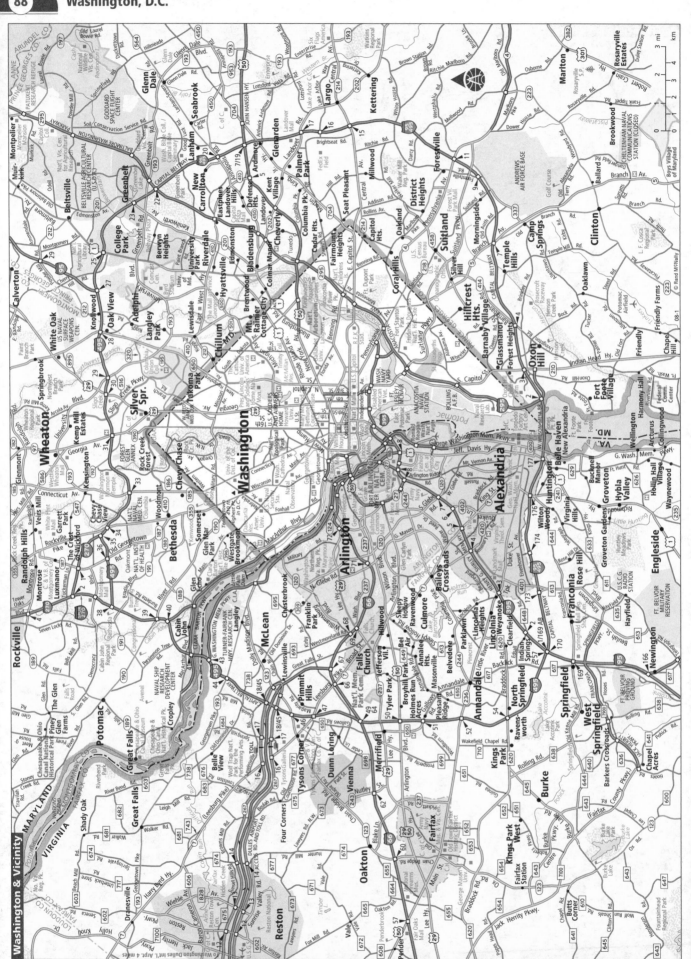

Tourism Concierge

On the road or before you go, log on to the official tourism website of your destination. These websites offer terrific ideas about organizing a visit and often include calendars of special events and activities. Prefer calling? Most states offer toll-free numbers.

United States

Alabama Bureau of Tourism & Travel
(800) 252-2262
www.800alabama.com

Alaska Travel Industry Association
(907) 929-2200
www.travelalaska.com

Arizona Office of Tourism
(866) 239-9712
www.arizonaguide.com

Arkansas Department of Parks & Tourism
(800) 628-8725
www.arkansas.com

California Travel & Tourism Commission
(800) 862-2543*
(916) 444-4429
www.visitcalifornia.com

Colorado Tourism Office
(800) 265-6723
www.colorado.com

Connecticut Tourism
(800) 282-6863
www.ctbound.org

Delaware Tourism Office
(866) 284-7483
(302) 739-4271
www.visitdelaware.com

Visit Florida
(888) 735-2872
www.visitflorida.com

Georgia Office of Tourism
(800) 847-4842
www.georgiaonmymind.org

Hawaii Visitors & Convention Bureau
(800) 464-2924
www.gohawaii.com

Idaho Tourism
(800) 847-4843
www.visitid.org

Illinois Bureau of Tourism
(800) 226-6632
www.enjoyillinois.com

Indiana Tourism Division
(888) 365-6946
www.enjoyindiana.com

Iowa Tourism Office
(800) 345-4692*
(888) 472-6035
(515) 242-4705
www.traveliowa.com

Kansas Travel & Tourism
(800) 252-6727
www.travelks.com

Kentucky Department of Travel
(800) 225-8747
(502) 564-4930
www.kentuckytourism.com

Louisiana Office of Tourism
(800) 334-8626
www.louisianatravel.com

Maine Office of Tourism
(888) 624-6345
(225) 342-8100
www.visitmaine.com

Maryland Office of Tourism
(800) 634-7386
www.visitmaryland.org

Massachusetts Office of Travel & Tourism
(800) 227-6277
(617) 973-8500
www.massvacation.com

Travel Michigan
(888) 784-7328
www.michigan.org

Minnesota Office of Tourism
(800) 657-3700
(651) 296-5029
www.exploreminnesota.com

Mississippi Division of Tourism
(800) 927-6378
(601) 359-3297
www.visitmississippi.org

Missouri Division of Tourism
(800) 810-5500
(573) 751-4133
www.visitmo.com

Travel Montana
(800) 847-4868
(406) 841-2870
www.visitmt.com

Nebraska Division of Travel & Tourism
(877) 632-7275
(800) 228-4307
(402) 471-3796
www.visitnebraska.org

Nevada Commission on Tourism
(800) 638-2328
www.travelnevada.com

New Hampshire Division of Travel and Tourism Development
(800) 386-4664
(603) 271-2665
www.visitnh.gov

New Jersey Office of Travel & Tourism
(800) 847-4865
(609) 777-0885
www.visitnj.org

New Mexico Department of Tourism
(800) 733-6396
www.newmexico.org

New York State Tourism
(800) 225-5697
(518) 474-4116
www.iloveny.com

North Carolina Division of Tourism
(800) 847-4862
(919) 733-8372
www.visitnc.com

North Dakota Tourism Division
(800) 435-5663
(701) 328-2525
www.ndtourism.com

Ohio Division of Travel & Tourism
(800) 282-5393
www.discoverohio.com

Oklahoma Tourism & Recreation Department
(800) 652-6552
www.travelok.com

Oregon Tourism Commission
(800) 547-7842
www.traveloregon.com

Pennsylvania Center for Travel & Marketing
(800) 847-4872
www.visitpa.com

Rhode Island Tourism Division
(888) 886-9463
(800) 556-2484
(401) 222-2601
www.visitrhodeisland.com

South Carolina Department of Parks, Recreation & Tourism
(888) 727-6453*
(803) 734-1700
www.discoversouthcarolina.com

South Dakota Department of Tourism
(800) 732-5682
(605) 773-3301
www.travelsd.com

Tennessee Department of Tourist Development
(800) 462-8366*
(615) 741-2159
www.tnvacation.com

Texas Tourism Division
(800) 888-8839*
www.traveltex.com

Utah Travel Council
(800) 200-1160
(801) 538-1030
www.utah.com

Vermont Department of Tourism and Marketing
(800) 837-6668
www.vermontvacation.com

Virginia Tourism Corporation
(800) 321-3244
(800) 847-4882
www.virginia.org

Washington State Tourism
(800) 544-1800
www.experiencewashington.com

Washington, D.C. Convention & Tourism Corporation
(800) 422-8644*
(202) 789-7000
www.washington.org

West Virginia Division of Tourism
(800) 225-5982
www.callwva.com

Wisconsin Department of Tourism
(800) 432-8747
www.travelwisconsin.com

Wyoming Travel & Tourism
(800) 225-5996
www.wyomingtourism.org

Canada

Travel Alberta
(800) 252-3782
www.travelalberta.com

Tourism British Columbia
(800) 435-5622
www.hellobc.com

Travel Manitoba
(800) 665-0040
www.travelmanitoba.com

Tourism New Brunswick
(800) 561-0123
www.tourismnbcanada.com

Newfoundland & Labrador Department of Tourism
(800) 563-6353
(709) 729-2830
www.gov.nf.ca/tourism

Nova Scotia Department of Tourism & Culture
(800) 565-0000
novascotia.com

Ontario Travel
(800) 668-2746
www.ontariotravel.net

Prince Edward Island Tourism
(888) 734-7529
www.peiplay.com

Tourisme Québec
(877) 266-5687
www.bonjourquebec.com

Tourism Saskatchewan
(877) 237-2273
www.sasktourism.com

Mexico

Mexico Tourism Board
(800) 446-3942
www.visitmexico.com

*To request travel materials only

Mile Markers
Mileage Chart

This handy chart offers more than 2,500 mileages covering 77 North American cities. Want more mileages? Visit go.randmcnally.com/MC and type in any two cities or addresses.

From \ To	Atlanta, GA	Billings, MT	Boston, MA	Charlotte, NC	Chicago, IL	Cincinnati, OH	Cleveland, OH	Dallas, TX	Denver, CO	Detroit, MI	Houston, TX	Indianapolis, IN	Kansas City, MO	Los Angeles, CA	Memphis, TN	Miami, FL	Milwaukee, WI	Minneapolis, MN	New Orleans, LA	New York, NY	Omaha, NE	Philadelphia, PA	Phoenix, AZ	Pittsburgh, PA	Portland, OR	St. Louis, MO	Salt Lake City, UT	San Francisco, CA	Seattle, WA	Tulsa, OK	Washington, DC	Wichita, KS
Albany, NY	1014	2076	166	777	820	727	478	1682	1814	648	1770	791	1287	2833	1230	1407	921	1236	1441	153	1274	238	2544	472	2927	1040	2206	2953	2899	1433	365	1477
Albuquerque, NM	1406	994	2247	1629	1341	1397	1606	644	439	1591	890	1290	783	799	1014	1960	1424	1222	1170	2019	979	1939	463	1649	1385	1041	626	1097	1456	650	1886	593
Amarillo, TX	1121	971	1962	1344	1056	1112	1321	359	424	1306	605	1005	604	1084	729	1675	1139	1043	885	1734	716	1654	748	1463	1666	756	911	1382	1737	365	1601	417
Atlanta, GA		1890	1100	243	712	463	715	791	1415	723	797	529	810	2205	393	661	811	1132	468	896	1000	816	1862	686	2604	556	1883	2503	2675	798	635	972
Baltimore, MD	673	1960	407	436	704	523	379	1366	1693	532	1454	592	1088	2681	914	1080	805	1120	1125	203	1158	102	2345	251	2811	841	2090	2837	2783	1234	38	1278
Billings, MT	1890		2242	2055	1247	1547	1598	1429	555	1534	1676	1433	1078	1239	1606	2551	1176	843	1954	2067	896	2017	1206	1716	891	1333	549	1179	821	1238	1961	1064
Birmingham, AL	148	1839	1185	391	661	467	719	647	1364	727	671	478	759	2058	246	783	760	1081	342	981	949	901	1722	753	2553	505	1832	2356	2624	651	743	825
Bismarck, ND	1558	417	1828	1610	833	1133	1184	1274	709	1120	1521	1019	790	1595	1318	2219	762	429	1709	1653	608	1603	1515	1302	1310	1045	927	1598	1240	1037	1547	802
Boise, ID	2184	621	2673	2349	1702	1959	2029	1704	830	1965	1951	1852	1372	846	1900	2845	1741	1466	2229	2498	1233	2448	995	2147	425	1627	338	648	496	1513	2392	1339
Boston, MA	1100	2242		863	986	893	644	1768	1980	814	1856	957	1453	2999	1316	1483	1087	1402	1527	211	1440	313	2710	586	3093	1206	2372	3119	3065	1599	441	1643
Buffalo, NY	896	1787	461	659	531	438	189	1376	1525	359	1495	502	998	2544	924	1381	632	947	1243	417	985	412	2255	216	2638	751	1917	2664	2610	1144	388	1188
Charleston, SC	321	2196	966	207	911	619	721	1112	1721	850	1113	730	1116	2526	714	580	1010	1325	784	762	1306	661	2183	654	2910	862	2189	2824	2981	1119	525	1306
Charlotte, NC	243	2055	863		770	478	516	1034	1580	645	1040	589	975	2428	617	724	869	1184	711	659	1165	534	2092	449	2769	721	2048	2726	2840	1021	398	1165
Cheyenne, WY	1450	455	1939	1615	968	1225	1295	974	100	1231	1221	1118	638	1102	1166	2111	1007	878	1499	1764	499	1714	906	1413	1155	893	434	1181	1226	783	1658	609
Chicago, IL	712	1247	986	770		293	342	933	1009	278	1089	179	529	2028	536	1373	92	407	927	811	469	761	1804	460	2122	300	1401	2148	2070	693	705	719
Cincinnati, OH	463	1547	893	478	293		252	938	1208	260	1057	112	603	2196	486	1124	392	707	805	660	726	580	1860	290	2379	356	1658	2405	2370	749	524	793
Cleveland, OH	715	1598	644	516	342	252		1190	1336	170	1309	316	812	2355	738	1238	443	758	1081	486	796	473	2069	135	2449	565	1728	2475	2421	958	380	1002
Columbus, OH	574	1606	783	433	352	111	142	1049	1276	204	1168	175	671	2264	597	1155	451	766	916	553	794	473	1928	183	2447	424	1726	2473	2429	817	417	861
Dallas, TX	791	1429	1768	1034	933	938	1190		882	1198	247	882	552	1440	454	1316	1016	991	526	1564	664	1484	1069	1228	2124	633	1403	1741	2195	262	1326	365
Davenport, IA	792	1166	1135	898	175	421	491	915	843	427	1095	314	363	1862	550	1453	214	359	941	960	303	910	1609	609	1956	266	1235	1982	1989	612	854	553
Denver, CO	1415	555	1980	1580	1009	1208	1336	882		1272	1129	1101	605	1022	1097	2076	1048	919	1407	1805	540	1750	809	1460	1250	858	529	1276	1321	691	1694	517
Des Moines, IA	961	997	1867	1580	333	590	660	746	674	596	926	483	194	1693	623	1622	372	243	1014	1129	134	1397	991	1463	1446	350	1066	1813	1820	443	1023	384
Detroit, MI	723	1534	814	645	278	260	170	1169	1272		1317	310	792	2291	746	1367	379	694	1065	639	732	589	2054	288	2385	350	1664	2411	2357	943	533	955
Duluth, MN	1189	861	1459	1241	464	764	815	1145	1073	751	1325	650	593	2092	965	1850	393	157	1356	1284	533	1234	1839	933	1754	681	1465	2042	1684	842	1178	783
El Paso, TX	1426	1178	2394	1669	1488	1544	1753	633	623	1738	753	1437	930	807	1087	1939	1571	1369	1100	2197	1016	2117	436	1796	1627	1188	868	1188	1698	797	1959	740
Fargo, ND	1369	607	1639	1421	644	944	995	1087	901	931	1334	830	603	1785	1131	2030	573	240	1522	1464	421	1414	1707	1113	1590	858	1117	1788	1430	850	1358	725
Flagstaff, AZ	1733	1070	2574	1956	1668	1724	1933	971	673	1918	1217	1617	1110	472	1341	2287	1751	1549	1497	2346	1210	2266	136	1796	1279	1368	520	770	1350	977	2213	920
Houston, TX	797	1676	1856	1040	1089	1057	1309	247	1129	1317		1025	732	1560	573	1190	1179	1171	351	1652	911	1572	1189	1347	2371	837	1650	1941	2442	505	1414	612
Indianapolis, IN	529	1433	957	589	179	112	316	882	1101	310	1025		496	2089	472	1190	278	593	816	729	619	649	1753	359	2272	249	1551	2298	2256	642	593	686
Jackson, MS	383	1817	1424	626	747	692	944	408	1225	952	442	683	737	1850	212	908	837	1119	180	1220	927	1140	1479	982	2467	495	1746	2149	2538	534	982	708
Jacksonville, FL	346	2236	1142	383	1058	795	897	1001	1761	1026	875	875	1156	2431	712	341	1157	1478	546	938	1346	837	2060	830	2950	902	2229	2742	3021	1117	701	1291
Kansas City, MO	810	1078	1453	975	529	603	812	552	600	792	732	496		1626	521	1471	568	439	917	1225	188	1145	1246	855	1792	251	1071	1818	1863	249	1089	190
Knoxville, TN	215	1826	928	229	542	250	502	840	1351	510	928	361	746	2199	388	876	641	956	599	724	936	644	1863	496	2540	492	1819	2497	2611	792	486	936
Las Vegas, NV	1982	966	2726	2205	1755	1956	2082	1220	749	2018	1466	1849	1353	275	1590	2536	1794	1665	1746	2551	1286	2498	292	2208	1021	1606	416	569	1122	1226	2462	1265
Lexington, KY	386	1669	935	401	375	83	335	874	1194	343	993	188	589	2175	422	1047	474	789	741	731	779	645	1839	373	2383	335	1662	2409	2454	728	543	779
Little Rock, AR	531	1513	1453	754	655	623	875	315	966	883	434	591	389	1682	139	1165	745	826	441	1249	577	1169	1346	913	2487	246	1352	1980	2279	275	1101	449
Los Angeles, CA	2205	1239	2999	2428	2028	2196	2353	1440	1022	2291	1560	2089	1626		1813	2746	2067	1938	1907	2824	1509	2738	371	2448	967	1840	689	381	1141	1449	2685	1392
Louisville, KY	415	1595	996	475	297	103	355	835	1120	363	954	114	515	2101	383	1076	396	711	702	763	705	683	1765	393	2309	261	1588	2335	2380	654	617	705
Memphis, TN	393	1606	1316	617	536	486	738	454	1097	746	573	472	526	1813		1027	626	908	392	1132	716	1032	1477	776	2320	284	1599	2111	2391	406	874	580
Miami, FL	661	2551	1483	724	1373	1124	1238	1316	2076	1367	1190	1190	1471	2746	1027		1472	1793	861	1279	1661	1178	2375	1171	3265	1217	2544	3057	3336	1432	1042	1606
Milwaukee, WI	811	1176	1087	869	92	392	443	1016	1048	379	1179	278	568	2067	626	1472		336	1017	912	508	862	1887	561	2069	383	1440	2187	1999	776	806	758
Minneapolis, MN	1132	843	1402	1184	407	708	753	991	919	661	1411	593	439	1938	908	1793	336		1299	1227	379	1177	1685	876	1736	624	1311	2058	1666	688	1121	629
Mobile, AL	329	2003	1429	572	920	726	978	598	1415	986	472	737	923	2028	398	718	1019	1305	143	1225	1113	1145	1657	1009	2657	681	1936	2339	2728	724	964	898
Montréal, QC	1227	1909	324	990	848	829	590	1767	1842	575	1886	879	1362	2861	1315	1632	949	1264	1654	384	1302	463	2632	617	2955	1128	2234	2981	2732	1521	590	1525
Nashville, TN	242	1650	1106	407	472	278	530	663	1175	538	782	289	570	2022	211	903	571	892	527	902	760	822	1686	568	2364	316	1643	2320	2435	615	664	760
New Orleans, LA	468	1954	1527	711	927	805	1057	526	1407	1065	351	816	917	1907	392	861	1017	1299		1323	1107	1243	1536	1095	2649	675	1928	2267	2720	679	1085	890
New York, NY	896	2067	211	659	811	660	486	1564	1805	639	1652	729	1225	2824	1112	1279	912	1227	1323		1265	109	2482	388	2918	978	2197	2944	2890	1371	237	1415
Norfolk, VA	557	2147	577	320	891	601	566	1348	1781	719	1384	713	1176	2729	918	948	992	1307	1055	373	1366	276	2393	438	2970	922	2249	2996	3041	1315	196	1366
Odessa, TX	1147	1204	2122	1390	1244	1292	1509	354	649	1494	546	1193	792	1088	808	1672	1327	1231	882	1918	904	1838	717	1552	1784	944	1025	1469	1855	553	1680	605
Oklahoma City, OK	862	1221	1702	1085	796	852	1061	208	674	1046	455	745	344	1343	470	1496	879	783	733	1474	456	1394	1007	1104	1916	496	1195	1641	1987	105	1342	157
Omaha, NE	1000	896	1440	1165	469	726	796	664	540	732	911	619	188	1559	716	1661	508	379	1107	1265		1215	1346	914	1653	443	932	1679	1724	435	1159	302
Orlando, FL	440	2330	1284	525	1152	903	1039	1095	1855	1163	969	969	1250	2525	806	229	1251	1572	640	1080	1440	979	2154	972	3044	996	2323	2836	3115	1211	843	1385
Philadelphia, PA	816	2017	313	534	761	580	436	1484	1750	589	1572	649	1145	2738	1032	1178	862	1177	1243	109	1215		2402	308	2868	898	2147	2894	2840	1291	136	1335
Phoenix, AZ	1862	1206	2710	2092	1804	1860	2069	1069	809	2054	1189	1753	1246	371	1477	2375	1887	1685	1536	2482	1346	2402		2112	1338	1504	656	752	1486	1113	2349	1056
Pittsburgh, PA	686	1716	586	449	460	290	135	1228	1460	288	1347	359	855	2448	776	1171	561	876	1095	388	914	308	2112		2567	608	1846	2593	2539	1001	252	1045
Portland, ME	1229	2343	117	964	1087	994	745	1897	2081	915	1985	1058	1554	3103	1656	1541	1058	312	1541	414	2811	687	3194	1307	2473	3220	3166	1700	542	1744		
Portland, OR	2604	891	3093	2769	2122	2379	2449	2124	1250	2385	2371	2272	1792	967	2320	3265	2069	1736	2649	2918	1653	2868	1338	2567		2047	578	636	174	1933	2812	1759
Rapid City, SD	1521	373	1904	1686	909	1209	1260	1069	400	1196	1316	1095	709	1312	1237	2182	838	609	1628	1729	527	1679	1206	1628	1266	964	641	1391	1196	878	1623	704
Reno, NV	2406	955	2895	2571	1924	2181	2251	1665	1052	2187	1911	2074	1594	473	2122	3067	1963	1834	2193	2720	1455	2670	735	2369	578	1849	522	224	752	1735	2614	1561
Roanoke, VA	430	1917	678	193	663	370	429	1098	1550	558	1186	482	945	2457	646	915	762	1077	857	474	1135	394	2121	365	2739	691	2018	2765	2810	1050	236	1113
St. Louis, MO	556	1333	1206	721	300	356	565	633	858	550	837	249	253	1840	284	1217	383	624	675	978	443	898	1504	608	2047		1326	2073	2118	393	878	443
Salt Lake City, UT	1883	549	2372	2048	1401	1658	1728	1403	529	1664	1650	1551	1071	689	1599	2544	1440	1311	1928	2197	932	2147	656	1846	758	1326		746	829	1212	2091	1038
San Antonio, TX	992	1483	2051	1235	1210	1215	1467	277	936	1475	199	1159	817	1365	731	1385	1293	1256	561	1767	994	1505	2100	910	1341	746	2171	539	1609	630		
San Diego, CA	2154	1299	3064	2397	2088	2214	2423	1361	1082	2351	1481	2107	1600	124	1831	2667	2127	1998	1828	2836	1619	2756	354	2466	1091	1858	749	505	1265	1467	2703	1410
San Francisco, CA	2503	1179	3119	2726	2148	2405	2475	1741	1276	2411	1941	2298	1818	381	2111	3057	2187	2058	2267	2944	1679	2894	752	2593	636	2073	746		810	1747	2838	1785
Sault Ste. Marie, ON	1047	1282	943	960	452	584	506	1357	1446	350	1510	537	966	2465	957	1708	404	549	1347	939	906	925	2228	624	2175	724	1838	2585	2105	1117	869	1129
Seattle, WA	2675	821	3065	2840	2070	2370	2421	2195	1321	2357	2442	2256	1863	1141	2391	3336	1999	1666	2720	2890	1724	2840	1486	2539	174	2118	829	810		2004	2784	1830
Shreveport, LA	605	1614	1646	848	851	819	1071	186	1067	1079	239	787	566	1628	335	1130	941	1005	347	1442	752	1362	1257	1109	2309	599	1588	1927	2380	339	1204	550
Sioux Falls, SD	1177	717	1564	1342	569	876	920	849	654	856	1096	769	365	1673	893	1838	498	269	1284	1385	183	1339	1460	1038	1610	620	989	1736	1540	612	1283	487
Spokane, WA	2431	539	2783	2596	1788	2088	2139	1970	1096	2075	2217	1974	1619	1215	2147	3092	1717	1384	2495	2608	1437	2558	1377	2257	352	1874	720	885	282	1779	2502	1605
Springfield, MO	684	1247	1418	849	512	568	777	423	761	762	666	461	169	1630	283	1345	595	606	674	1190	357	1110	1294	820	1961	212	1240	1928	2032	183	1090	262
Tallahassee, FL	270	2143	1301	470	965	733	985	839	1668	993	713	782	1063	2269	550	478	1064	1385	384	1097	1253	996	1898	917	2857	809	2136	2580	2928	955	860	1129
Tampa, FL	458	2348	1340	581	1170	921	1095	1113	1873	1181	987	987	1268	2543	824	273	1269	1590	658	1136	1458	1035	2172	1028	3062	1014	2341	2854	3133	1229	899	1403
Toronto, ON	961	1773	566	766	517	498	296	1436	1511	244	1555	548	1031	2530	984	1488	618	933	1303	528	971	517	2301	323	2624	797	1903	2650	2596	1190	495	1194
Tulsa, OK	798	1238	1599	1021	693	749	958	262	691	943	505	642	249	1449	406	1432	776	688	679	1371	435	1291	1113	1001	1993	393	1212	1714	2004		1271	174
Washington, DC	635	1961	441	398	705	524	380	1326	1694	513	1414	593	1089	2685	874	1042	806	1121	1085	237	1159	136	2349	252	2812	878	2091	2838	2784	1271		1279
Wichita, KS	972	1064	1635	1165	719	793	1002	365	517	955	612	686	190	1392	580	1606	758	629	890	1415	302	1335	1056	1045	1759	443	1038	1785	1830	174	1279	

Mileages ©Rand McNally